Broadcasting

The New Law

Nicholas Reville, LLB, MA
*Senior Lecturer, School of Law,
Leicester Polytechnic*

Butterworths
London, Dublin & Edinburgh
1991

United Kingdom	Butterworth & Co (Publishers) Ltd , 88 Kingsway, LONDON WC2B 6AB and 4 Hill Street, EDINBURGH EH2 3JZ
Australia	Butterworths Pty Ltd, SYDNEY, MELBOURNE, BRISBANE, ADELAIDE, PERTH, CANBERRA and HOBART
Canada	Butterworths Canada Ltd, TORONTO and VANCOUVER
Ireland	Butterworth (Ireland) Ltd, DUBLIN
Malaysia	Malayan Law Journal Sdn Bhd, KUALA LUMPUR
New Zealand	Butterworths of New Zealand Ltd, WELLINGTON and AUCKLAND
Puerto Rico	Equity de Puerto Rico, Inc, HATO REY
Singapore	Malayan Law Journal Pte Ltd, SINGAPORE
USA	Butterworth Legal Publishers, AUSTIN, Texas; BOSTON, Massachusetts; CLEARWATER, Florida (D & S Publishers); ORFORD, New Hampshire (Equity Publishing); ST PAUL, Minnesota; and SEATTLE, Washington

A CIP Catalogue record for this book is available from the British Library.

ISBN 0 406 00137 5

Printed and bound by Dotesios Ltd, Trowbridge, Wiltshire

Preface

The Broadcasting Act 1990 sets up a new system of independent broadcasting regulation in the United Kingdom. Important provisions also relate to the BBC, whose present charter expires at the end of 1996. In the words of Earl Ferrers, (minister of state, Home Office), the Broadcasting Act 1990 is 'enormous' and covers a 'huge and complicated area'. This explains, in part, the approach adopted in this book of setting a comprehensive statement of the provisions of the Broadcasting Act 1990 in the context of the policy considerations that led to their formulation. The Broadcasting Act 1990 had an unusually long gestation period. Consequently, reference is made to the official reports and government announcements made before the Broadcasting Bill was produced. There was an exceptionally large number of government amendments to the Bill as it progressed through Parliament. Hence, there is frequent reference to parliamentary considerations, particularly at the committee stages in the House of Commons and House of Lords. Likewise, account is taken of the international obligations that are acknowledged (expressly or impliedly) in the Broadcasting Act 1990, especially the European Directive 'Television without Frontiers' and the Council of Europe Convention on Transfrontier Television.

A further factor that influenced the approach adopted in a book of this size is that readers will have widely differing interests in broadcasting. An overall view of the Broadcasting Act 1990 is given in which those interests can be set. The transitional provisions relating to the change-over from the old independent broadcasting regime to the new are considered only in outline in chapter 2.

One prominent characteristic of the Broadcasting Act 1990 is its enabling nature and the large amount of discretion that it gives to the Secretary of State and the various regulatory bodies that it sets up. Public opinion can be influential in its implementation.

The discretion given to me by the publishers of this book as to its format is much appreciated, as are the enabling skills of its editorial team.

On a more personal note, I would thank Jill, Thomas and Matthew for their forbearance and encouragement.

Nicholas Reville
March 1990

CONTENTS

Contents

Contents

ADDRESSES OF BODIES SET UP OR RE-ESTABLISHED BY THE 1990 ACT

The Independent Television Commission
70 Brompton Road
London SW3 1EY

The Radio Authority
70 Brompton Road
London SW3 1EY

Broadcasting Complaints Commission
Grosvenor Gardens House
35 - 37 Grosvenor Gardens
London SW1W 0BS

Broadcasting Standards Council
5 - 8 The Sanctuary
London
SW1P 3JS

Chapter 1

INTRODUCTION

Outline of the Broadcasting Act 1990

1.1   The Broadcasting Act 1990 sets up a comprehensive new system of independent broadcasting regulation in the United Kingdom. It repeals the two major preceding broadcasting statutes [1] and provides for a far wider range of matters than did those statutes. Parts I and II set up the Independent Television Commission (ITC) and reform the legal framework for independent television and cable. Direct broadcasting by satellite (DBS) and non-domestic satellite broadcasting (non-DBS) are also covered. DBS operates on frequencies allocated to the United Kingdom for broadcasting. Non-DBS services use other frequencies. Provision is made for microwave transmission as well as 'additional services' which are data, text and other services which use the spare capacity of broadcasting signals. Part I also covers 'licensable programme services' such as a channel delivered in tape form to a cable system. Part III sets up the Radio Authority and provides for a far wider range of independent radio stations, including three new national services and many new small stations catering for local communities. Part IV deals with the privatisation of the Independent Broadcasting Authority's transmission system. Part V re-establishes the Broadcasting Complaints Commission. Part VI sets up the Broadcasting Standards Council on a statutory basis. Part VII deals with the extension to broadcasting of the law of obscenity and incitement to racial hatred. Part VIII has measures against pirate broadcasting. Part IX is concerned with the copyright issues of 'needle time' and programme listings. Part X ranges over unacceptable foreign satellite services, unauthorised decoders, television licensing, listed events of national interest, the funding of Gaelic television programmes, a national television archive, independent producers and the implementation of the United Kingdom's international obligations.

1   The Broadcasting Act 1981, which concentrated on independent terrestrial broadcasting and the Cable and Broadcasting Act 1984 which focused on cable.

1.2   References in this book to 'the 1990 Act' or to any section are references to the Broadcasting Act 1990 or to a section of it, unless the contrary is apparent.

1.3   Reference is made in this book to the Parliamentary debates on the Broadcasting Bill. The reports of these debates are as follows:

House of Commons
1st Reading:
    HC Deb, Vol 163, 6 December 1989, col 336.
2nd Reading:
    HC Deb, Vol 164, 18 December 1989, cols 40-148.

Standing Committee F:
>The Committee met on 38 occasions between 9 January and 15 March 1990. Its deliberations are recorded in cols 1-1522 of the Official Report.

Report:
>HC Deb, Vol 172, 8, 9 May 1990, cols 49-169 and 195-368.

3rd Reading:
>HC Deb, Vol 172, 10 May 1990, cols 412-450.

House of Lords
1st Reading:
>HL Deb, Vol 519, 15 May 1990, col 230.

2nd Reading:
>HL Deb, Vol 519, 5 June 1990, cols 1220-1357.

Committee [1] :
>HL Deb, Vol 521, 9 July 1990, cols 10-74 and 77-103.
>>Vol 521, 11 July 1990, cols 300-426.
>>Vol 521, 18 July 1990, cols 900-1006.
>>Vol 521, 19 July 1990, cols 1016-1066 and 1071-1110.
>>Vol 521, 24 July 1990, cols 1334-1402 and 1419-1440.
>>Vol 521, 25 July 1990, cols 1463-1472, 1486-1545 and 1577-1608.
>>Vol 521, 26 July 1990, cols 1655-1783.

Report:
>HL Deb, Vol 522, 9 October 1990, cols 153-226 and 240-268.
>>Vol 522, 11 October 1990, cols 414-524.
>>Vol 522, 16 October 1990, cols 727-876.

3rd Reading:
>HL Deb, Vol 522, 22 October 1990, cols 1142-1227.

House of Commons – Consideration of Lords Amendments
>HC Deb, Vol 178, 25 October 1990, cols 520-619.

House of Lords – Consideration of Commons Amendments
>HL Deb, Vol 522, 30 October 1990, cols 1772-1799.

1 References to House of Lords and House of Commons debates from the commencement of the House of Lords stage of the Broadcasting Bill are references to the weekly and not the bound volumes of those reports because only the former were available at the time of writing this book.

Official Reports and Announcements

1.4 The 1990 Act was preceded by the 1986 Peacock Report [1], the 1987 radio Green Paper [2] and, in 1988, the Home Affairs Committee reports [3] and the Broadcasting White Paper [4]. In 1989, before the Broadcasting Bill was produced, the Government made a number of announcements proposing major changes to its White Paper's proposals. They were concerned with such topics as cable [5], ownership [6], quality requirements [7], Channel 4 [7], independent radio [8], night hours [9] and transmission [10].

1 'Report of the Committee on Financing the BBC' (Cmnd 9824).
2 'Radio: Choices and Opportunities' (Cmnd 92).
3 'The Future of Broadcasting' (HCP 262, 1987-88) and 'The Financing of Channel 4' (HCP 185, 1988-89).
  'The Financing of Channel 4' (15 March 1989); 'The Future of Broadcasting'(22 June 1989).
4 'Broadcasting in the 90's: Competition, Choice and Quality' (Cmnd 517).

5   HC Deb, Vol 151, 27 April 1989, cols 637-640 w.
6   HC Deb, Vol 153, 19 May 1989, cols 317-319 w.
7   HC Deb, Vol 154, 13 June 1989, cols 710-713.
8   HC Deb, Vol 156, 4 July 1989, cols 100-101w.
9   HC Deb, Vol 156, 4 July 1989, col 101w.
10 HC Deb, Vol 156, 4 July 1989, cols 102-103w.

Application of the 1990 Act

1.5   Generally, the 1990 Act applies to the United Kingdom [1]. It comes into force on such day as the Secretary of State appoints by order. Different days may be so appointed for different provisions or for different purposes (s204(2)). At the time of this book going to press one commencement order [2] had been made and most of the 1990 Act is either in force (as of 1 December 1990 or 1 January 1991) or a date has been appointed for commencement. The book is written on the basis that the whole Act is in force.

1   Section 204(3). Section 162 and Sch 15 apply to England and Wales, s163 applies to Scotland, s164 applies to England, Wales and Scotland, s165 applies to Northern Ireland and the amendments and repeals in Schs 20 and 21 apply to the extent as did the legislation to which they refer. Her Majesty may by Order in Council direct that any provisions of the 1990 Act apply to the Isle of Man or any of the Channel Islands with such modifications, if any, as appears to Her Majesty to be appropriate (s204(4) - (6)).

2   S.I. 1990/2347 (C. 61). A number of repeals in Sch 21 have yet to be given a commencement date.

The BBC and the 1990 Act

1.6   Traditionally, the public broadcasting authorities were appointed as trustees for the public interest in the effective use of the finite resource, the spectrum. The British Broadcasting Corporation (BBC) and Independent Broadcasting Authority (IBA), acting independently of government, provided a public service of high quality and wide range, which informed, educated and entertained. While the 1990 Act provides for the most major reorganisation of independent television and radio since their introduction in the United Kingdom, there is comparatively little provision for the BBC, whose present charter expires at the end of 1996. The 1990 Act provides, inter alia, for television or sound programmes broadcast by the BBC to be within the remit of the Broadcasting Complaints Commission and the Broadcasting Standards Council. Also, the provision on 'needletime' [1] and programme schedules [2] apply to the BBC. It will have an interest in compliance with the new offence relating to unauthorised decoders for encrypted services [3] and the provisions relating to wireless telegraphy [4]. The BBC is directly affected by the requirements relating to their duties in relation to independent productions [5]. The power of the Secretary of State to give it directions relating to international obligations [6], the transfer to it of functions connected with television licences [7] and the provisions on 'listed events' [8]. The government reconsidered its 1988 White Paper proposals on 'night hours broadcasting' and decided to permit the BBC to retain both sets on condition that it makes full use of them for raising subscription income [9].

1   Section 175. See paras 5.1 - 5.9.
2   Section 176. See para 5.10.
3   Section 179. See para 5.15.
4   Sections 168 - 174. See Chapter 6.
5   Section 186 and 187. See paras 5.29 - 5.34.
6   Section 188. See para 5.36.
7   Section 180. See para 5.21.
8   Section 182.
9   HC Deb, Vol 156, 4 July 1989 col 101w.

The BBC and Public Service Broadcasting

1.7   The Government acknowledged in its 1988 White Paper [1] that 'the BBC will continue as the cornerstone of public service broadcasting'. This fact explains, in part, the policy of the 1990 Act in imposing on all independent services, other than Channel 4, programming requirements that fall short of those found in public service broadcasting.
1   Cmnd 517, para 1.3.

The IBA System

1.8   The IBA was required by the Broadcasting Act 1981 to provide public service broadcasting. Programme contractors, selected by the IBA, discharged this function. The pre 1990 Act television contracts were extended until the end of 1992 by the Broadcasting Act 1987. Rentals were paid to the IBA to finance its network of television transmitters by the ITV companies who also subscribed to the financing of Channel 4 and the Welsh Fourth Channel (S4C). A levy was paid by companies making a sufficient profit.

The Need for Change

1.9   Much of the debate on the framework of broadcasting into the third millennium starts with the 1986 Peacock Report. It suggested a move away from a highly regulated television duopoly towards a more competitive system [1]. Technical advances will enable viewers and listeners to receive a multiplicity of programme services from a variety of services transmitted by different means. In 1988 both the White Paper and the Homes Affairs committee (the Committee) considered the potential for additional programme services.
1   Cmnd 9824, chapter 12.

Further Terrestrial Channels

1.10   The Committee assumed that for the foreseeable future the four pre-1990 Act terrestrial channels will remain the dominant forces in British television [1]. The Government's White Paper considered that a fifth terrestrial channel capable of covering 50-70% of the population could be technically feasible by 1993 if Ultra High Frequencies (UHF) were reallocated. A sixth terrestrial channel at UHF, covering up to 50% of the population, although perhaps feasible, could require considerable technical problems to be solved [2].
1   'The Future of Broadcasting' (HCP 262, 1987-88) Vol I (22 June 1988), para 52.
2   Cmnd 517, paras 5.6 and 5.7.

Satellite Services

1.11   The government intends to 'safeguard absolutely' any services in the five Direct Broadcasting by Satellite (DBS) channels allocated to the United Kingdom at the World Administrative Radio Conference in 1977 and whose franchise was originally awarded to British Satellite Broadcasting (BSB) [1]. The Committee considered that a number of services available on cable (transmitted originally by low-powered satellite) were likely to become available direct to home receiving dishes via the medium-powered Astra satellite or Eutelsat. Consumer base inertia made it likely that no satellite service would quickly obtain a major share of viewers. However, it acknowledged that by the year 2000 satellite television would be an accepted feature of broadcasting [2].
1   The 1988 White Paper (Cmnd 517), para 5.10.
2   'The Future of Broadcasting' (HCP 262, 1987-88) Vol 1 (22 June 1988), paras 55 and 57.

Cable

1.12   At the time of the Cable and Broadcasting Act 1984 the Department of Trade and Industry anticipated that British cabling would be entertainment-led. The Committee found that the process of cabling had been markedly slower than foreseen and was unlikely to transform the television market within the short to medium term [1].
1   'The Future of Broadcasting' (HCP 262, 1987-88) Vol 1 (22 June 1988), para 58.

Multipoint Video Distribution Systems (MVDS)

1.13   For some time the United States has used MVDS as a delivery system for multi-channel services direct to the customer. Terrestrial transmitters use microwave frequencies to transmit television and sound channels to aerials on individual homes. Cable operators may be attracted to MVDS as a means of cheaply expanding the cable services market [1].
1   'The Future of Broadcasting' (HCP 262, 1987-88) Vol 1 (22 June 1988), para 58.

Features of the 1990 Act

1.14   Two traditional features of broadcasting legislation are found in the 1990 Act. First, the regulators are normally independent of government control [1]. During the progress of the Broadcasting Bill there was acknowledged the 'need to ensure that government stands at arm's length from the regulation of broadcasting' [2]. The annual report remains the main form of communication between Parliament and the regulator [3]. Second, the 1990 Act generally provides for the regulation of broadcasting in broad terms. Wide administrative powers are conferred on the Independent Television Commission (ITC) and Radio Authority, as they were on the IBA by the Broadcasting Act 1981, so that, for example, within a framework set by Parliament, the ITC is given as much discretion as possible to go about its business [2]. This happens, inter alia, in relation to the general code for programmes and the code for advertisements and sponsorship that the ITC and Radio Authority must respectively draw up [4]. The purpose of such codes is 'to enable the relevant regulatory bodies to set out detailed rules for their licensees on aspects of broadcasting which Parliament wants to be regulated' [5]. While the 1990 Act prescribes the codes' subject matter, how the subjects are covered and the wording used is left to the expertise of the ITC and Radio Authority. The drawn up codes do not require Parliamentary approval, so avoiding the possibility of ministers being responsible for them.
1   Government control over licensed services is provided for in ss10 and 94. See paras 3.39, 3.40 and paras 8.39 and 8.40.
2   Mr David Mellor (minister of state, Home Office) House of Commons Committee, col 447.
3   For the ITC and Radio Authority annual report see para 15 of Schs 1 and 8 respectively. See paras 3.1 and 8.5.
4   Under ss7(1), 9(1), 91(1) and 93(1). See paras 3.32, 3.36, 8.35 and 8.37.
5   Earl Ferrers (minister of state, Home Office) House of Lords Committee, col 399.

1.15   In carrying out their statutory duties under the 1990 Act the ITC and Radio Authority are often required to 'do all that they can to' ensure certain objectives are met. For example, compliance with their respective codes for programmes and advertisements under ss7(1), 9(1), 91(1) and 93(1) [1]. The interpretation of such provisions leaves them with much freedom and may be pragmatically justified as the best that can be expected of them. The 1990 Act does not require the setting up of advisory councils to assist the ITC and Radio Authority. This is left to their discretion. Public participation in the decision-making procedures is required on occasion. For example, both bodies are required to make arrangements for ascertaining the state of public opinion concerning programmes included in licensed services and the types of programme members of the public would like to be included [2]. Apart from the pressures of public opinion, the ITC and Radio Authority, like other regulatory agencies, are subject to judicial review. The practice of judicial review of policy decisions involves two dangers. In the absence of necessary judicial intervention, regulatory bodies would be able to exercise arbitrary power. Excessive judicial intervention would prevent them from adequately performing the functions allocated to them by statute.

1   See para 1.14, footnote 4.
2   Sections 12 and 96. See paras 3.42 and 8.42.

Judicial Review

1.16   The courts have an inherent power to review the actions and decisions of broadcasting regulatory agencies should it be alleged that they have not duly performed their statutory duties or have usurped, exceeded or abused their statutory powers. Agencies may do this in a number of ways. Consequently, there are various 'grounds of challenge' but each is merely one aspect of the general supervisory jurisdiction and cases can often be explained on more than one ground. While the court reviews the legality of conduct, it does not have a roving commission to scrutinise and than quash any conduct or decision of which it disapproves. Judicial review merely allows a court to measure what has, or has not, been done against the relevant statutory provision.

1.17   There was comparatively little judicial intervention in the activities of the IBA. This is partly explained by the fact that many of its powers arose out of contract and not statute. The use of administrative law to ensure a degree of accountability was restricted when the IBA exercised private contractual rights in its relationship with a broadcasting company. When judicial review was possible the courts looked favourably on the expertise of the IBA. In a 1973 case [1] the Court of Appeal considered the IBA duty under s3(1)(a) of the Television Act 1964 [2] to satisfy itself about the content of programmes. It held that the court could only question its decision to transmit a particular programme if it were shown that it had misdirected itself in law or that its decision was unreasonable. There was sufficient evidence to require the court to hold that the decision in this case was one which the IBA could reasonably make. Twelve years later the same court considered s4(1) of the Broadcasting Act 1981 which required the IBA to satisfy itself that, so far as possible, the programmes broadcast by it complied with certain requirements [3]. The court found that this allowed the IBA to adopt a system which, in its opinion, was best adapted to ensure compliance with s4(1). That system, which allowed the Director General of the IBA to decide whether programmes should be referred to IBA members for their personal decision, was an administrative set up with which the court would not interfere. In 1988 the Scottish National Party petitioned for judicial review and conceded that it could only succeed in establishing a breach of duty imposed on the IBA by s2(2)(b) of the Broadcasting Act 1981 [4] if no reasonable authority could have acted in the way that the IBA acted.

1   *Attorney-General, ex rel McWhirter v Independent Broadcasting Authority* [1973] 1 QB 629.
2   Television Act 1964 s3: '(1) It shall be the duty of the authority to satisfy themselves that, so far as possible, the programmes broadcast by the authority comply with the following requirements, that is to say - (a) that nothing is included in the programme which offends against good taste or decency or is likely to encourage or incite to crime or lead to disorder or be offensive to public feeling . . .'.
3   *R v Independent Broadcasting Authority, ex p Whitehouse* (1985) Times, 4 April.

4   Section 2(2)(b) of the 1981 Act provided that it was the duty of the IBA to ensure that the programmes broadcast by it in each area mentioned a proper balance in their subject matter. See *Wilson v Independent Broadcasting Authority (No 2)* (OH), 1988 SLT.

Broadcasting and International Obligations

1.18   The Secretary of State may by order direct the BBC, ITC, the Welsh Authority, Radio Authority and the Broadcasting Standards Council to carry out any functions enabling the government to give effect to any international obligations of the United Kingdom. An order is subject to annulment by resolution of either House of Parliament (s188). Two European instruments which may provide the subject matter for such an order are the 1989 European Community Directive 'Television without Frontiers' and the European Convention on Transfrontier Television.

The 1989 European Directive 'Television Without Frontiers'

1.19   The regulation of broadcasting originated prior to, and clearly took no account of, the existence of the European Economic Community (EEC) or the opportunities made available by new communications technology. The pursuit of a protectionist broadcasting policy by individual member states could be incompatable with the freedom of information exchange laid down by Art 10 of the European Convention on Human Rights [1], and the EEC Treaty. The main aims of the Treaty include 'the abolition, as between member states, of obstacles to freedom of movement for services' [2] and 'the establishment of a common market' for all services [3]. The member states 'shall abstain from any measure which could jeopardise the attainment of the [Treaty's] objectives' [4]. As stated by the European Court of Justice in various judgments, broadcasting is a service under Art 59 of the Treaty which, in effect, eliminates restrictions on trans-border services [5].

1   Article 10(1) guarantees the right to impart information and ideas, to receive them and to disseminate them, in each case regardless of frontiers. Article 10(2) enumerates the permissible grounds for restriction of the rights guaranteed by Art 10(1), adding that these restrictions must be 'prescribed by law' and 'necessary in a democratic society'.
2   Articles 3(c), 7 and 59 - 66.
3   Article 2.
4   Article 5(2).
5   Article 59 abolishes 'all restrictions on freedom to provide services within the Community . . . in respect of nationals of member states who are established in a state of the Community other than that of the person for whom the services are provided.'

The Directive's Effect

1.20   The Directive will have co-ordinated certain broadcasting laws, regulations and administrative provisions of member states by 3 October 1991. This takes the form of rules constituting the minimum required to guarantee freedom of transmission. Consequently, member states are free to require television broadcasters in their jurisdiction to establish stricter rules in the areas covered by the Directive (Art 3). The Directive provides for television advertising, sponsorship, the protection of minors, the right of reply and promotion of distribution and production of television programmes. It takes account of the technological changes in broadcasting systems so that 'television broadcasting' means the initial transmission by wire or over the air, including that by satellite, in unencoded or encoded form, of television programmes intended for reception by the public.

1.21 Article 4 of the Directive requires member states to ensure that 'where practicable . . . broadcasters reserve for European works [1] . . . a majority proportion of their transmission time.' Designed to limit programme imports from the United States, it is a compromise because the United Kingdom had favoured no EEC restrictions on imported programmes while France and Italy sought a more demanding requirement [2]. Article 5 requires member states to ensure that broadcasters reserve at least 10% of their transmission time (which is restricted as in Art 4) or programming budget for European works created by independent producers. The Directive's rules on the placing of advertising mainly accord with United Kingdom practice, but television films can only be interrupted after a period of 45 minutes for the first 90 minutes of transmission. Member states must institute a procedure for the prior examination of broadcasts, which may exist within the broadcasting bodies. Broadcasts likely, because of their nature or time of transmission to 'seriously impair the physical, mental or moral development of minors' are prohibited (Art 22) [3]. A 'right of reply' is provided by Art 23 when a person's 'legitimate interests, in particular reputation . . . have been damaged by an assertion in a television programme.'

1 Article 6 defines 'European works' for the purposes of Arts 4 and 5 as including, in certain circumstances, work originating from member states, European third states party to the European Convention on Transfrontier Television and other European third countries.

2 Article 4 does not cover news, sport, advertising, game shows or teletext services and is stricter than it may seem. However, the meeting of foreign ministers that gave final approval was reported as agreeing that Art 4's requirement is more of a 'political objective' than a legal obligation the breach of which would lead to prosecution in the European Court of Justice (*The Independent*, 4 October 1989).

3 This provision is particularly aimed at programmes involving pornography, gratuitous violence or incitement to hatred on grounds of race, sex, religion or nationality.

Reasons for the European Convention of Transfrontier Television [1]

1.22 The traditional European concept of television is being transformed by the use of a variety of new transmission techniques. Relatively limited technical capacity meant that the availability of television programme services in individual European states was restricted in number and generally could not be received by viewers in other states. The present widespread use of communications satellites and wide-band cable systems as well as services via direct broadcasting satellites (DBS) have changed the European broadcasting landscape. Services are of an increasingly transfrontier nature. The same service can, with the appropriate transmission and reception equipment, be received in many European states. Services via DBS and intermediate satellites will contribute to this trend. The development of technical capacity also means a major increase in the number of television channels available, resulting in a multiplication of programme services and competition between them. Concerns about the future of European transfrontier broadcasting focus on the risk of a market approach detrimentally affecting viewer choice, the public service concept of broadcasting (be it publicly or privately organised) and European cultural identities.

1 See 'Explanatory Report on the European Convention on Transfrontier Television' Directorate of Human Rights, Strasbourg, 1990, paras 21 - 25.

Main Features of the Convention

1.23 The Convention provides for common basic standards, confines the guarantee of freedom of reception and establishes the principle of non-restriction of the retransmission of television programme services conforming to those standards. A party to the Convention is free to apply stricter standards to services transmitted from within his jurisdiction [1]. However, those stricter rules do not entitle the restriction on retransmission on his territory of services complying with the Convention and transmitted from the jurisdiction of another party [2]. The standards in the Convention relate to the protection of certain industrial rights [3], the broadcasters' responsibility in maintaining programme standards [4], advertising [5] and sponsorship [6]. Although it emphasises the need for co-operation for the implementation of its provisions, provision is made for arbitrations [7]. The United Kingdom is a signatory to the Convention.

1   Article 28.
2   See art 4.
3   For example, Article 8 (right of reply).
4   Chapter II.
5   Chapter III.
6   Chapter IV.
7   Chapter IX.

The Directive and the Convention

1.24   The objectives of the 1989 Directive and the European Convention on Transfrontier television are different. The aim of the Directive is a common market for television, covering all transmissions, not only transfrontier broadcasts, within an individual member state. The Convention is limited to facilitating transfrontier transmission and retransmission of programmes. Another significant difference is that while the EEC legal system is empowered to enforce the Directive's provisions, the Convention lacks any juridical means to secure its enforcement. The minimum legal framework for European broadcasting provided by the two instruments seeks to develop the European audio-visual industry and satisfy the 'information society' viewer.

General Provisions in the 1990 Act

Offences by Bodies Corporate (s195)

1.25   When a body corporate is guilty of an offence under the 1990 Act and that offence is proved to have been committed with the consent or connivance of, or to be attributable to any neglect on the part of, a director, manager, secretary or other similar officer of the body corporate or a person who was purporting to act in such a capacity, then he, as well as the body corporate, is guilty of that offence and is liable to be proceeded against and punished accordingly (sub-s(1)) When the affairs of a body corporate are managed by its members, s195 applies in relation to a member's acts and defaults in connection with his functions of management as if he were a director of the body corporate (sub-s(2)).

Entry and Search of Premises (s196) [1]

1.26   If a justice of the peace is satisfied by information on oath that (a) there is reasonable ground for suspecting that an offence under ss13 [2], 82 [3] or 97 [4] has been or is being committed on any premises specified in the information and (b) evidence of the commission of the offence is to be found on those premises, he may grant a search warrant conferring power on any person(s) authorised in that behalf by the relevant authority to enter and search the specified premises at any time within one month from the date of the warrant (sub-s(1)). The 'relevant authority' in relation to an offence (a) under ss13 or 82, means the ITC and (b) under s97, means the Radio Authority (sub-s(2)). A person who intentionally obstructs a person in the exercise of powers conferred on him under s 196 is guilty of an offence and liable to a fine on summary conviction (sub-s(3)). A person who discloses, otherwise than for the purposes of legal proceedings or of a report of them, any information obtained by means of an exercise of powers conferred by s196 is guilty of an offence and liable on summary conviction to a fine or on conviction on indictment to two years' imprisonment and/or a fine (sub-s(14)).

1   In the application of s196 to Scotland and Northern Ireland respectively the reference to a justice of the peace is to be taken as a reference to the sheriff and a resident magistrate, respectively and any reference to information on oath is to be taken as a reference to evidence on oath and a complaint on oath, respectively (sub-ss(5), (6)).
2   See para 3.13.
3   See para 7.39.
4   See para 8.19.

Restriction on disclosure of information (s197)

1.27   No information with respect to a particular business which has been obtained under or by virtue of the 1990 Act must, so long as that business continues to be carried on, be disclosed without the consent of the person for the time being carrying on that business (sub-s(1)) [1]. A person who discloses any such information is guilty of an offence and liable on summary conviction to a fine or on conviction on indictment to two years' imprisonment and/or a fine (sub-s(6)).

1   This does not apply to information disclosed (a) to facilitate the performance of any functions of (i) the ITC, Welsh Authority or Radio Authority under the 1990 Act or the Control of Misleading Advertisements Regulations 1988 or (ii) the Director General of Fair Trading, the Secretary of State or the Monopolies and Mergers Commission under the Fair Trading Act 1973 (excluding Parts II, III and XI), the Restrictive Trade Practices Act 1976, the Competition Act 1980, the 1990 Act or the 1988 regulations, (b) in the investigation of a criminal offence or for the purposes of criminal proceedings or a report of them (c) for the purposes of any civil proceedings brought under or by virtue of the Fair Trading Act 1973 (excluding Part III), the Restrictive Trade Practices Act 1976, the 1990 Act, the 1988 regulations or a report of such proceedings or (d) in pursuance of any Community obligation (sub-s(2)). Section 197 does not (a) limit matters which may be included in, or made public as part of, a report under s186 or Sch 4 or (b) apply to information made public as part of the report (sub-s(3)). Nor does it apply to information obtained as mentioned in s196(4) (sub-s(4)). Section 133(1) of the Fair Trading Act 1973, s41(1) of the Restrictive Trade Practices Act 1976 and s19(1) of the Competition Act 1980 do not apply to information disclosed to facilitate the performance of any functions of the ITC, the Welsh Authority or the Radio Authority under the 1990 Act or the 1988 Regulations (sub-s(5)).

Financial Provisions (s198)

1.28   There must be paid out of money provided by Parliament any increase attributable to the 1990 Act in the sums payable out of money so provided under any other Act (sub-s(1)). Any sums received by the Secretary of State by virtue of the 1990 Act are to be paid into the Consolidated Fund (sub-s(2)).

Notices (s199)

1.29   Certain requirements must be met in relation to a notice required or unauthorised by or under the 1990 Act to be served on or given to any person other than the Secretary of State (sub-s(1)). The notice must be in writing and may be served or given to the person by (a) delivering it to him (b) leaving it at his proper address or (c) sending it by post to him at that address (sub-s(2)). It may, in the case of (a) a body corporate be served on or given to its secretary or clerk (b) a partnership, be served on or given to a partner or person having the control or management of its business (c) an unincorporated association other than a partnership, be served on or given to a member of its governing body (sub-s(3)). The proper address of a person is his last-known address except that where it is to be served on or given to (a) a body corporate, its secretary or clerk, it is the address of the body's registered or principal office or (b) a partnership, partner or person having control or management of a partnership business, it is the address of the principal office of the partnership [1]. A notice served by (a) the ITC under ss21, 41, 42 or 45 or (b) the Radio Authority under ss103, 109, 110, 111 or 120, must be published in the manner that that body considers appropriate and as soon as reasonably practicable after it is served (sub-s(5)).

1   In relation to a company registered, or a partnership carrying on business, outside the United Kingdom, the reference in para (a) or (b) to its principal office includes a reference to its principal office within the United Kingdom (if any) (s199(4)).

Regulations and Orders (s200)

1.30   The power of the Secretary of State to make regulations or an order under the 1990 Act is exercisable by statutory instrument (sub-s(1)). Such a regulation or order may make (a) different provision for different cases and (b) such supplemental, incidental, consequential or transitional provision or savings as he considers appropriate (sub-s(2)).

Chapter 2

TRANSMISSION AND TRANSITIONAL PROVISIONS

Privatisation of Terrestrial Broadcasting Transmission System

2.1   In its 1988 White Paper the Government stated that the ultra high frequency transmission networks owned and operated by the BBC and the IBA reached 99.4 % of UK households and stated its objective to move the system progressively into the private sector and separate transmission (ie service delivery) from service provision [1]. In a 1989 announcement [2] the then Home Secretary stated that the government's approach would be to set up two national transmission networks. The BBC, if it so wishes, is to retain its transmission responsibilities, including for the world service, until the expiry of its charter at the end of 1996 when the position would be reviewed with a view to privatisation. In the meantime, the BBC may only transmit its own services and may not compete for the transmission of new broadcasting or telecommunication services.

1   Cmnd 517, para 9.1.
2   HC Deb Vol 156, 4 July 1989, col 102w.

2.2   After the 1988 White Paper, the Government decided to privatise the IBA's transmission operation as soon as possible. Sections 127, 135 to 140 and Sch 9 provide for the IBA to be given powers, subject to the Secretary of State's approval, to make a scheme dividing its assets and liabilities between the ITC, Radio Authority and a shell company nominated by the Secretary of State for the purpose of having vested in it the IBA's transmission assets and liabilities. The shell company is the privatisation vehicle. Clearly, the new private transmission company is in a powerful market position and Schs 20 and 21 allow the Director General of Telecommunications to carry out its economic regulation under a Telecommunications Act 1984 licence. In his 1989 announcement the then Home Secretary [1] proposed that, because of the wide regional variations in the cost of transmission, there should be a uniform tariff for Channel 3 companies based on their share of the total Channel 3 income, taking account of subscription, sponsorship and net advertising revenue. This tariff will be laid down in the Telecommunications Act licence [2]. To enable this cross-subsidy system to work s66 [3] empowers the ITC to have conditions in a regional Channel 3 licence requiring licensees to go to a single transmission operator for a period specified by the Secretary of State.

1   HC Deb, Vol 156, 4 July 1989, col 103w.
2   House of Commons Committee, col 1404.
3   See paras 2.12 to 2.15

Transfer of IBA Undertakings

Division of Assets of IBA and its Dissolution (s127)

2.3   On such day as the Secretary of State may be order appoint as the transfer date, there must come into force a scheme made under Sch 9 providing for the division of the property, rights and liabilities of the IBA between (a) the ITC (b) the Radio Authority and (c) a company nominated for the purposes of s127 by the Secretary of State (sub-s(1)). He may, by order made before the transfer date, nominate any company formed and registered under the Companies Act 1985. It must be a company limited by shares which is wholly owned by the Crown (sub-s(2)). The IBA continues in existence after the transfer date until it is dissolved by order made by the Secretary of State (sub-s(3)). He is not to make the order unless he is satisfied, after consultation with the IBA, ITC, Radio Authority and nominated body, that nothing remains to be done by the IBA under or by virtue of Sch 9 (sub-s(6)). On the transfer date the chairman and members of the IBA cease to hold office. As from that date the IBA will (a) consist only of a chairman appointed by the Secretary of State and, if he thinks fit, such other person(s) as he may appoint as members of the IBA and (b) only have the functions which fall to be carried out by it under or by virtue of Sch 9 (sub-s(4)). If requested by the chairman, the ITC must furnish the IBA with any assistance required by it to carry out those functions (sub-s(5)).

Scheme Providing for Division of Assets of IBA

2.4   Schedule 9 provides for the making and modification of the transfer scheme (para 2), the scheme's content (para 3), the effect of the scheme (para 4), third parties affected by the scheme (para 5) and supplemental provisions of the scheme (para 6). Provision is also made for the vesting of the IBA's property after the scheme comes into force (para 7), certification by the Secretary of State as to vesting of property etc (para 8), the power of the Secretary of State to control division of the IBA's pension fund (para 9), the discharge by the IBA of contingent and other liabilities (para 10) and the final accounts and annual report of the IBA (para 11).

Provisions Relating to Nominated Company

Initial Government Holding in Nominated Company (s135)

2.5   As a consequence of the vesting in the nominated company, in accordance with the scheme made under Sch 9, of property, rights and liabilities of the IBA, that company must issue to the Secretary of State those securities of it as he may from time to time direct (sub-s(1)). He is not to give a direction once the company has ceased to be wholly owned by the Crown (sub-s(2)). Securities required to be issued in pursuance of s135 must be issued at such time(s) and on such terms as the Secretary of State may direct (sub-s(3)). The shares must be (a) of such nominal value as the Secretary of State may direct and (b) issued as fully paid and treated for the purposes of the Companies Act 1985 as if they had been paid up by virtue of the payment to the nominated company of their nominal value in cash (sub-s(4)). The Secretary of State is not to exercise any power conferred on him by s135, or dispose of any securities issued to him in pursuance of it, without Treasury consent (sub-s(5)). Any dividends or other sums received by him in right of or on the disposal of any securities acquired by virtue of s135 must be paid into the Consolidated Fund (sub-s(6)).

Exercise of Functions Through Nominees (s136)

2.6   The Secretary of State may, with Treasury consent, appoint any person to act as his nominee, or one of his nominees, for the purpose of s135 [1] (sub-s(1)). However, any issue of securities to a nominee in pursuance of s135 must be effected in accordance with such directions as may be given from time to time by the Secretary of State with Treasury consent (sub-s(1)). Any person holding securities as a nominee of the Secretary of State must hold and deal with them on the terms and in the manner as the Secretary of State may direct with Treasury consent (sub-s(2)).

1   See para 2.5.

Target Investment Limit for Government Shareholding in Nominated Company (s137)

2.7   As soon as he considers it expedient, and in any case not later than six months after the nominated company ceases to be wholly owned by the Crown, the Secretary of State must by order [1] fix a target investment limit in relation to the aggregate of the shares for the time being held in the company with legislative authority by a Crown Minister [2] or his nominee ('the Government shareholding') (sub-s(1)). This limit is to be expressed as a proportion of the voting rights exercisable in all circumstances at the company's general meetings ('the ordinary voting rights') (sub-s(2)). The first limit must be equal to the proportion of ordinary voting rights which is carried by the Government shareholding in the company when the order fixing the limit is made (sub-s(3)). The Secretary of State may by order fix a new limit but (a) the new limit must be lower than the one it replaces and (b) a s137 order may only be revoked by an order fixing a new limit (sub-s(4)). A Crown Minister must exercise (a) any legislative power to dispose of shares in the company and (b) his power to give directions to his nominee(s), so as to ensure that the Government shareholding does not carry a proportion of ordinary voting rights exceeding the current target investment limit (sub-s(5)). Notwithstanding this duty, a Crown Minister may take up, or direct any nominee of his to take up, any rights available to him, or the nominee, as a holder of securities of the company. However if, as a result, the target investment limit is exceeded, the Minister must comply with the requirement of not exceeding the limit as soon as is reasonably practicable (sub-s(6)).

1   A s137 order is subject to annulment in pursuance of a resolution of either House of Parliament (sub-s(8)).
2   References to a Crown Minister in s137 include references to the Treasury. For the purposes of s137 the temporary suspension of ordinary voting rights is disregarded.

Reserves of Nominated Body (s138)

2.8   If the Secretary of State so directs at any time before the nominated company ceases to be wholly owned by the Crown, such sums as specified in the direction must be carried by the company to a reserve ('the statutory reserve') (sub-s(1)). The statutory reserve may only be applied by the company in paying up unissued company shares to be allotted to company members as fully paid bonus shares (sub-s(2)). For the purpose of determining under s264(3)(d) of the Companies Act 1985 (restriction on distribution of assets) whether the company may make a distribution at any time, any amount standing to the credit of the statutory reserve is treated for the purposes of s264(3)(c) as if it were unrealised profits of the company (sub-s(3)).

Loans by Secretary of State to Nominated Company (s139)

2.9   As from the transfer date the Secretary of State may, with Treasury consent, make loans to the nominated company out of money provided by Parliament. A loan cannot be made under s139 when the company has ceased to be wholly owned by the Crown (sub-s(1)). The aggregate amount outstanding in respect of the principal of a loan must not exceed £20m or such greater sum not exceeding £100m as the Secretary of State may from time to time specify by order [1] with Treasury consent (sub-ss(2), (3)). The loan is to be repaid at times and rates the Secretary of State may direct with Treasury consent (sub-s(4)).

1   An order is not to be made unless a draft of it has been approved by a resolution of the House of Commons (sub-s(5)).

Temporary Restrictions on Borrowings of Nominated Body (s140)

2.10   The aggregate amount outstanding in respect of the principal of any relevant borrowing of the nominated company must not, when the company is wholly owned by the Crown, exceed the sum determined by the Secretary of State with Treasury consent (sub-s(1)). 'Relevant borrowing' means (a) loans to the company or subsidiary of it, other than loans made (i) by the subsidiary or (as the case may be) by the company and (ii) loans made under s139 [1] and (b) loans treated as being made to the company, including loans treated as being made by virtue of the issue of debentures under s135 (sub-s(2)).

1   See para 2.9.

Requirements Relating to Transmission and Distribution of Services (s66(1), (2))

2.11   During such period [1] as the Secretary of State may by order [2] specify, all Channel 3 services must be broadcast for general reception by a single person under arrangements made with him by the persons licensed to provide those services. Every Channel 3 licence must include conditions which appear to the ITC to be appropriate for securing that (a) the result and (b) the costs incurred in respect of the broadcasting of those services (taken as a whole) during that period in accordance with those arrangements are shared by those persons in a manner approved by the Secretary of State (sub-s(1)). A Channel 3 licence must include conditions appearing to the ITC to be appropriate for securing that the costs incurred in respect of the distribution [3] of Channel 3 services (taken as a whole) during such period as the Secretary of State may by order specify are shared by the persons licensed to provide those services in the manner approved by the Secretary of State (sub-s(2)).

1   The Secretary of State may by order provide for the period to be extended by a further specified period. Any conditions included in a Channel 3 licence must then have effect in relation to the extended period (sub-s(3)).
2   A s66 order is subject to annulment by resolution of either House of Parliament (sub-s(8)).
3   'Distribution' means the conveyance of Channel 3 services (by whatever means and whether directly or indirectly) to the broadcasting stations from which they are broadcast for general reception (sub-s(2)).

2.12   A Channel 3 licence or licence to provide Channel 4 or 5 must include such conditions as appear to the ITC to be appropriate for requiring the signals carrying the licensed service to attain high standards in terms of technical quality and reliability throughout so much of the relevant area as is for the time being reasonably practicable (s66(4)). Before imposing conditions the ITC must consult the Secretary of State as to how much of the relevant area is to be specified in the conditions as being where the required standards are to be attained (s66(5)). The 'relevant area' in relation to (a) a Channel 3 or Channel 5 licence, is the area for which the licensed service is to be provided and (b) the licence to provide Channel 4, is England, Scotland and Northern Ireland (s66(6)).

2.13   The Welsh Authority must do all it can to ensure that the signals carrying S4C attain high standards in terms of technical quality and reliability throughout so much of Wales as is for the time being practicable (s66(7)).

2.14   Section 66 seeks to achieve the maintenance of high technical transmission standards after privatisation. The ITC are empowered to impose conditions to the licences for Channel 3, 4 and 5 requiring licensees to maintain high standards of technical quality and reliability and to achieve a specified level of coverage of their franchise areas. It is then the responsibility of licensees to enter into transmission contracts to fulfil these requirements. The private transmission company will be required, under its Telecommunication Act licence, to provide the service required by the ITC licence conditions [1]. The transmission company must, because of its contract with ITC licensees and its Telecommunication Act 1984 licence, provide a high quality service.

1   House of Commons Committee, col 1403.

Transitional Arrangements Relating to IBA's Broadcasting Services (In Outline)

2.15   Schedule 11 contains major provisions for the transitional arrangements for independent television and radio. Additional provision is found not only in s129 [1], but also s130 (variation of programme contracts to take account of the new transmission arrangements), s131 (supplementary provisions relating to the variation of programme contracts), s132 (disposal by IBA of DBS transmitting equipment etc) and s133 (functions exercisable by the IBA before the transfer date in connection with local sound broadcasting) which were mainly introduced at the House of Lords' committee stage [2] of the Broadcasting Bill. In particular, transitional arrangements for direct broadcasting by satellite (DBS) is provided for because the IBA was responsible for broadcasting not only ITV and Channel 4 but also the services for its DBS contractor, British Satellite Broadcasting (BSB). The Government decided that BSB continue as DBS contractors until the end of 1992, with the ITC standing in the place of the IBA, but then the former DBS contractors would become domestic satellite service licensees under s44. The intention is to place them on generally the same regulatory footing as non-domestic satellite services licensees such as Sky. The Government decided to sell the transmission equipment which transmits the signals from the earth to the satellite used by BSB to BSB. The transitional provisions allow for the privatisation of the IBA's terrestrial transmission system. In 1991 and 1992 the ITC inherits the IBA's responsibilities, including those in relation to transmission, for ITV and Channel 4. The ITC must, because it does not provide a transmission system, require ITV contractors to enter into a transmission contract with the new private transmission company for that period. A similar arrangement is made for Channel 4 and S4C. A similar duty is imposed on the Radio Authority in relation to independent local radio stations remaining as contractors. The IBA is permitted to sell, with the Secretary of State's approval, assets used or held by the IBA in connection with the transmission of local sound broadcasts at less than market value to radio companies

1   Section 129(1) gives effect to Sch 11, see para 2.16.
2   House of Lords Committee, cols 1508 - 1526.

2.16   Schedule 11 has effect (a) with respect to the provision by the ITC and Welsh Authority, during the period from the transfer date [1] until 31 December 1992 (the 'interim period') of television broadcasting services formerly provided by the IBA under the Broadcasting Act 1981 (b) for the purpose of the regulation by the ITC after that period's end of services provided in succession to the DBS services provided by it during that period and (c) in the case of local sound broadcasting services formerly provided by the IBA until the transfer date by the Radio Authority (i) with respect to their provision on and after that date by the Radio Authority and (ii) for the purpose of the regulation by the Authority on and after that date of services provided in succession to those services (s129(1)).
1   See para 2.3.

Television Broadcasting Services to be Provided by ITC

2.17   Part II of Sch 11 provides for the IBA's television broadcasting services to be provided by the ITC during the interim period [1] (para 1), programme contracts and programme contractors (para 2), Channel 4 (para 3), teletext services (para 4), DBS services (para 5), S4C (para 6), broadcasting of advertisements on S4C (para 7), financing of S4C during the interim period [1] (para 8), delivery of programmes by means of local delivery services (para 9), the Broadcasting Complaints Commission (para 10) and the Broadcasting Standards Council (para 10). Supplementary provisions are contained in para 12.
1   See para 2.16.

Replacement of DBS Contracts by Licences Under 1990 Act

2.18   Part III of Sch 11 provides for the replacement of a DBS programme contract by a domestic satellite licence (para 1), the power to require the licence holder to make additional payments under the Broadcasting Act 1981 (para 2) and the replacement of a DBS teletext contract by an additional services licence (para 3).

Sound Broadcasting Services to be Provided by the Radio Authority

2.19   Part IV of Sch 11 provides for certain local sound broadcasting services of the IBA to be provided by the Radio Authority as from the transfer date [1] (para 1), the preservation of certain local sound broadcasting contracts (para 2), the delivery of programmes by means of local delivery services (para 3), the Broadcasting Complaints Commission (para 4) and the Broadcasting Standards Council (para 5). Supplementary provisions are contained in para 6.
1   See para 2.3.

Replacement of Programme Contracts by Local Licences

2.20   Part V of Sch 11 provides for the replacement of certain contracts by local licences (para 1), the replacement by local licences of certain contracts for the provision of local sound broadcasts in localities in which such broadcasts were already provided (para 2), common provisions applying to licences granted in pursuance of paras 1 or 2 (para 3) and the saving for liabilities under terminated contracts (para 4).

2.21   Schedule 11's primary effect is that from the transfer date [1] until the end of 1992 responsibility for ITV and Channel 4 will rest with the ITC. It will also assume the IBA's contractual liabilities for the ITV contracts which terminate on 31 December 1992. Until that date the pre-1990 Act financial arrangements for Channel 4 and S4C will be unchanged. All pre-1990 Act independent radio contractors could become

licensees of the Radio Authority on a common changeover date but certain independent local radio contractors may complete their IBA contracts under the Radio Authority's supervision. The necessary provisions of the Broadcasting Act 1981 are preserved for this purpose.
1   See para 2.3.

Transfer of Cable Authority Undertakings

Vesting in ITC of Assets of Cable Authority and Dissolution of Authority (s 128)

2.22   On the transfer date [1] all the property, rights and liabilities to which the Cable Authority (the Authority) were entitled or subject immediately before that date [2] become property, rights and liabilities of the ITC (sub-s(1)). The Authority continues in existence after the transfer date until it is dissolved by order made by the Secretary of State (sub-s(2)). He is not to make the order unless he is satisfied, after consultation with the Authority and the ITC, that nothing remains to be done by the Authority under or by virtue of Sch 10 which supplements the provisions of s128 (sub-ss(1)(5)). On the transfer date the chairman and members of the Authority cease to hold office. As from that date the Authority shall (a) consists only of a chairman appointed by the Secretary of State and,if he thinks fit, such other person(s) as he may appoint members of the Authority and (b) only have the functions which fall to be carried out by it under or by virtue of Sch 10 (sub-s(3)). If requested by the chairman, the ITC must furnish the Authority with any assistance required by it to carry out those functions (sub-s(4)).
1   See para 2.3.
2   These include property, rights and liabilities which are not capable of being transferred by the Authority (sub-s(6)).

Supplementary Provisions Relating to Dissolution of Cable Authority (Sch 10)

2.23   Schedule 10 supplements the provisions of s128 [1] concerning the vesting in the ITC of the Cable Authority's assets and its dissolution. It contains provisions as to vesting of property etc of the Authority (paras 1 and 2), the transfer of employees (para 3) and the final accounts and annual reports of the Authority (para 4).
1   See para 2.22.

Transitional Arrangements Relating to Existing Cable Services

2.24   Schedule 12 has effect for the purpose of the regulation (a) by the ITC on and after the transfer date [1] of (i) diffusion services (within the meaning of Part I of the Cable and Broadcasting Act 1984) which immediately before that date, were authorised to be provided under Part I of the 1984 Act and (ii) services provided in succession to such services and (b) by the ITC or the Radio Authority on and after the transfer date of services provided in succession to restricted services (within the meaning of Part I of the 1984 Act) which, immediately before that date, were authorised to be provided under the 1984 Act (s134).
1   See para 2.3.

Licensing of Existing Cable Services

2.25   Part II of Sch 12 provides for prescribed diffusion services, in particular the continuation in force of existing licences (para 1), the replacement of cable licences by local delivery licences (para 2), the grant of new licences to provide existing services (para 3) and that cable licences are to be succeeded on their expiry by local delivery licences (para 4). Provision is made for other diffusion services, in particular the continuation in force of existing licences (para 5), the replacement of cable licences by local delivery licences (para 6), that certain licences are to cease to have effect (para 7), that certain unlicensed services are to be licensed as cable services or local delivery services (para 8) and when services fall partly within and partly outside franchise areas (para 9). Also provided for are the replacement of existing restricted services licences (para 10), requests made under Part II of Sch 12 (para 11) and the saving for liabilities under terminated licences (para 12).

Provisions Relating to Licences in Force Under or by Virtue of Sch 12

2.26   Part III of Sch 12 provides for the effect of relevant licences (para 1), general provisions about them (para 2), restrictions on the holding of certain relevant licences (para 3), the inclusion of broadcasts in licensed services (para 4), the inclusion of local material in prescribed diffusion services (para 5) and the revocation of licences (para 6). Supplementary provisions are contained in para 7.

2.27   Schedule 12 is based on the 1988 White Paper's [1] proposals for the transitional arrangements for broadband cable franchise holders, a parliamentary written answer concerning other categories of cable system [2] and amendments introduced in the House of Lords [3]. Broadband operators with a pre-1990 Act franchise may choose to retain their existing rights (to retail and deliver cable services) and obligations (to install cable) for the remainder of their licence period. Similar renewal provisions to those in s78 [4] apply to those broadband franchise holders who make this choice under Sch 12 and retain their status under the Cable and Broadcasting Act 1984. On renewal, they are granted a local delivery licence provided they meet the necessary criteria. Alternatively, they may opt to become 'technology-neutral' operators [5] in their franchise area. They forfeit their effective local retailing of services monopoly but, if the ITC agree, are permitted to retail a number of services if their system is available to other retailers. The government proposes a designation order be made under s72(1)(b) [6] that local delivery systems covering less than 1,000 homes will not be required to be licensed by the ITC. Consequently, SMATV [7] licences for systems covering less than 1,000 homes lapse. Unlicensed systems covering less than 1,000 homes continue in operation. Any system covering less than 1,000 homes, whether previously licensed by the Cable Authority or not, can carry BBC services, S4C, services regulated by the ITC and services from a Council of Europe or convention country.

1   Col 517, para 6.40.
2   HC Deb, Vol 168, 2 March 1990, cols 349 - 350w.
3   House of Lords Committee, cols 1526 - 1533.
4   See para 7.31.
5   For example, by using Multi-point Video Distribution Service (MVDS). See para 1.13.
6   See para 7.2.
7   Satellite master antenna television. See para 7.7.

SMATV Systems Licensed to Cover 1,000 Homes or More

2.28   If the SMATV systems fall wholly outside any cable franchise area [1], they are deemed to have a local delivery licence for five years which is renewable under s78 after three years. If they fall wholly or partly within a cable franchise area, they continue under their pre-1990 Act licence which the ITC may extend until it is satisfied that the broadband cable operator can offer an alternative service to the homes passed by the SMATV system.

1   An area covered by a prescribed diffusion service licence issued by the Cable Authority when the designation order becomes effective.

Unlicensed Systems Covering More than 1,000 Homes

2.29   If the systems carry only the four terrestrial channels, they continue to require no licence. Other unlicensed systems (including those that carried the IBA's DBS services) and not licensed as SMATV systems by the Cable Authority, if they fall wholly or partly in a cable franchise area are deemed to have a SMATV licence under the terms of the Cable and Broadcasting Act 1984 for five years. The ITC is empowered to extend the licence until it is satisfied that the broadband cable operator can offer an alternative service to the homes passed by the system. Unlicensed systems satisfying the same criteria which fall wholly outside cable franchise areas are deemed to have a local delivery licence.

Restricted Services

2.30   A restricted services licence granted under the Cable and Broadcasting Act 1984 ceases to have effect on the transfer date [1] . Their holders are to have the right to be granted by the ITC (or Radio Authority) a licensable programme service licence (or a licensable sound programme service licence) for their services.

1   See para 2.3.

CHAPTER 3

REGULATION BY ITC OF TELEVISION SERVICES GENERALLY

Establishment of ITC (s1)

3.1   The ITC was set up by the 1990 Act (sub-s(1)). It consists of a chairman and a deputy chairman, appointed as such, and between eight and ten other members (sub-s(2)). All appointments are made by the Secretary of State. Further provisions for the ITC's constitution and procedure are found in Sch 1. Some of the more relevant ones are mentioned here. It is within the ITC's capacity as a statutory corporation to do such things and enter into such transactions as are 'incidental or conducive' to the discharge of its functions under the 1990 Act (para 1(3)). A person is disqualified from being a member if he is a governor or employee of the BBC or is a member or employee of the Channel Four Television Corporation, Broadcasting Complaints Commission or Broadcasting Standards Council. Nor may the membership include more than one person who is either a member or an employee of the Welsh Authority. Three members, other than the chairman and deputy chairman, must be people who appear to the Secretary of State to be suited to make the interests of Scotland, Wales and Northern Ireland respectively their special care (para 2(1), (2), (3)). Appointments are made for a maximum period of five years (para 3(2)). ITC members are disqualified from sitting in the House of Commons and Northern Ireland Assembly (para 5). The public accountability of the ITC is demonstrated by the requirement that at the end of each financial year it must prepare a general report of its proceedings during that year and transmit it to the Secretary of State who must lay copies of it before Parliament. The report must include a report by the ITC on the extent to which holders of Channel 3 or Channel 5 licences have failed to comply with the conditions included in their licences to deliver service in pursuance of s 33(1)(a). So the ITC will publicly hold to account any Channel 3 or 5 licensee who fails to realise his programme promises. It must have attached to it the statement of accounts for the year, a copy of any report made by the auditors on that statement and include such information as the Secretary of State may direct (para 15(1), (2), (3)).

3.2   The appointment of ITC (and Radio Authority) members is an example of the exercise of delegated legislation. The first chairman of the ITC, which replaces the Cable Authority and IBA, is the former IBA chairman and this can be seen as an attempt to maintain continuity in the licensing and regulation of a rapidly developing industry in a new legal environment. ITC members require business expertise to deal with licence application, and, in particular, must have knowledge about business plans to decide whether programme proposals are viable. No mandatory provision is made in the 1990 Act for advisory councils, whereas under the Broadcasting Act 1981 the IBA had to appoint them. They gave advice on, for example, religious, advertising and medical matters. The ITC may appoint advisory councils (para 16 of Sch 1). The

Shadow ITC planned to set up viewer consultative committees in different parts of the country [1]. Also the 1990 Act provides for public consultation by the ITC on the award of Channel 3 and Channel 5 franchises. Programme Plans, with the applicants' names, must be published. The ITC must take into account any public views before deciding whether the programme quality threshold has been passed by an applicant. There is no requirement in the 1990 Act that the ITC (or Radio Authority) seek the Secretary of State's approval whenever it wishes to delegate its functions to its members or employees (para 6(2) of Schs 1 and 8). The borrowing powers of the ITC (and Radio Authority) are subject to the Secretary of State's approval (para 13 of Schs 1 and 8). Both bodies can fund working and capital expenditure borrowing requirements by advances from the Exchequer at Treasury rates. They are expected eventually to finance their expenditure in full from their licence fee income [2]. One essential difference between the ITC and the IBA is that whereas the IBA was, being a broadcaster, obliged to consider whether or not to broadcast material, the ITC is not obliged to determine what is included in a programme service, as it is a licensing and regulatory body.

1 House of Lords Committee, col 32.
2 House of Lords Committee, col 25.

Representation by ITC of Government and Other Interests in Broadcasting Matters (s70)

3.3 The functions of the ITC include representing, at the request of the Secretary of State (a) Her Majesty's government in the United Kingdom and (b) persons providing television programmes, on bodies concerned with the regulation (whether nationally or internationally) of matters relating to television broadcasting.

Assignment of Frequencies by the Secretary of State (s65)

3.4 The Secretary of State may assign by notice to the ITC, for the purpose of the provision of services licensed by it under the 1990 Act [1], such frequencies as he may determine. They must be taken to be assigned for the purpose only of being used for the provision of one or more of those services and used only in the area(s) specified by the Secretary of State when making the assignment (sub-s(1), (2)). He may revoke the assignment of any specified frequency whether or not it is for the time being one on which there is being provided a licensed service (sub-s(4)). The interests of the BBC will be taken into account by the Secretary of State before assigning frequencies to the ITC [2].

1 See paras 3.6 and 3.10.
2 House of Commons Committee, col 900.

Frequency Planning and Research and Development (s69)

3.5 The ITC may make arrangements for such work relating to frequency planning to be carried out as it considers appropriate in connection with the discharge of its functions (sub-s(1)). The work must be directed towards securing that the frequencies assigned to the ITC under the 1990 Act are used as efficiently as is reasonably practicable (sub-s(2)). The ITC may also (a) make arrangements for such research and development work to be carried out as it considers appropriate in connection with the discharge of its functions and (b) promote the carrying out by other persons of research and development work relating to television broadcasting (sub-s(3)). It must consult its licence holders as to the former arrangements (sub-s(4)). The ITC must ensure that, so far as is reasonably practicable, (a) any work carried out under any arrangement is done under the ITC's supervision by persons who are neither members nor employees of the

ITC and (b) any research and development work other than that relating to television broadcasting is to a substantial extent financed by persons other than the ITC (sub-s(5)).

ITC's Regulatory Function (s2(1))

3.6 The function of the ITC is to regulate the provision of (a) television programme services provided from places in the United Kingdom by persons other than the BBC and the Welsh Authority [1]; (b) additional services provided from places in the United Kingdom [2]; and (c) local delivery services [3] (s2(1)). The ITC is not responsible for the Welsh Fourth (S4C) Channel; hence there is the reference to the Welsh Authority.
1   See para 3.8 for meaning.
2   See para 4.152 for meaning.
3   See para 7.2 for meaning.

3.7 The regulation of these three categories of service involves the ITC in discharging a general duty [1] and duties specific to the particular services. Whereas the need for the regulation of television programme services and local delivery services seems clear, such a need may not be so obvious for additional services. Sections 48 - 55 are concerned with additional services provided on television broadcasting frequencies. These provisions permit the ITC to license those additional lines, which are unused by television broadcasting, to be utilised for an assortment of purposes. An example of their use are the teletext services on BBC and commercial television channels. Under the Cable and Broadcasting Act 1984 a licence was required for the provision of a visual service consisting of moving pictures which was regulated. Consequently, other services consisting, for example, of still pictures and text were only subject to the general regulation which applied to the medium of print, for example, the Obscene Publications Act 1959. Parliament recognised that there was growing concern over computer-produced pornographic bulletin boards [2]. The 1990 Act now provides that a computer service consisting of still pictures requires an ITC licence and ITC regulation. An unlicensed service could result in a s 13 prosecution [3], which can be brought for abuses of computerised transmission systems. Harmless services may be subject to exemption orders made by the Secretary of State under s 13(2) [3].
1   See para 3.6.
2   House of Commons Committee, col 222.
3   See para 3.13.

Meaning of Television Programme Service (s2(4) - (6), 43(1), 46(1))

3.8 A 'television programme service' has three meanings (s2(4)). First, it means a 'television broadcasting service' which is a service consisting in the broadcasting of television programmes for general reception in, or in any area in, the United Kingdom, including a domestic satellite service (s2(5)). A domestic satellite service is a television broadcasting service where the television programmes included in the service are transmitted by satellite from a place in the United Kingdom (a) on an allocated frequency and (b) for general reception in the United Kingdom (s43(1)). 'Allocated frequency' means a frequency allocated to the United Kingdom for broadcasting by satellite (s43(4)). An example would be the five channels originally awarded to British Satellite Broadcasting. Not included in the meaning of 'television broadcasting service' is any teletext service or any other service where the visual images broadcast in the service consist wholly or mainly of non-representational images, that is to say visual images which are neither still pictures nor comprised within sequences of visual images capable of being seen as moving pictures (s2(6)). Second, 'television programme service' means a 'non-domestic satellite service' [1]. Third it means a 'licensable programme service' [2].

1   See para 4.126 for meaning.
2   See para 4.138 for meaning.

3.9   The basic approach of the 1990 Act is to categorise the different types of commercial television services by regard to their means of delivery. A distinction is made between terrestrial broadcasting and satellite transmission, and both differ from licensable programme services delivered by cable or Multipoint Video Distribution Systems (MVDS) [1]. However, all these services will contain television programmes provided by the licensees or others, like independent producers. The 1990 Act makes no provision for the ITC or the government to create an industry training body, funded by a levy. This is essentially the responsibility of the programme-making companies. The 1990 Act does provide that an applicant for a Channel 3 or 5 licence must include in his application his proposals for training or retraining people employed or to be employed by him in programme making [2]. An applicant must also set out his proposals for providing a service which would comply with the requirement for a regional Channel 3 or national service [3]. The effect of s 33(1) is that the ITC can require that the programme promises made by the applicant together with the undertakings given as regards training and use of regional facilities be licence conditions.

1   See para 7.6.
2   Section 15(3)(d), see para 4.6.
3   Section 16(2)(3), see paras 4.13, 4.17.

ITC's Licensing Duty (s2(2))

3.10   The ITC must discharge its functions as respects the licensing of television programme services, additional services and local delivery services in the manner in which it considers is best calculated to ensure that (i) a wide range of services is available throughout the United Kingdom and (ii) the competition in the provision of such services and services connected with them is fair and effective (s2(2)(a). The duty to ensure fair and effective competition does not affect the discharge by the Director General of Fair Trading, the Secretary of State or the Monopolies and Mergers Commission of their functions in connection with competition (s2(3)). Specific requirements for particular services are set out later in the 1990 Act. The ITC duty to ensure fair and effective competition in the provision of licensed services extends to services connected with them. The section makes no reference to competition between licensees only, so the ITC can act should a non-licensee be affected by a licensee's anti-competitive practices. To facilitate the execution of its duty, the ITC can require, and subsequently enforce, licence conditions concerning abuses of a dominant market position. For example, a licence condition can prevent Channel 3 licensees abusing their domination of advertising on commercial television should they impose exclusive conditions on advertisers. Such a practice would hinder the development of Channels 3 and 5, as well as satellite services. The ITC duty is clearly not intended to exempt ITC-licensed services from the Fair Trading Act 1973 or the restrictive trade practices legislation. Nor does it replace the powers and duties of the Office of Fair Trading. It is a second order duty and allows for ITC scrutiny of the propriety of arrangements made between an independent producer and a television company. Each licence granted by the ITC is subject to the ITC exercising its duty and the fairness of two licences being granted to one holder is to be examined in the context of each individual licence.

3.11   The ITC does not have power to circumscribe intellectual property rights enjoyed by, for example, authors of literary, dramatic and musical works and their publishers as well as artistes, except in certain circumstances. This would be where the owners of the rights agree in writing and also where compliance of a court order is required. Such orders may be given by the Comptroller General of Patents and Trade Marks, the High Court, the Patent Court and the Copyright Tribunal set up by the Copyright, Designs and Patents Act 1988.

3.12   The ITC must also discharge its functions as respects the licensing of television programme services in the manner which it considers is best calculated to ensure the provision of such services which (taken as a whole) are of high quality and offer a wide range of programmes calculated to appeal to a variety of tastes and interests (s2(2)(b)). The ITC general duty in respect of the range and quality of television services applies to services taken as a whole. All services are not expected separately to meet these requirements. The ITC must discharge its licensing of television programmes in the manner that it, and not a government department, considers appropriate. This is in the tradition of governments keeping their distance from the licensers. In this respect 'one likes to get the government out of it and give responsibility to the [ITC] to set the standards as far as possible. This is the whole purpose of [the Broadcasting Bill]' [1]. The government considered it 'unnecessary and undesirable' to impose a public service remit on all ITC licensed services. A number of reasons can be given for this [2]. The public service remit of informing, entertaining and educating the public originated when the number of television (and radio) services were very limited. Dependence on availability of spectrum meant that it seemed reasonable to ensure, by somewhat detailed regulation, that each channel catered for a wide range of interests. Today television (and radio) services are burgeoning. Other channels must compete with the public service broadcasting required of BBC1 and 2 and Channel 4, whose remit is to appeal to a range of minority audiences. It can be argued that the television services are beginning to deliver the diversity of programming which originally depended on heavier regulation than that found in the 1990 Act. For example the Cable and Broadcasting Act 1984 did not impose a public service requirement and yet specialised cable and satellite services are developing so as to cater for such particular interests as sports and news. The policy of the 1990 Act is that with more television services available there is less need for a regulatory body to ensure that each is of public service broadcasting standard and that poor quality channels which do not attract an audience (and consequently advertising and sponsorship) be allowed to become economically unviable. Also ITC scheduling commitments should be kept at a realistic level [3].

1   Earl Ferrers, House of Lords Committee, col 17.
2   House of Lords Committee, col 19.
3   House of Lords Committee, col 88.

Prohibition on Providing Unlicensed Television Services (s13)

3.13   Any person who provides a relevant service without being authorised to do so by or under a licence under the 1990 Act is guilty of an offence. The relevant services are television programme services provided from places in the United Kingdom by persons other than the BBC and the Welsh Authority which fall within s2(1)(a) and additional services provided from places in the United Kingdom which fall within s2(1)(b)(sub-s(1)). The Secretary of State may, after consultation with the ITC, by order provide that an offence is not committed with respect to such services or descriptions of service as are specified in the order (sub-s(2)). The order is subject to annulment by a resolution of either House of Parliament (sub-s(6)). In England and

Wales no prosecution can be brought except by or with the consent of the Director of Public Prosecutions. In Northern Ireland it is the Director of Public Prosecutions for Northern Ireland (sub-s(4)). On conviction a fine may be imposed and there is no limit to that fine if the conviction is on indictment (sub-s(3)). Compliance with the prohibition on providing unlicensed television services can also be enforceable by civil proceedings by the Crown for an injunction, interdict or other appropriate relief (sub-s(5)). On occasion, a civil remedy may be a quick and effective measure to prevent an unlicensed service being provided.

General Provisions about Licenses

Overarching Duty of ITC (s3(3))

3.14   The ITC must (a) not grant a licence to provide a television programme service, additional service or local delivery service, unless it is satisfied that the applicant is a fit and proper person to hold it and (b) do all that it can to ensure that, if it ceases to be so satisfied in the case of any person holding a licence, that person does not remain the holder of the licence (s3(3)). The ITC is required to carefully scrutinise both applicants for, and holders of, licences for licensed services. The requirement that he be a 'fit and proper' person applies at the licensing stage and throughout the period that the licence is in force. The concept of a 'fit and proper' person is undefined in the 1990 Act and is to be determined by the ITC. The ITC is obliged to act in the public interest when determining whether to withhold a licence from unfit persons, despite the merits of their programme proposals and/or cash bid. The holding of an ITC licence does not relieve the holder of the requirements to hold a licence under s 1 of the Wireless Telegraphy Act 1949 or s 7 of the Telecommunications Act 1984 in connection with the provision of the licensed service (s3(8)).

Form, Scope, Duration, Variation and Transfer of a Licence (s3)

3.15   A licence granted by the ITC must be in writing and, unless the 1990 Act provides otherwise, continues in force for such period as is provided in relation to a licence of the kind in question by the relevant provisions in the Act (sub-s(1)). The duration of a Channel 3 licence is 10 years (s20(1)) and is 10 years for the Channel 4 licence beginning on 1 January 1993 (s24(4)), 10 years for a Channel 5 licence (s29(1)), 10 years for a domestic satellite service licence (s44(3)), 10 years for a non-domestic satellite service licence (s45(4)), 10 years for a licensable programme service (s47(3)) and 10 years for a licence to provide additional services on a frequency assigned by the Secretary of State under s65(1) or the period specified by the Secretary of State when the additional service is provided on a frequency notified to the ITC by the him under s48(1)(b) (s53(1)). A licence may be granted for the provision of such a service as is specified in the licence or for the provision of a service of such a description as is specified (sub-s(2)). The ITC may vary a licence by a notice served on the licence holder if (a) in the case of a variation of the period for which the licence is to continue in force, the licence holder consents or (b) in the case of any other variation, the licence holder had been given a reasonable opportunity of making representations to the ITC about the variation (sub-s(4)). Should the ITC wish to invoke its powers under s41 [1] to shorten a licence period, no consent of the licence holder is required, and licence conditions as to additional payments made in pursuance of ss 19(1) [2] and 52(1) [3] still apply (sub-s(5)). The ITC is given some discretion as to what constitutes a 'reasonable opportunity' to make representations about the variation. It may wish to raise a number of matters with a licence holder and for practical reasons there is no mention of a definite period in the 1990 Act. A licence granted to any person is not transferable to any other person without the previous consent in writing of the ITC (sub-s(6)). The ITC must not grant its consent unless it is satisfied that the proposed licence holder would be in a position to comply with the conditions included in the licence throughout the remainder of the period for which it is to be in force (sub-s(7)). Takeovers are as normal a risk of commercial life for companies holding ITC licences (except that for Channel 4) as they are for other commercial companies. Although it may be said that ITC licence holders should, in this respect, be no more protected than other companies, it would be bizarre if someone who would not have been granted a licence had he applied for it as being 'unfit' was able to obtain one simply by buying it from the licence holder. A takeover may occur when an entire company wishes to take over from the franchise holder. The new person must apply for ITC consent to the licence transfer. The ITC must be satisfied that the new person is 'fit and proper' and that his assertion to honour the conditions is credible. A takeover may also happen when there is a change in the controlling shareholder of a licence holder. In circumstances where there was a change in the persons having control over or interest in the licence holder such that the ITC believed the new controlling shareholder was not a fit and proper person to hold the licence, it could refuse its consent to the transfer under s5 [4] which imposes restrictions on the holding of ITC licences.

1   See para 4.112.
2   See para 4.31.
3   See para 4.165.
4   See paras 3.20 to 3.26.

General Licence Conditions (s4)

3.16   The basic principle underlying the terms of licences for a television programme service, additional services and local delivery services is that the licences may include such conditions as appear to the ITC to be appropriate having regard to any duties which are or may be imposed on it or on the licence holder by or under the 1990 Act (sub-s(1)(a), (b)). The ITC has power to impose these general licence conditions and a specific power to require licence holders to comply with its directions under s 4(2) [1]. Thus the 1990 Act provides a means whereby the ITC can enforce licence conditions. Examples of licence conditions required by the 1990 Act are to be found in ss 146(5) [2], 147(3) [3] and 156(5) [4].

1   See para 3.18.
2   See para 9.10.
3   See para 9.11.
4   See para 9.22.

3.17   A licence may also include conditions requiring the payment by the licence holder to the ITC (whether on the grant of the licence or at such times afterwards as may be determined by or under the licence or both) of a fee(s) (sub-s(1)(b)). These fees must be in accordance with a tariff from time to time fixed by the ITC. The amount of any fee which is to be paid by the licence holder of a particular class or description must be such as to represent what appears to the ITC to be the appropriate contribution of the licence holder towards meeting the sums which the ITC regards as necessary in order to discharge its duty under Sch 1, para 12(1)(sub-s(3)). This duty is to conduct its affairs as to ensure that its revenues are at least sufficient to enable it to meet its obligations and discharge its functions under the 1990 Act. The ITC tariff may specify different fees in relation to different cases and circumstances. The ITC must publish every tariff in the manner it considers appropriate (sub-s4).

3.18   A licence may also include conditions requiring the licence holder to provide the ITC with such information as it may require in exercising the functions assigned to it by or under the 1990 Act (sub-s(1)(c)). Likewise it may include conditions providing for such incidental and supplemental matters as appear to the ITC appropriate (sub-s(1)(d)). Apart from these general conditions, a licence may in particular include conditions requiring the licence holder (a) to comply with any direction given by the ITC as to such matters as are specified in the licence or are of a description so specified or (b) not to do or do such things as are specified in the licence or are of a description so specified (except to the extent that the ITC consents otherwise) (sub-s(2)). Finally, where the licence holder (a) is required by any condition imposed under the 1990 Act to provide the ITC with any information and (b) in purported compliance with that condition provides it with information which is 'false in a material particular' he is to be regarded for the purposes of ss 41 and 42 to have failed to comply with that condition (sub-s(5)). Such a failure means that the ITC has the general power to impose a financial penalty or shorten the licence period (s41). It can likewise revoke a Channel 3 or 5 licence (s42). Under the doctrine of vicarious liability, the breach of a licence condition by an employee of the licence holder is regarded as a breach by the licensee. There is no need for the 1990 Act to direct employers to bring any licence conditions to their employees' attention and ensure compliance.

Conditions Relating to Technical Standards

3.19   Apart from commercial pressures to attain high technical standards, s 66(4) [1] gives the ITC power to impose licence conditions about picture quality, coverage and reliability in the licences for Channel 3, 4 and 5 services. Section 66(7) [2] places an analogous duty on the Welsh Authority in relation to S4C. The 1990 Act does not provide the ITC with similar powers in relation to other television services.
1   See para 2.12.
2   See para 2.13.

Restrictions on the Holding of Licences (s5(1))

3.20   The ITC must do all that it can to ensure that (a) a person does not become or remain a licence holder if he is a 'disqualified person' in relation to that licence by virtue of Part II of Sch 2 and (b) any requirements imposed by or under Parts III - V of Sch 2 are complied with by or in relation to licence holders to whom these requirements apply (sub-s(1)). The provisions of Part II, as to who is a 'disqualified person', and Parts III - V of Sch 2 as to the requirements to be complied with by or in relation to licence holders restricting the holding of licences are examined later [1]. The diversity of media opportunities made possible by technological developments is likely to be frustrated should licences be held by few people. The ITC are to enforce the ownership rules set out in Sch 2.
1   See paras 10.13 to 10.23 and 10.24 to 10.53.

Enforcement Powers (s5(2))

3.21   Section 5(2) provides the means by which the ITC may carry out its duty to ensure compliance with the ownership rules in s 5(1). The ITC is given a discretion as to its use of the enforcement powers which can be employed across a spectrum of issues, from the comparatively small, like requiring a potential licensee who is only technically in breach of the ownership rules to make necessary changes under s 5(2)(c), to the big, like the issues involved in Channel 3 licences. The ITC is consequently not obliged to follow a particular process in enforcing the ownership rules each time it is required to act. To facilitate the discharge of its s 5(1) duty on licence ownership, the ITC may require the applicant for a licence to provide it with such information as it may reasonably require to determine (i) whether he is a 'disqualified person', (ii) whether any requirements imposed by Parts III - V of Sch 2 would preclude it from granting a licence to him, and (iii) if so, the steps to be taken by him, or in relation to him, so that the requirements are met (s5(2)(a)). To secure compliance with these requirements the ITC may make the grant of a licence conditional on the taking of any specified steps that appear to it necessary (sub-s(2)(c)). This provides a prospective licensee with the opportunity of remedying something that should be remedied when there is no bad faith. When the ITC determines that any condition imposed by it has not been satisfied, the effect is as if the person to whom the licence was awarded or granted had not made an application for it (sub-s(3)(b)). However the ITC may decide that it is more desirable to publish a notice proposing to grant a licence (or, if appropriate, a further licence) to provide the service (sub-s(4)). The power to require information enables the ITC to enquire into the real ownership of companies and satisfy itself on every material point on which it has a discretion to refuse a licence. It is the applicant's responsibility to satisfy the ITC, which can draw adverse conclusions if it is not satisfied. Should it not be able to ascertain the real purposes of, for example, a blind trust in favour of General Noriega's cat in Hong Kong which made use of Philippines company law [1], the ITC could refuse or revoke a licence on the 'fit and proper' person requirement in s 3(3) [2].

1   An example given in the House of Commons Committee, col 284.
2   See para 3.14.

3.22   The ITC may, to ensure compliance with the requirements imposed by Parts III - V of Sch 2, impose conditions in a licence enabling it to give the licence holder directions requiring him to take, or arrange for the taking of, any specified steps appearing to it to be required in the circumstances (sub-s(2)(e)).

Relevant Change (s5(7))

3.23   A body to which a licence has been awarded or granted may undergo a 'relevant change'. A 'body' means a body of persons whether incorporated or not and includes a partnership (s202(1)). A 'relevant change' means any change (a) affecting the nature or characteristics of the body or (b) in the persons having control over or interests in the body, being (in either case) a change which is such that if the ITC had to determine whether to award the licence to that body in the new circumstances of the case, it would be induced by the change to refrain from awarding the licence (sub-s(7)). Certainly a 'relevant change' would be when a body holding a licence becomes disqualified in relation to that licence by virtue of Part II of Sch 2 or any requirements imposed by or under Parts III - V of that Schedule are not complied with by it. What else constitutes a 'relevant change' may, in part, be determined by the ITC's overarching duty, first, to facilitate the provision of licensed services to ensure a wide range of them is available throughout the United Kingdom and fair and effective competition in the provision (s2(2)(a)) [1]. And, second, to ensure that the provision of television programme delivery services (taken as a whole) are of high quality and offer a wide range of programmes calculated to appeal to a variety of tastes and interests (s2(2)(b)) [2].

1   See para 3.10.
2   See para 3.12.

3.24   The ITC may revoke the award of a licence to a body where the 'relevant change' takes place after the award but before the grant of it (s5(2)(b)). Should it do this, the effect is as if the person to whom the licence was awarded had not made an application for it (s5(3)(a)). However, the ITC may decide that it is more desirable to publish a notice proposing to grant a licence (or, if appropriate, a further licence) to provide the service (s5(4)). It must adopt the latter course of action if a licence is revoked after it comes into force.

3.25   To facilitate the provisions on 'relevant change' the ITC must include in every licence conditions that it considers necessary or expedient to ensure that where (a) the licence holder is a body and (b) a 'relevant change' takes place after the grant of the licence the ITC may revoke the licence by a notice served on the licence holder. The revocation takes effect on a date specified in the notice (s5(5)). The ITC must give the licence holder a reasonable opportunity of making representations to it, about the matters complained of, before serving the notice (s5(6)).

3.26   A more particular power is given to the ITC where the licence holder is a body corporate. The ITC may impose licence conditions requiring the body corporate to give to it advance notice of proposals affecting (i) shareholdings in the body or (ii) the directors of the body, where such proposals are known to the body (s5(2)(d)).

General Provisions about Licensed Services

General Requirements as to Licensed Services [1] *(s6(1), (2), (3))*

3.27   The ITC must do all that it can to ensure that every licensed service complies with five requirements (sub-s(1)). The methods employed can range from the use of informal correspondence and discussions to formal licence conditions. The ITC has a number of methods of enforcing licence conditions [2] . The first requirement is that nothing is included in a programme which offends against good taste or decency or is likely to encourage or incite crime or to lead to disorder or to be offensive to public feeling (sub-s(1)(a)). These regulatory principles date back to the BBC Charter of 1927 and the Television Act 1954 which established the Independent Television system. Reproducing s 4(1)(a) of the Broadcasting Act 1981, it seeks to provide viewers with a minimum standard of programme content and 'catch those matters which might not be caught under the criminal law' [3]. If a programme has little or no merit the Broadcasting Standards Council can make or receive complaints and consider them in certain circumstances [4]. News given, (in whatever form) in programmes is to be presented with due accuracy and impartiality (sub-s(1)(b)). There is no requirements that all services licensed by the ITC (or Radio Authority) provide news, although news requirements for Channels 3, 4 and 5 are to be found in ss 25(2)(d) and 31(1). The need for every cable programme service, satellite channel or local radio station to devote time to news was seen to run counter to the government's desire to foster expansion and diversity in those areas [5]. Due impartiality is to be preserved on the part of the service provider as respects matters of political or industrial controversy or relating to current public policy (sub-s(1)(c)). In applying this requirement a series of programmes may be considered as a whole (sub-s(2)). It may be that the ITC will not regard programmes as part of a series when on the face of it '[they] are entirely unrelated and not linked in any way' [6]. The requirement for a code of practice on impartiality is laid down in s 6(3) [7]. Due responsibility is to be exercised with respect to the content of religious programmes and in particular they are not to involve (i) improper exploitation of any susceptibilities of viewers or (ii) abusive treatment of the religious views and beliefs of the those belonging to a particular religion or religious denomination (sub-s(1)(d)). The 1990 Act makes no reference to 'no editorialising' and no 'undue prominence' rules in religious broadcasting which are replaced by the above requirement. Finally, programmes must not include any technical device which, by using images of very brief duration or by any other means, exploit the possibility of conveying a message to, or otherwise influencing the minds of, viewers without their being aware or fully aware, of what has occurred (sub-s(1)(e)). The potential dangers of subliminal messages in programmes are recognised in this requirement.

1   Nothing in ss6 - 12 has effect in relation to any licensed service which is an additional service other than the teletext service referred to in s 49(2)(s6(8)).
2   See ss40 - 42. See paras 4.111 to 4.117.
3   Earl Ferrers, House of Lords Committee, col 360.
4   See para 9.19.
5   House of Lords Committee, col 364.
6   House of Commons Committee, col 418 (Mr Mellor, minister of state, Home Office).
7   See para 3.29.

Editorialising (s6(4))

3.28   The ITC must do all that it can to ensure that there are excluded from programmes all expressions of the views and opinions of the service provider on matters (other than the provision of programme services) which are of political or industrial controversy or relate to current public policy (s6(4)). This provision is intended to ensure that licensees do not present an equivalent of a newspaper editorial column. It is unnecessary to place this restriction on producers because they are subject to the impartiality rules [1], to the extent that should a producer breach the 'editorialising rule', the licensee for whom he works will be in breach of s6.

1   See paras 3.29 to 3.31.

Impartiality Code (s6(3)(7))

3.29   The ITC must (a) draw up, and from time to time review, a code giving guidance as to the rules to be observed in connection with the application of the s6(1)(c) requirement for due impartiality in relation to licensed services; and (b) do all that it can to ensure that code's provisions are observed in the provisions of licensed services. The ITC may make different provision in the code for different cases or circumstances (s6(3)). It must publish the code and every revision of it in the manner that it considers appropriate (s6(7)).

Subject Matter of Impartiality Code (s6(5), (6))

3.30   The rules in the code must, in particular, take account of the facts (a) that due impartiality should be preserved by the service provider as respects the major matters, within s6(1)(c), of political or industrial controversy or relating to current public policy as well as matters falling within that provision taken as a whole; and (b) the need to determine what constitutes a series of programmes for the purposes of s6(2) [1] (s6(5)). This impartiality provision is not designed merely to imply that programmes can be completely biased on some minor matters of political or industrial controversy or of current public policy. Its purpose is to make it clear that impartiality is not expected to be achieved over every nuance of these matters. For example, the crisis precipitated by Iraq's invasion of Kuwait in 1990 should be impartially handled. However, every statement on that crisis need not receive an equal and opposite rejoinder. It is for the ITC to determine what might be regarded as a major matter and set out guidelines in its code [2]. The rules in the code must, in addition, indicate, to the extent that the ITC considers appropriate, the following matters: what due impartiality does and does not require, either generally or in relation to particular circumstances (s6(6)(a)); the ways in which due impartiality may be achieved in connection with programmes of particular descriptions (s6(6)(b)); the period within which a programme should be included in a licensed service if its inclusion is intended to ensure that due impartiality is achieved for the purposes of s6(1)(c) [1] in connection with that programme and any programme previously included in that service taken together (s6(6)(c)). Here, the code is to indicate the timescale within which programmes must be included if impartiality is to be achieved over a series. In relation to an inclusion in a licensed service of a series of programmes which is of a description specified in the rules (i) the dates and times of the other programmes comprised in the series should be announced when the first programme is included in the service or (ii) if this is not practicable, advance notice should be given by other means of subsequent programmes so comprised which include material intended to ensure, or assist in ensuring, that due impartiality is achieved in connection with the series as a whole (s6(6)(d)). Here, the code is to indicate the means by which the audience is informed that impartiality will be achieved over a series rather than in a single programme. Section 6 requires that the rules in the code must, in particular, indicate that due impartiality does not require absolute neutrality on every issue or detachment from fundamental democratic principles. Although s6(5), (6) prescribes the subject matter of the code, it is for the ITC to determine how the subjects are covered, what wording is used, the strength of the coverage and the severity of the enforcement. The Welsh Authority must apply the code to programmes broadcast on S4C (s59(5)). The ITC must draw up and publish a code for licensable programme services. These services are subject to the lighter undue prominence test rather than the due impartiality requirement (s47(4)).

1   See para 3.27.
2   House of Lords, Third Reading, col 1144.

3.31   Broadly speaking, the requirement of impartiality has been in broadcasting legislation since 1954. The introduction, by the 1990 Act, of the subject matter to be covered by the impartiality code can be explained by the fact that whereas the IBA was both broadcaster and regulator, now the licensee is the broadcaster and the ITC the regulator. Consequently, the licensee should know the sorts of guidelines to which he is expected to adhere [1]. Critics of s6(5), (6) regard it as a serious interference with free speech whose vice is its uncertainty: 'It will be suspended over [the heads of the programme makers] like a sword of Damocles and undoubtedly referred to constantly by the management who are more timid than [them]' [2]. It may be noted that the BBC is not a licensing body and operates under a Royal Charter with the consent of Parliament. Decisions on impartiality matters rests with the BBC governors who perform a regulatory and a managerial role and they may be expected to take into account s6 [3].

1   House of Lords Report, col 421.
2   Lord Goodman, House of Lords, Third Reading, col 1151.
3   House of Lords Report, col 460, 461.

General Code for Programmes (s7)

3.32   The ITC must draw up, and from time to time review a code giving guidance as to (a) the rules to be observed with respect to the showing of violence, or the inclusion of sounds suggestive of violence, in programmes included in licensed services, particularly when large numbers of young children and young persons may be expected to be watching the programmes; (b) the rules to be observed with respect to the inclusion in such programmes of appeals for donations; and (c) such 'other matters' concerning standards and practice for such programmes as the ITC may consider suitable for inclusion in the code (sub-s1). In considering what 'other matters' ought to be included in the code the ITC must have special regard to programmes included in licensed services in circumstances such that large numbers of children and young persons may be expected to be watching the programmes (sub-s2). When drawing up or revising the code the ITC must take account of such international obligations of the United

Kingdom as the Secretary of State may notify to them (sub-s3). The ITC must not only publish the code and every revision of it in the manner it considers appropriate (sub-s4) but also do all it can to ensure that the provisions of the code are observed in the provision of licensed services (sub-s1). The phrase 'large numbers of children' was preferred to 'many children' as the latter may be interpreted as meaning only a few dozen. In that event, the generally accepted 9pm watershed for the point when programmes unsuitable for children may begin would have to be moved to a later time. The government considered that while broadcasters must take into account the impact of their programmes on children, parents also have a responsibility to circumscribe their childrens' viewing within reasonable hours [1]. More generally the ITC should take care not to cross the line from being a regulatory body to being a censor. Programme judgments are best left to programme makers who are accountable for their decisions in accordance with s6 [2].

1   House of Lords Committee, col 396.
2   House of Commons Committee, col 422.

General Provisions as to Advertisements (s8)

3.33   The ITC must do all that it can to ensure that, in relation to licensed services, the following rules are complied with: (a) a licensed service must not include (i) any advertisement which is inserted by or on behalf of any body whose objects are wholly or mainly of a political nature (ii) any advertisement which is directed towards any political end or (iii) any advertisement which has any relation to any industrial dispute (other than an advertisement of a public service nature inserted by, or on behalf of, a government department); (b) in the acceptance of advertisements for inclusion in a licensed service there must be no unreasonable discrimination either against or in favour of any particular advertiser; and (c) a licensed service must not, without the previous approval of the ITC, include a programme which is sponsored by any person whose business consists, wholly or mainly, in the manufacture or supply of a product, or in the provision of a service, which the licence holder is prohibited from advertising by virtue of any provision in s9 which requires an advertising and sponsorship code [1] (sub-s(1), (2)). The Secretary of State may, after consultation with the ITC, make regulations amending, repealing or adding to these rules. Such regulations require approval by a resolution of each House of Parliament (sub-s4). Section 8(2) does not prohibit the inclusion in a licensed service of a party political broadcast which complies with the rules (so far as applicable) made by the ITC for the purposes of s36 (s8(3)). Not surprisingly, the ITC must not act as an advertising agent [2] (s8(5)).

1   See paras 3.36 to 3.38.
2   See para 10.3, footnote 1.

3.34   The s8 prohibitions constitute an apparent blanket ban, and may in certain circumstances, operate unfairly [1]. 'Political' is undefined in the 1990 Act. The pre-1990 Act advice from the IBA was that the term covered any material that sought to secure a change in some aspect of public policy. Anything that attempts such a change inevitably impinges on political party purposes. The words in brackets in s8(2)(a)(iii) are intended to exempt public service advertisements from the general ban on advertisements relating to an industrial dispute and may allow, for example, the Department of Social Services to sponsor a television advertisement showing how social services claimants could receive payment during a postal strike. In the event of a rail strike, the government could place a public service announcement giving details of additional car parking or alternative travel arrangements but would be prevented from advertising their version of the dispute [2]. The government intended that the rules on sponsorship of programmes be liberalised, provided the sponsored programme did not become an extended advertisement. Also the ITC (and Radio Authority in s92(2)(c)) are given some discretion to permit sponsorship if it considers the product ban need not be extended to a sponsorship ban on the company making or supplying the product. The consequential ban remains when a whole class of product is banned from advertising by international convention. An example is cigarette advertising. However, if the ITC (or Radio Authority) place a ban on a product, it is for it to determine whether the consequential ban on sponsorship by the manufacturers or suppliers of the product should follow through. For example, a medical product supplied by a pharmaceutical company may be subject to an advertising ban. The ITC (or Radio Authority) may consider that a sponsorship ban on that company would be unjustified [3].

1   House of Commons Committee, col 428.
2   House of Lords Committee, col 400.
3   House of Lords Committee, col 404.

Religious Advertising

3.35   The removal of the Broadcasting Act 1981 ban on religious advertising is an example of the deregulation of religious broadcasting. However, religious programmes, which include advertisements, must not involve any improper exploitation of the audience or any abusive treatment of the religious views of others (s6(1)(d)) [1]. Appeals for money are dealt with under s7(1)(b) [2] which requires the ITC to draw up a code giving guidance on the rules to be observed in this connection. Should it be considered necessary by the Secretary of State to amend, repeal or add to the s8 rules on religious or other advertising, he may, subject to Parliament's approval, make changes to the rules [3].

1   See para 3.24.
2   See para 3.32.
3   See para 3.33.

Advertisements and Sponsorship Code (s9)

3.36   The ITC must draw up, and from time to time review, an advertising and sponsorship code. This is after consultation with (a) the Radio Authority; (b) every ITC licence holder except a local delivery services licence holder; (c) such bodies or persons appearing to the ITC to represent (i) viewers (ii) advertisers and (iii) professional organisations qualified to give advice in relation to the advertising of particular products, as the ITC think fit; and (d) such other bodies or persons who are concerned with standards of conduct as the ITC think fit (sub-s(1), (2)). The code must (i) govern standards and practice in advertising and in the sponsoring of programmes and (ii) prescribe the advertisements and methods of advertising or sponsorship to be prohibited, or to be prohibited in certain circumstances (sub-s1(a), (b)). The ITC may make different provision in the code for different kinds of licensed service (sub-s(1). In drawing up or revising the code it must take account of such relevant international obligations as the Secretary of State may notify it (sub-s(9)). It must publish the code and every revision of it in the manner it considers appropriate and do all that it can to ensure that the provisions of the code are observed in the provision of licensed services (s9(1)(b), (3)).

3.37   The 1990 Act avoids prescribing specific items for inclusion in the code because it was felt that, as a matter of principle, this was best left to the ITC's discretion [1]. However, s9 empowers the ITC to draw up different provisions for different kinds of licensed service. So it may be anticipated that the code will place tighter advertisement and sponsorship requirements on Channels 3, 4 and 5 than on cable and satellite services. The government expects the ITC, when drawing up a code on sponsorship for Channels 3, 4 and 5 to ensure that there is a clear separation of sponsored programmes and advertisements and that editorial control of sponsored programmes remains with the broadcasters [2]. The code can also be expected to address the way the provisions relating to political advertising found in s8 are implemented. Section 9(8) requires the ITC, in drawing up the code, to take account of the international obligations of the United Kingdom, which is subject to the EC Directive 'Television Without Frontiers' [3] and is a signatory to the Council of Europe convention on transfrontier television. Whereas the convention is limited to facilitating transfrontier transmission and retransmission of television programmes, the Directive is concerned with all transmissions, not only transfrontier transmission, within a single member state. The ITC must therefore take into account the provisions relating to advertising and sponsorship which are to be found in these two instruments. Channel 3 is a transfrontier programme as it can be received in Belgium and the Netherlands, and there is likely to be Irish or continental 'overspill' from Channel 5. Consequently both channels fall within the provisions of the Convention. Even if they do not, they fall within the provisions of the Directive which is not confined to transfrontier broadcasting and is drawn in similar terms as those found in the convention. For example, Art 11.3 of the Convention provides that nothing in advertising addressed to, or using children, should harm their interests or exploit their special susceptibilities. Article 14.1 provides that 'advertisements may . . . be inserted during programmes in such a way that the integrity and value of the programme and the rights of the right holders are not prejudiced.' Article 14.3 states 'Transmission of audio-visual works such as feature films and films made for television . . . provided their duration is more than 45 minutes, may be interrupted once for each complete period of 45 minutes. A further interruption is allowed if their duration is at least 20 minutes longer than two or more complete periods of 45 minutes.' Article 17.1 states that sponsored programmes 'shall be clearly identified as such by the appropriate credits at the beginning and/or end of the programme.' Editorial control is the concern of Art 17.2 which provides 'The content and scheduling of sponsored programmes may in no circumstances be influenced by the sponsor in such a way as to affect the responsibility and editorial influence of the broadcaster in respect of programmes.' Undue advertising is the concern of Art 17.3.

1   House of Commons Committee, col 435.
2   House of Lords Committee, col 404.

Compliance with Advertisements and Sponsorship Code and Further Requirements (s9)

3.38   The ITC may, in the discharge of its general responsibility for advertisements and methods of advertising and sponsorship, impose requirements as to advertisements or methods of advertising or sponsorship which go beyond the requirements imposed by the code (sub-s(5)). The methods of control exercisable by the ITC for the purpose of ensuring that the provisions of the code are complied with, and for the purpose of securing compliance with requirements which go beyond the requirements of the code, include a power to give directions to a licence holder with respect to (a) the classes and descriptions of advertisements and methods of advertising or sponsorship to be excluded, or to be excluded in particular circumstances or (b) the exclusion of a particular advertisement, or its exclusion in particular circumstances (sub-s(6)). Also, the ITC may give directions to persons holding any class of licences with respect to the times when advertisements are to be allowed (sub-s(7)). When giving directions the

ITC must take account of any international obligations of the United Kingdom as the Secretary of State may notify it (sub-s(9)). Section 9 directions may be either general or specific and qualified or unqualified. In particular, directions as to the times of advertisements may relate to (a) the maximum amount of time to be given to advertisements in any hour or other periods (b) the minimum interval which must elapse between any two periods given over to advertisements and the number of such periods to be allowed in any programme or in any hour or day, and (c) the exclusion of advertisements from a specified part of a licensed service. Such directions may make different provisions for different parts of the day, different days of the week, different types of programme or for other differing circumstances (sub-s(8)).

Government Control over Licensed Services (s10)

3.39   If it appears to him to be necessary or expedient to do so in connection with his functions, the Secretary of State or any other Crown Minister [1] may at any time by notice require the ITC to direct the holders of any licence specified in the notice to publish in their licensed service, at times specified in the notice, a specified announcement, with or without visual images of any picture, scene or object mentioned in the announcement (sub-s(1)). The ITC must comply with this notice and where the licence holder publishes the announcement he may announce that he is doing so in pursuance of a s10 direction (sub-s(1), (2)). The Secretary of State may also at any time by notice require the ITC to direct the holders of any licences specified in the notice to refrain from including in the programmes included in their licensed services any matter or classes of matter specified in the notice (sub-s(3)). The ITC must comply with the notice and where it has given the licence holder the direction, revoked the direction because the Secretary of State has revoked the notice or the notice has expired, the licence holder may publish in the licensed service an announcement of the giving or revocation of the direction or the expiration of the notice (sub-s(3), (4)). The 1990 Act provides that the s10 powers are in addition to any power specifically conferred on the Secretary of State elsewhere in the 1990 Act (sub-s(5)).

1   In relation to a licensed service provided from a place in Northern Ireland, the head of any Northern Ireland department may issue a notice (s10(6)).

3.40   Section 10(1) announcements can be used in cases of civil emergency, for example when water pollution and toxic gases are presenting a health hazard. It may be anticipated that a request, rather than a direction, will suffice to secure such announcements. The provision may also be used in a period of preparation for war when the government wishes to have an announcement made. A s10(3) direction relates to what may or may not be included in a programme. A similar wide and censorial power was part of the original licensing arrangement for the BBC in 1927 and has been part of the legislation relating to commercial television since 1954. Rarely used, the most recent example of a direction being made, under legislation pre-dating the 1990 Act was the 1988 prohibition on the broadcasting of direct statements by members of the Irish Republican Army. Previously, it had been used on only five occasions. Advocates of the existence of this power may say that a distinction is to be drawn between its existence and its exercise [1].

1   House of Commons Committee, col 475.

ITC Monitoring of Programmes (s11)

3.41   For the purpose of maintaining supervision over the programmes included in licensed services the ITC may make and use recordings of those programmes or any part of them (sub-s(1)). Also, a licence must include conditions requiring the licence holder (a) to retain, for a period not exceeding 90 days, a recording of every programme included in the licensed service (b) at the request of the ITC to produce to it any recording for examination or reproduction and (c) again at the request of the ITC, to produce to it any script or transcript of a programme included in the licensed service which he is able to produce to it (sub-s(2)). Section 11 facilitates the supervisory role of the ITC and the consideration of complaints by the Broadcasting Complaints Commission [1] and the Broadcasting Standards Council [2]. The ITC is not required to preview programmes included in licensed services (sub-s(3)). In the case of monitoring, by the Radio Authority, of programmes included in its licensed services the maximum period of retention is 42 days under s95 [3].

1   See para 9.8.
2   See para 9.19.
3   See para 8.41.

Audience Research (s12)

3.42   The ITC must make arrangements for (a) ascertaining (i) the state of public opinion concerning programmes included in a licensed service and (ii) any effects of those programmes on the attitudes or behaviour of viewers; and (b) the purpose of assisting it to perform its functions in connection with the programmes to be included in Channels 3, 4 and 5 for ascertaining the types of programme that members of the public would like to be included (sub-s(1)). These arrangements must (a) ensure that, so far as is reasonably practicable, any research in pursuance of them is undertaken by people who are neither members nor employees of the ITC and (b) include provision for full consideration by the ITC of the results of the research (sub-s(2)). The duty to commission research into the types of programmes which the public like to see is limited to assisting the ITC perform its statutory functions in relation to Channel 3, 4 and 5 programmes. The ITC has a power to make positive programme requirements for the three channels, but not, for example, for non-domestic satellite channels. Similarly the Radio Authority is not assisted by research into what people would like included in additional services which may only carry data transmissions. However, before it needs to take account of public demand when licensing national and local services so as to provide the diversity it is statutorily obliged to seek. Consequently, s96(1)(b) [1] only requires research as to programmes that the public like to hear for the purpose of licensing national and local radio services. Neither the ITC nor the Radio Authority is obliged to publish the results of any research.

1   See para 8.42.

CHAPTER 4

INDEPENDENT TELEVISION SERVICES

Channel 3

Establishment of Channel 3 (s14(1), (2), (5), (6), (7))

4.1   The ITC must do all that it can to ensure the provision of a nationwide system of television broadcasting services to be known as Channel 3 (s14(1)). Channel 3 is to be structured on a regional basis, with each of the services comprised within it ('Channel 3 services') being provided for such area in the United Kingdom as the ITC may determine in the case of that service (s14(2)). The area must not comprise or include the whole of either England or Scotland (s14(7)). A service provided for a particular area is a 'regional Channel 3 service' (s14(6)). If the ITC so determine, a Channel 3 service may be provided for two or more areas for which regional Channel 3 services are provided, but it may only be provided between particular times of the day (s14(5)). This Channel 3 service is a 'national Channel 3 service' (s14(6)).

4.2   This regulatory framework permits, but does not prescribe, that the ITC advertise for applicants for the 15 ITV franchises that existed before the 1990 Act came into effect. The chairman-designate of the ITC has indicated a preference for retaining the former ITV regions for Channel 3 [1]. However, the ITC must consider the regional map in the light of the 1990 Act's provision. The acknowledgment of a national Channel 3 service is in relation to the breakfast national service and national news service. It is not in relation to the mainstream of Channel 3 [2].

1   House of Lords Committee, col 425.
2   House of Commons Committee, col 496.

4.3   If it appears to the ITC appropriate, it may determine that a particular Channel 3 service must include the provision of different programmes for such (a) different parts of the area for which it is provided or (b) different communities living within that area, as it may determine (s14(3)). A 'programme' does not include an advertisement (s14(8)). The ITC may determine that a particular Channel 3 service be provided for a particular area only between certain times of the day or on certain days of the week (or both) (s14(4)).

4.4   The power to impose a sub-regional requirement allows the ITC to view Wales, for example, as a single entity. It is unlikely that it would wish to establish a Channel 3 region smaller than the whole of Wales as this may well be economically unviable. It would also not want to divide Wales between two larger regions unless this was thought to be the only way of providing a viable services for Wales. Almost certainty, given the regional ethos of Channel 3 as demonstrated in the regional programme requirements of s16(2) [1], Wales will form part of a complete regional service including the Bristol area [2]. Section 202 (1) provides that a 'programme' includes an advertisement

38

unless the context requires otherwise. In ss14, 15 and 16 a programme does not include an advertisement and this fact anticipates that the quality threshold requirements are meant to refer to programmes other than advertisements.

1   See para 4.13.
2   House of Lords Committee, col 425.

Licensing of Channel 3 Services

Proposal Notice (s15(1), (2))

4.5   When the ITC propose to grant a licence to provide a Channel 3 service, it must publish, in the manner that it considers appropriate, a notice. The notice must (a) state that it proposes to grant a Channel 3 licence (b) specify (i) if the service is to be a regional Channel 3 service, the area in the United Kingdom for which the service is to be provided, (ii) if the service is to include the provision of programmes mentioned in s14(3) [1], the different parts of that area or (as the case may be) the different communities living within it, for which the programmes [2] are to be provided (iii) if the service is to be provided as mentioned in s14(4) [3], the times of the day or the days of the week (or both) between or on which it is to be provided and (iv) if the service is to be a national Channel 3 service, the areas in the United Kingdom for which it is to be provided and the times of the day between which it is to be provided (c) invite applications for the licence and specify the closing date for applications and (d) specify the (i) application fee and (ii) percentage of qualifying revenue for each accounting period that would be payable by an applicant in pursuance of s19(1)(c) [4] if he were granted the licence (s15(1)). The ITC must publish with the proposal notice general guidance to the applicants which contains examples of the kinds of programme whose inclusion in the service proposed by them in their application under s15(3)(b) [5] would be likely to result in a finding by the ITC that the service would comply with the programme and other requirements specified in s16(2) [6] for a regional Channel 3 service or s16(3) [7] for a national Channel 3 service (as the case may be) (s15(2)). It may be anticipated that the illustrative guide to potential applicants will state that applicants are expected broadly to follow the range of programming on pre-1990 Act ITV [8].

1   See para 4.3.
2   In ss 14 and 15 'programme' does not include an advertisement (s14(8)).
3   See para 4.3.
4   See para 4.31.
5   See para 4.6.
6   See para 4.13.
7   See para 4.17.
8   House of Commons Committee, col 535.

Applications (s15(3) to (5)).

4.6   The written application must be accompanied by (a) the application fee (b) the applicant's proposals for providing a service that would comply with the regional programme and other requirements in s16(2) or the national programme and other requirements in s16(3) (as the case may be) [1] (c) the applicant's proposals for promoting the understanding and enjoyment by people who are (i) deaf or hard of hearing and (ii) blind or partially sighted, of the programmes to be included in his proposed service [2] (d) the applicant's proposals for training or retraining people employed or to be employed by him in order to help fit them for employment in, or in connection with, the programmes to be included in his proposed service, together with his proposals for encouraging the training or retraining of people employed or to be employed by people providing programmes for inclusion in that service [1] (e) if the application is for a licence to provide a regional Channel 3 service, the applicant's proposals as to the use, in connection with his proposed service of (i) offices and studios situated within the area for which that service is to be provided and (ii) the services of people employed (whether by him or someone else) within that area [1] (f) the applicant's cash bid for the licence (g) such information as the ITC may reasonably require as to the applicant's present financial position and his projected financial position during the period for which the licence would be in force [1] and (h) any other information which the ITC may reasonably require for the purpose of considering the application [1] (s15(3)). Any information to be furnished to the ITC must, if it so requires, be in the form or verified in the manner that it specifies (s15(4)).

1   Between receiving the application and before determining it, the ITC may require additional information from the applicant on this matter (s15(5)).

Cash Bid

4.7   The 'cash bid' is an offer to pay to the ITC a specified amount of money for the first complete calendar year falling within the period for which the licence is in force (being an amount which, as increased by the appropriate percentage, is also to be payable in respect of subsequent years falling wholly or partly within that period (s15(7))). Indexation makes the annual licence payments equal in real terms. It does away with uncertainty in formulating a cash bid and should prevent overbidding because of miscalculation of the role of inflation. The 1990 Act provides for the concept of competitive tender. There is no government-determined price for a Channel 3 (or Channel 5 or national commercial radio licence). Three policy reasons may be given for having a cash bid [1]. The presence of a cash bid for licences is a market test for its value. It does away with the pre-1990 Act system which would have required the ITC (or Radio Authority) to make sometimes fine value judgements on the quality of programming offered by applicants ready to pay a fixed licence price. The combination of market-based cash bids and ITC (or Radio Authority) determined percentages of additional payments under s19 (or s102) are more likely to reflect the licence value than the imposition of a revenue levy.

1   House of Lords Committee, col 909.

4.8   One feature of the application requirements is their general nature. For example, an applicant must indicate the extent to which he would seek to promote greater access to his programmes for people with hearing and sight disabilities. The 1990 Act does not specifically refer to the provision of an audio descriptive service for those with sight difficulties or the provision of sign language for the deaf. The nature of the technology associated with audio descriptive services, screen usage of sign language and the uncertainty about their demand led the government to conclude that it was not sensible to have the same kind of statutory provision for them as for subtitling services as found in s35 [1]. The expectations of the disabled were to be balanced against the right of licensees not to commit themselves to an additional financial commitment in circumstances of uncertainty. Should an applicant propose an audio descriptive service, the ITC may exercise its power under s48(3)(c) to reserve spare capacity within signals for services which are ancillary to programmes included in the service and allocate it for an audio descriptive service.

1   House of Lords Report, col 215.

Publication of Application (s15(6))

4.9   The ITC must, as soon as reasonably practicable after the closing date for applications, publish in the manner it considers appropriate (a) the following matters

(i) the name of every applicant (ii) his proposals under s15(3)(b) for providing a service that would comply with the regional or national programme and other requirements in s16(2) [1] or (3) [2] (as the case may be) and (iii) any other information connected with his applications as the ITC consider appropriate and (b) a notice (i) inviting representations to be made to it with respect to the above last two published matters and (ii) specifying the manner in which, and the time by which, any representations are to be made (s15(6)).

1   See para 4.13.
2   See para 4.17.

4.10   The 1990 Act seeks public participation in the application process for Channel 3 (and 5) licences. This helps the ITC ascertain whether the regional programme requirements have been satisfied. The discretion given to the ITC enables it not to publish commercially confidential information supplied by applicants.

Consideration of Applications (s16(1))

4.11   The ITC must not proceed to consider whether to award an applicant the licence on the basis of his cash bid in accordance with s17 [1] unless it appears to it that (a) his proposed service would comply with either the regional or the national and other programme requirements specified in s16(2) [2] or (3) [3] (as the case may be) and (b) he would be able to maintain that service throughout the period for which the licence would be in force (s16(1)).

1   See paras 4.20 to 4.27.
2   See para 4.13.
3   See para 4.17.

4.12   Applicants for a Channel 3 (and Channel 5 by virtue of s29(1)) licence must pass a quality threshold before the ITC considers them eligible to bid. The quality hurdle presented by s16(2) or (3) (as the case may be) consists of a requirement for news, high-quality programmes, regional programmes, religious programmes and children's programmes and programmes catering for a wide variety of different interests. In the normal course of events, and in the absence of exceptional circumstances [1], the eligible applicant who submits the highest cash bid is awarded the licence. The Broadcasting Bill provided for a security requirement, or performance bond. This was to provide a financial incentive for licensees to comply with their service proposals. The requirement was removed from the Bill because it might place an unnecessary financial burden on licensees and so be counter-productive to its original purpose [2]. No security requirement is imposed by the 1990 Act on Channels 3 and 5 and national radio licences. Should the licensees fail to provide the promised service, a penalty amounting to 7% of the qualifying revenue of his actual or estimated last complete accounting period can now be imposed (ss18, 29 and 101). Failure to keep to their programming and other proposals, which are incorporated into their licences as conditions under s33 (1) and s106 (1) attracts the range of sanctions in ss40 - 42 for Channels 3 and 5 licensees (and ss109 - 111 for national licensees). These provisions are intended to act as the sword of Damocles to ensure that licensees keep to their programme proposals and include the possibility of imposing financial penalties of up to 3% of qualifying revenue for the first breach of a licence condition and up to 5% for a subsequent breach. Should the ITC consider the amount of the cash bid raises doubts as to the applicant's ability to satisfy the programme requirement, it can refuse to proceed with his application. Therefore, the applicant's business plan is of crucial importance because money spent on the bid cannot be used on programme proposals.

1   See paras 4.20, 4.21.
2   House of Lords Committee, col 900.

Regional Programme and other Requirements (s16(2))

4.13   Where a regional Channel 3 service is to be provided, the programme requirements are that (a) a sufficient amount of time is given in the programmes [1] to news and current affairs programmes which (in each case) are of high quality and each with both national and international matters, and that news programmes are broadcast at intervals throughout the period for which the services is provided and, in particular, at peak viewing times (b) a sufficient amount of time is given to programmes (other than news and current affairs programmes) which are of high quality (c) a sufficient amount of time is given (i) to a suitable range of regional programmes (including news programmes) which are of particular interest to people living within the area for which the service is provided and (ii) if the service is to include the provision of programmes mentioned in s14(3) [2], to a suitable range of programmes for each of the different parts of that area or (as the case may be) for each of the different communities living within it, being in each case a range of programmes (including news programmes) which are of particular interest to persons living within the relevant part of that area or (as the case may be) the relevant community, and that news programmes are of high quality (d) a suitable proportion of the above regional programmes are made within the area for which the service is to be provided (e) a sufficient amount of time is given to religious programmes and programmes are calculated to appeal to a wide variety of tastes and interests (f) (taken as a whole) the programmes are calculated to appeal to a whole variety of tastes and interests (g) a proper proportion of the matter included in programmes is of European origin and (h) in each year not less than 25% of the total amount of time allocated to the broadcasting of 'qualifying programmes' is allocated to a range and diversity of 'independent productions' [3] (s16(2)). 'Qalifying programmes and 'independent productions' are programmes of the description specified in an order by the Secretary of State (s16(5)). He may by order substitute a different percentage for the time allocated to independent productions (s16(6)). Before making either order he must consult with the ITC and no order is to be made unless a draft of it has been approved by a resolution of each House of Parliament (s16(7)).

1   In s 16 'programme' does not include an advertisement (s16(8)).
2   See para 4.3.
3   The range is to be interpreted in terms of cost of acquisition and types of programme involved (s16(5)).

4.14   The general thrust of broadcasting legislation since the beginning of commercial television has been to set out in primary legislation broad requirements about he range and quality of standards and to allow the regulatory bodies to interpret them in practical terms. The 1990 Act continues this traditional approach. Those wishing to be awarded a Channel 3 (or 5) licence must satisfy the ITC on many points and s16(2) may be regarded not so much as a shopping list of specific items of limited meaning but as a list of items that enables the licensee and not the legislator to determine the precise programme mix on Channel 3 (or 5) [1]. Under the 1990 Act the ITC is not required to involve itself in its licensees' programme scheduling. Generally, Channel 3 (and 5) licensees are responsible for their own schedules, except in the case of news bulletins which are required throughout the day and at peak times. Whether a regional Channel 3 service is to be provided for the whole of Scotland or an area the greater part of which is Scotland, the provisions on Gaelic programmes in s184 [2] are to be included in the s16(2) requirements (s184(1)). More generally, the ITC must do all it can to ensure that a suitable proportion of programmes included in Channel 3 (as well as Channel 4 and 5) (taken as a whole) are schools programmes (s34).

1   House of Lords Committee, col 935.
2   See para 5.25.

4.15 The provisions on regional programmes and their being made in the region reflect the importance of the regional integrity of Channel 3. Together with the requirement that an applicant must state under s15(3)(e) what regional facilities he would use, they are not found in previous legislation but similar conditions were found in IBA contracts. The 25% requirement for independent productions may facilitate the growth of regional production facilities. Under s2(2)(a)(ii) [1] the ITC has the duty of ensuring fair and effective competition in the provision of licensed services and services connected with them. As the ITC can deal with anti-competitive practices, it can intervene should competition be frustrated by undue collusion between independent production companies and licence holders. The Director General of Fair Trading can investigate and the Secretary of State for Trade and Industry can intervene to protect the public interest when monopolies or mergers lead to a company having more than 25% of any market, including that of independent production. General competition legislation also provides against anti-competitive practices. Independent production should be spread across a range of programming and that range should be interpreted in terms of cost and type of programming [2]. The background policy is that the example of the pre-1990 Act Channel 4 in establishing and maintaining an independent sector producing programmes for both the United Kingdom and other markets should be developed so as to avoid an introverted duopoly of terrestrial channels in the United Kingdom. The 25% provision makes, or should make, it easier than before for a non-television company, for example a film company, to provide facilities and make programmes for television.

1   See para 3.10.
2   House of Commons Committee, cols 660, 661.

4.16 The regulatory tradition of religious broadcasting is that it should strike a balance between taking account of long standing Christian beliefs and recognising a wide range of other beliefs. Before the 1990 Act religious programmes accounted for only 2% of ITV's programming output. This percentage is unlikely to increase on Channels 3 and 5 when many more channels offer potential outlets for religious programmes [1].

1   House of Lords Committee, col 981.

National Programme and other Requirements (s16(3))

4.17 Where a national Channel 3 service is to be provided the programme and other requirements that must be met are those requirements (if any) specified in s16(2) [1] which the ITC determine to be appropriate having regard to the nature of the service (s16(3)).

1   See para 4.13.

4.18 The basic philosophy of the 1990 Act is to permit the ITC to interpret the requirements on the programme range, quality and standards required. The 1990 Act seeks to balance giving it too wide a discretion, which may result in failure to provide the minimum requirements expected of commercial television, with imposing too detailed a specification of the requirements, which may constrict the development of television broadcasting [1]. One incentive for attractive programming is that advertisers are concerned about the fact that in the five years before the 1990 Act the number of television owning homes tuned into Channel 3 at peak viewing times fell from 21% to 16%.

1   House of Commons Committee, col 640.

Other Considerations Relating to Programme Requirements (s16(4))

4.19   In deciding whether an applicant's proposed service would comply with the regional or national and other requirements specified in s16(2) [1] or (3) [2] (as the case may be) the ITC must take into account any representations made to it in pursuance of s15(6)(b) [3] when it published a post application notice inviting the public's views on the applications (s16(4)). The ITC must have regard to the international obligations of the United Kingdom, notified to it by the Secretary of State, when applying the requirement in s16(2)(g) [4] that a proper proportion of the matter included in programmes is of European origin (s16(4)). One example is Art 4 of European directive 'Television Without Frontiers' which requires co-ordination of the laws of member states by not later than 3 October 1991. Article 4 requires member states to ensure 'where practicable . . . broadcasters reserve for European works . . . a majority proportion of their transmission time'. This requirement is more onerous than it may seem as it does not cover news, sport, game shows, advertising or teletext services. However, the meeting of foreign ministers that gave final approval was reported as agreeing that this requirement should be regarded more as a 'political objective' than a legal obligation, the non-respect of which would lead to proceedings in the European Court of Justice [5].

1   See para 4.13.
2   See para 4.17.
3   See para 4.13.
4   See para 4.9.
5   *The Independent*, 4 October 1989.

Award of Channel 3 Licence (s17(1), (3), (4))

4.20   The general principle is that the ITC must, after considering all the cash bids submitted by the applicants for a Channel 3 licence who have satisfied the ITC as required by s16(1) [1], award it to the applicant who submitted the highest bid (s17(1)). However, the ITC may disregard this requirement and award the licence to an applicant who has not submitted the highest bid if it appears to it that there are 'exceptional circumstances' which make it appropriate for it to award the licence to him (s17(3)). Although the 1990 Act does not define 'exceptional circumstances', it does provide an example. The ITC may regard 'exceptional circumstances' exist when it appears to it that (a) the quality of a proposed service is exceptionally high and (b) the quality of that service is substantially higher than the quality of the service proposed (i) by the applicant who has submitted the highest cash bid or (ii) in a case falling within s17(2) [2], each of the applicants who have submitted equal highest bids. Where it appears to the ITC, in the context of the licence, that circumstances are to be regarded as 'exceptional circumstances', they may be so regarded despite the fact that similar circumstances have been so regarded by it in the context of another licences (s17(4)).

1   See para 4.11.
2   See para 4.22.

4.21   Whenever the 1990 Act confers a licensing function on the ITC it is to be exercised in accordance with the overarching obligation in s2(2)(b) [1] that it discharge its functions as respects the licensing of television programme services in the manner it considers is best calculated to ensure the provision of services which (taken as a whole) are of high quality and offer a wide range of programmes calculated to appeal to a variety of tastes and interests. This requirement is especially relevant when the 1990 Act confers a discretion on the ITC, as it does as regards 'exceptional circumstances'. The wide meaning that can be applied to this phrase facilitates the exercise of a discretion in relation to matters other than quality. The other occasion when the ITC is not to grant the licence to the highest bidder who has passed the s16(1)[2] quality threshold is when this is not in the public interest because of its source of funds [3].

1   See para 3.10.
2   See para 4.11.
3   See para 4.23.

Identical Cash Bids (s17(2))

4.22   When two or more applicants for a particular licence have submitted cash bids specifying an identical amount which is higher than the amount of any other cash bid submitted, then the ITC must invite those applicants to submit further cash bids in respect of that licence. However, the ITC may propose to exercise their power under s17(3) [1] and award the licence to an applicant because it appears to it that there are exceptional circumstances which make this appropriate (s17(2)).

1   See para 4.20.

The Public Interest (s17)(5), (6), (7), (10), (14))

4.23   Channel 3 licences should not be awarded to an applicant if this is contrary to the public interest. Accordingly, if it appears to the ITC, in the case of the applicant to whom it would otherwise award the licence, that there are grounds for suspecting that any 'relevant source of funds' is such that it would not be in the public interest for the licence to be awarded to him, it must (a) refer his application to the Secretary of State, together with (i) a copy of all documents submitted to it by the applicant and (ii) a summary of its deliberations on the application and (b) not award the licence to him unless the Secretary of State has given his approval (s17(5)). On such a reference the Secretary of State may only refuse to give his approval if he is satisfied that any 'relevant source of funds' is such that it would not be in the public interest to award the licence to him (s17(6)). A 'relevant source of funds' is any source of funds to which an applicant might (directly or indirectly) have recourse for the purpose of (a) paying any additional payments in respect of the licence under s19(1) [1] or (b) otherwise financing the provision of the proposed service (s17(7)). When the ITC are precluded from awarding the licence to an applicant because his relevant source of funds is such that to do so would not be in the public interest, the effect is as if he had not made an application for the licence unless the ITC decides that it would be more desirable to publish a fresh notice under s15(1) [2] proposing to grant the licence and again invite applications for it (s17(10), (14)).

1   See para 4.31.
2   See para 4.5.

Non-Compliance With Parts III - V of Schedule 2 (s17(8), (9))

4.24   In a case where a requirement imposed by or under Parts III - V of Sch 2 and mentioned in s5(1)(b) [1] precludes the ITC from awarding a licence to the applicant to whom it would otherwise have awarded it, the ITC must award the licence in accordance with rules made by it for regulating the award of licences in such cases. These rules may provide for the awarding of licences by reference to orders of preference notified to the ITC by applicants at the time of making their applications (s17(8)). Any rules must be published by the ITC in the manner that it considers appropriate, but they do not come into force unless they have been approved by the Secretary of State (s17(9)).

1   See para 3.20.

Grant of Licence (s17(11), (12), (13))

4.25   When the ITC have awarded a Channel 3 licence to any person, it must, as soon as is reasonably practicable (a) publish certain matters in the manner that it considers appropriate and (b) grant the licence to that person (s17(11)). The matters to be published are (a) the name of the person to whom the licence has been awarded and the amount of his cash bid (b) the name of every other applicant in whose case it appeared to the ITC that his proposed service would comply with the regional or national programme and other requirements specified in s16(2)[1] or (3)[2] (as the case may be) (c) when the licence has, by virtue of s17(3)[3] been awarded, in exceptional circumstances, to an applicant who has not submitted the highest cash bid, the ITC's reasons for the licence having been so awarded and (d) such other information as the ITC consider appropriate (s17(12)). When a licence has been awarded to a person on the revocation of an earlier grant of it, the ITC must publish the above matters (bar the names of applicants who satisfied the programme and other requirements of s16(2) or (3)) and an indication of the circumstances in which the licence has been awarded (s17(13)).
1   See para 4.13.
2   See para 4.17.
3   See para 4.20.

4.26   When a licence has been revoked and subsequently granted to another applicant in the original competition there is no point in publishing again the names of the applicants who passed the quality threshold in that competition. There is a need to publish the reasons for revoking the licence and granting it to another person.

4.27   Every year the ITC must make a report which is laid before Parliament on the extent to which holders of Channel 3 (or Channel 5) licences have failed to comply with the conditions included in their licences in pursuance of s33(1)(a)[1] (para 15(2) of Sch 1). This requires the ITC to comment on how licensees have fulfilled their undertakings given during the application process and included in their licences as conditions. The ITC may make a general comment and refer to particular licensees when it considers that it is appropriate so to do.
1   See para 4.77.

Failure to Begin Providing Channel 3 Service (s18(1), (2))

4.28   If, after a Channel 3 licence has been granted to a person but before the licence has come into force (a) he indicates to the ITC that he does not intend to provide the service or (b) the ITC for any other reason have reasonable grounds for believing that he will not provide the service once the licence has come into force, then (i) the ITC must serve on him a notice revoking the licence as from the time the notice is served on him and (ii) the effect is as if he had made no application for the licence unless the ITC consider it desirable to publish a fresh notice, under s15(1)[1], proposing to grant the licence and inviting applications (s18(1)). When the ITC reasonably believe that he will not begin to provide the Channel 3 service, it must serve on the person awarded the licence, a notice stating the ground for its belief after giving him a reasonably opportunity of making representations to it about the matter complained of (s18(2)).
1   See para 4.5.

4.29   Section 18 empowers the ITC to revoke the licence and impose a financial penalty of 7% of the qualifying revenue of his actual or estimated last complete accounting period if the licence holder fails to provide the promised service.

Financial Penalties on Licence Revocation (s18(3), (4), (5))

4.30   When the ITC revoke a Channel 3 licence under s18 or under any other provision in the 1990 Act, it must serve on the licence holder a notice requiring him to pay to it, within a specified period, a financial penalty of the 'prescribed amount' (s18(3)). Where (i) the licence is revoked under s18 or (ii) the first complete accounting period of the licence holder falling within the period for which the licence is in force has not yet ended, the 'prescribed amount' is 7% of the amount which the ITC estimate would have been the qualifying revenue for that accounting period. In any other case, it is 7% of the qualifying revenue for the last complete accounting period of the licence holder so falling. The 'qualifying revenue' is determined in accordance with s19(2) - (6) (s18(4)). Any financial penalty payable by a body is recoverable by the ITC from that body whether or not the licence is in force and from any person who controls that body (s18(5)).

Additional Payments for Channel 3 Licences (s19(1), (9), (10))

4.31   In addition to any fees required to be paid because of a licence condition under s4(1)(b) [1], a Channel 3 licence must include conditions requiring the licence holder to pay to the ITC additional payments that fall into three categories. The first, in respect of the first complete calender year falling within the period for which the licence is in force, is the amount specified in his cash bid (s19(1)(a)). The second, in respect of each subsequent year falling wholly or partly within that period, is the amount so specified as increased by the 'appropriate percentage' (s19(1)(b)). The 'appropriate percentage', in any relevant year, is the percentage corresponding to the percentage increase between (a) the retail prices index published by the Central Statistical Office of the Chancellor of the Exchequer for the November in the year preceding the first complete calender year falling within the period for which the licence is in force and (b) the retail prices index for the November in the year preceding the relevant year (s19(10)). The third category of payment, in respect of each accounting period of his falling within the period referred to in the first category, is an amount representing such percentage of the qualifying revenue for that accounting period as was specified in the notice proposing to grant a Channel 3 licence under s15(1)(d)(ii) [2] (s19(1)(c)). When (a) the first complete accounting period of the licence holder falling within the licence period in the first category of additional payments does not begin at the same time as the period or (b) the last complete accounting period of his falling within that licence period does not end with that period, an accounting period in the third category includes that part of the accounting period preceding the first complete accounting period, or (as the case may be) following the last complete accounting period as falls within the licence period. Other references to accounting periods are to be similarly construed (s19(9)).

1   See para 3.17.
2   See para 4.5.

Three Categories of Additional Payment

4.32   The above provisions relate to payment by licence holders of the cash lump sum that they bid for the first calender year of the licence (the first category). That sum is increased in the second and subsequent years of the licence by a percentage representing the year-on-year rise in the retail prices index for the November preceding that year (the second category). They must also make payments based on their qualifying revenue for the licence period (the third category).

Qualifying Revenue (s19(2), (6))

4.33   For the purposes of the above third category of additional payment, the 'qualifying revenue' for any accounting period of the licence holder consists of all payments received or to be received by him or by any connected person [1] (a) in consideration of inclusion in the Channel 3 service in that period of advertisements or other programmes or (b) in respect of charges made in that period for the reception of programmes included in that service (s19(2)). The purpose is to include all relevant income, not only from advertisements but also sponsorship. If, in any accounting period of the licence holder, he or any connected person [1] derives, in relation to any programme included in the Channel 3 service, any financial benefit (whether direct or indirect) from payments made by any person, by way of sponsorship, for the purpose of defraying or contributing towards costs incurred or to be incurred in connection with that programme, the qualifying revenue for that accounting period shall be taken for the purposes of the third category to include the amount of the financial benefit derived by the licence holder or the connected person (s19(6)). Consequently, a licensee cannot reduce his qualifying revenue by arranging for all or part of it to be paid into an associated company.

1   See para 10.11.

Further Rules Apply to the Determination of 'Qualifying Revenue' (s19(3) - (5))

4.34   If, in connection with the inclusion of any advertisement or other programmes whose inclusion is paid for by payment falling with s19(2)(a) [1], payments are made to the licence holder or any connected person [2] to meet payments payable by the licence holder for the third category of additional payment, they are to be regarded as made in consideration of the inclusion of the programmes (s19(3)). When an advertisement is included under arrangements made between (a) the licence holder or any connected person and (b) a person acting as an advertising agent, the amount of any receipt by the licence holder or any connected person that represents a payment by the advertiser from which the advertising agent has deducted any amount by way of commission must be the amount of the payment by the advertiser after the deduction of the commission (s19(4)). However, if the amount deducted by way of commission exceeds 15% of the payment by the advertiser, the amount of the receipt is taken to be the amount of the payment less 15% (s19(5)). Part I of Sch 7 contains provisions relating to the ITC duty to publish a statement of principles for the computation of qualifying revenue (para 1) and disputes (para 2).

1   See para 4.33.
2   See para 10.11.

Additional Payment Licence Conditions (s19(7), (8))

4.35   A Channel 3 licence may include conditions (a) enabling the ITC to estimate before the beginning of an accounting period the amount due for that period because of the existence of the third category of additional payment in s19(1)(c) and (b) requiring the licence holder to pay the estimated amount by monthly instalments throughout that period (s19(7)). In particular, there may be conditions (a) authorising the ITC to revise any estimate on one or more occasions, and to adjust the instalments payable by the licence holder to take account of the revised estimated and (b) providing for the adjustment of any overpayment or underpayment (s19(8)).

Duration and Renewal of Channel 3 Licences

Duration of Channel 3 Licence (s20(1))

4.36   A Channel 3 licence continues in force for 10 years and may, subject to the provisions of s20, be renewed on one or more occasions for 10 years beginning with the date of renewal (s20(1)). The 10 year duration of the licence should give reasonable security for the licensee and continuity of service for the viewer. Although technological progress in the future, such as the possibility of digital picture transmission, may make the provisions of the 1990 Act obsolete, 'it would be rash and undesirable to build a regulatory structure now on the basis of technological developments that may or may not happen within a particular time' [1].

1   Mr Mellor, (minister of state, Home Office) House of Commons Committee, col 693.

Renewal of Channel 3 Licences (s20(2), (10))

4.37   An application for the renewal of a licence under s20 may be made by the licence holder not earlier than four years before the date on which it would otherwise cease to be in force and not later than the 'relevant date' (s20(2)). The 'relevant date' is the date which the ITC determine to be that by which it would need to publish a proposal notice under s15(1) [1] if it were to grant, as from the date on which that licence would expire if not renewed, a fresh licence to provide the Channel 3 service formerly provided under that licence (s20(10)).

1   See para 4.5.

4.38   The presumption of licence renewal will be displaced should the ITC consider the licensee's performance has not been satisfactory and is unlikely to improve. The rationale for the renewal provisions in s20 is that after the competitive tender arrangements initially restructure the commercial television service, any insufficiencies will be dealt with by the normal market mechanisms of takeovers [1]. However, the ITC has the same rights on takeovers as it has to prevent an unsuitable applicant being initially awarded a licence. The ITC is under a duty not to grant a licence to anyone unless satisfied that he is a fit and proper person to hold it (s3(3)). There need be no threat to the continuity of the service if the ITC lacks confidence in the person making a successful takeover of the licence holder because it can request a neighbouring licensee to provide a temporary service under s22 [2]. Section 5(5) [3] imposes strict licence conditions enabling the ITC to revoke the licence if any relevant change occurs.

1   House of Commons Committee, col 698.
2   See para 4.47.
3   See para 3.25.

Formal Renewal (s20(3), (8))

4.39   When the ITC have granted a person's application under s20 it must formally renew his licence not later then the relevant date [1], or if that is not practicable, as soon after that date as is reasonably practicable. It must not renew his licence until it has notified him of (a) the amount determined and (b) any percentage specified by it under s20(6) [2], and he has, within the period specified in the notification, notified it that he consents to the licence being renewed on those terms (s20(8)). Provided the application is made before the relevant date, the ITC may postpone consideration of it for as long as it thinks appropriate having regard to s20(8) (s20(3)). If the renewal process were to extend unreasonably beyond the relevant date there is the possibility that, if it were to

come to naught, the ITC would not have sufficient time to award the licence to a new applicant before the licence period commenced.
1   See para 4.37.
2   See para 4.41.

Refusal to Renew Licence (s20(4), (5))

4.40   There is a presumption that a Channel 3 licence will be renewed. When an application for renewal of a licence has been duly made to the ITC, it may only refuse the application if (a) it is not satisfied that the applicant would, if his licence were renewed, provide a service which complied (i) with the conditions included in the licence in pursuance of s33(1) [1] requiring delivery of the promised service and (ii) with the regional or national programme or other requirements in s16(2) [2] or (3) [3] (as the case may be) or (b) it proposes to grant a fresh Channel 3 licence for the provision of a service which would differ from that provided by the applicant under his licence as respects either (i) the area for which it would be provided or (ii) the times of the day(s) of the week between or on which it would be provided, or both (s20(4)). The provisions safeguarding the public interest if there are grounds for suspecting that any 'relevant sources of funds' may be used by the applicant, and found in s17(5) - (7) [4], apply in relation to an applicant for the renewal of a licence (s20(5)).
1   See para 4.77.
2   See para 4.13.
3   See para 4.17.
4   See para 4.23.

Determination of Post Grant Payments (s20(6), (7))

4.41   On the grant of an application for licence renewal the ITC (a) must determine an amount which is to be payable to it by the applicant in respect of the first complete year falling within the period for which the licence is to be renewed and (b) may specify a different percentage from that specified in the notice proposing to grant a licence under s15(1)(d)(ii) [1] as the percentage of qualifying income for each accounting period of his that will be payable by him as the third category of additional payment in pursuance of s19(1)(c) [2] during the period for which the licence is to be renewed (s20(6)). The amount determined by the ITC above must be such as would, in its opinion, be payable to it as the first category of additional payment by virtue of s19(1)(a) [3] if it were granting a fresh licence to provide the Channel 3 service (s20(7)). Clearly, the provisions in s19 relating to licence payments apply equally to a renewed licence as to the original licence save in terms of the amounts of the payments.
1   See para 4.5.
2   See para 4.31.
3   See para 4.31.

Renewed Licence Conditions (s20(9))

4.42   The 1990 Act provides for three consequential effects on the conditions in a Channel 3 licence that has been renewed. Any conditions included in it concerning additional payments in pursuance of s19 have effect during the period for which the licence has been renewed (i) as if the amount determined by the ITC under s20(6)(a) [1] were an amount specified in a cash bid submitted by the licence holder and (ii) subject to any determination made under s20(6)(b) [2] (s20(9)(a)). Subject to this, s19 [3] has effect in relation to the period for which a Channel 3 licence has been renewed as it has effect in relation to the period for which it is originally in force (s20)(9)(b)). The reference in s42(4) [4] (which relates to the ITC's power to revoke a Channel 3 licence) to the end of the period for which a Channel 3 licence is to continue in force is to be construed as a reference to the end of the period for which it has been renewed (s20(9)(c)).

1   See para 4.41.
2   See para 4.41.
3   See paras 4.31 to 4.35.
4   See para 4.114.

Restrictions on Changes in Control over Channel 3 Licence Holders (s21)

4.43   Where (a) any change in the persons having control over (i) a body to which a Channel 3 licence has been awarded or transferred under the 1990 Act or (ii) an associated programme provider, takes place within the relevant period and (b) that change takes place without having previously been approved for the purposes of s21 by the ITC, then the ITC may, if the licence has not yet been granted, refuse to grant it to that body, or if it has already been granted, serve on that body a notice revoking it (s21(1)). The body is to be given a reasonable opportunity to make representations to the ITC about the complaint (s21(4)). An 'associated programme provider' is any body which is connected [1] to the body referred to in s21(1) and appears to the ITC to be, or to be likely to be, involved to any extent in the provision of programmes for inclusion in the Channel 3 service. The 'relevant period' is the period beginning with the date of the award of the licence and ending on the first anniversary of the date of its coming into force. Paragraph 3 in Part 1 of Sch 2 [2] has effect for the purposes of s21(1) as if a body to which a Channel 3 licence has been awarded but not yet granted were the holder of the licence (s21(2)).

1   See para 10.11.
2   See para 10.11.

4.44   The ITC must refuse, in two sets of circumstances, to approve for the purposes of s21 a change in the persons having control over (i) a body to which a Channel 3 licence has been awarded or transferred or (ii) an associated programme provider, taking place within the relevant period, and mentioned in s21(1)(a) [1]. First, if it appears to it that the change would be prejudicial to the provision under the licence, by that body, of a service which accords with the regional or national programme and other proposals submitted under s15(3)(b) [2] by it (or, as the case may be, by the person to whom the licence was originally awarded). Second, if it appears to it that the change would be prejudicial to the provision by Channel 3 of such a nationwide system of services as is mentioned in s14(1) [3]. The ITC may refuse to approve any change as is mentioned in s21(1)(a) [1] if, in circumstances other than the above two, it considers it appropriate to do so (s21(3)).

1   See para 4.43.
2   See para 4.6.
3   See para 4.1.

4.45   Section 21 provides a limited moratorium on takeovers involving a change in control of a body holding a Channel 3 (or Channel 5) licence. A body may be incorporated, unincorporated or a partnership (s202). The moratorium lasts for the first year of the licence period. Thereafter takeovers are regarded as an important market discipline [1] but are subject to overview by the ITC. The ITC can revoke the licence under s42 if it is not satisfied that the licence conditions are being honoured. Also s5(5) [2] may be utilised by the ITC.

1   House of Lords Committee, col 1017.
2   See para 3.25.

Refusal to Grant a Licence (s21(5))

4.46   When under s21(1) [1] the ITC refuse to grant a licence to any body, s17 [2] shall (subject to 17(14)) [3] have effect as if that body had not made an application for the licence (s21(5)). When under s21(1) [1] the ITC serve on any body a notice revoking its licence, the provisions of s42(6) [4] (on the taking of effect of the notice) and (7) [5] (on the delay of its notice taking effect) apply (s21(5)).

1   See para 4.36.
2   See paras 4.20 to 4.27.
3   See para 4.23.
4   See para 4.116.
5   See para 4.116.

Temporary Provision of Regional Channel 3 Service for Additional Area (s22)

4.47   Where it appears to the ITC that (a) (whether as a result of the revocation of an existing regional Channel 3 licence or for any other reason) there would be, in the case of a particular area determined under s14(2) [1], a temporary lack of any regional Channel 3 service licensed to be provided for that area, but (b) it would be reasonably practicable for the holder of a licence providing a regional Channel 3 service for any other area to provide his service for the above area as well, the ITC may invite that licence holder temporarily to provide his licensed service for that additional area (s22(1)). If that licence holder agrees to provide his licensed service, the ITC must authorise the provision of that service for the additional area during the period as it may determine, by means of a variation of the licence to that effect (s22(2)).

1   See para 4.1

Channel 4

Establishment of the Channel Four Television Corporation ('The Corporation') (s23))

4.48   The Corporation is set up by the 1990 Act (sub-s(1)). It consists of a chairman and a deputy chairman, appointed by the ITC, and between 11 and 13 other members (the actual number being determined from time to time by the ITC) (sub-s(2)). The other members consists of persons appointed by the ITC and ex-officio members of the Corporation, who are (a) the Corporation's chief executive and (b) other employees of the Corporation who are nominated by the Corporation's chief executive and chairman acting jointly (sub-s(3), (5)). All appointments made by the ITC require the approval of the Secretary of State and their total number of appointees must exceed the number of ex-officio members (sub-s(3)(4)). Further provisions for the Corporation's constitution and procedure are found in Sch 3. Some of the more relevant ones are mentioned here. It is within the Corporation's capacity as a statutory corporation to do such things and enter into such transactions as are 'incidental or conducive' to the discharge of its functions under the 1990 Act (para 1(3)). A person is disqualified from being a member if he is a governor or employee of the BBC or a member or employee of the ITC, Radio Authority, Broadcasting Complaints Commission or Broadcasting Standards Council (para 2(1)). Appointments are made for a maximum period of five years (para 3(2)). Corporation members are disqualified from sitting in the House of Commons and Northern Ireland Assembly (para 5). The public accountability of the Corporation is demonstrated by the requirement that at the end of each financial year it must prepare a general report of its proceedings during the year and transmit it to the Secretary of State who must lay copies of it before Parliament (para 13(1)). The report must have attached to it the statement of accounts for the year, any auditor's report on the statement, and such information as the Secretary of State may from time to time direct (para 13(2)).

4.49 Channel 4 is owned by the Channel 4 Corporation. The government retains the power to veto appointment by the ITC of members, which is envisaged as being used only in the remotest of circumstances and justified because the Corporation is a statutory body operating to a statutory programming remit [1].
1   House of Lords Committee, col 1028.

4.50 Before the 1990 Act, the Channel Four Television Company was primarily a commissioning, purchasing and editing body rather than a programme-making organisation [1]. A subsidiary of the IBA, it was funded out of subscriptions raised from the ITV companies. The IBA approved its schedules, broadcast its programmes and decided its income. The statutory remit of Channel 4 was to cater for tastes and interests not properly served elsewhere on ITV, to encourage innovation and experimentation in programming, and to devote a suitable proportion of its airtime to education programming. In a ministerial statement [2] on 13 June 1989 the government announced that it was not feasible for Channel 4 to become an independent commercial company competing with other broadcasters if, as it considered it essential, Channel 4 was to retain its remit. Acknowledging the difficulty in Channel 4 continuing to be owned by the ITC, who regulate its output, the government concluded that a public trust be set up, licensed by the ITC, to continue the provision of the services set out in its special remit. Certainly, the relationship between Channel 4 and the IBA was different to that which exists between Channel 4 and the ITC. Since the 1990 Act, the Corporation decides Channel 4 schedules, broadcasts its programmes and generally establishes the perimeters of its funding by selling its own advertising.
1   White Paper 'Broadcasting in the '90s: Competition, Choice and Quality' (Cmnd 517), (para 4.7).
2   House of Commons, Vol 154, col 712.

The Corporation's Provision of Channel 4 (s24)

4.51 The function of the Corporation is to secure the continued provision of the television broadcasting service known as Channel 4 (s24(1)). On 1 January 1993 the shares in the subsidiary company of the IBA [1], referred to in s12(2) of the Broadcasting Act 1981, and formed by the IBA to carry out activities involved in providing programmes for Channel 4, vest in the Corporation (s24(2)). Channel 4 is to be provided by the Corporation, under a licence granted to it by the ITC, for so much of England, Scotland and Northern Ireland as may from time to time be reasonably practicable (s24(3)). The licence continues in force for 10 years, beginning on 1 January 1993, and may be renewed by the ITC on one or more occasions for a period of 10 years beginning with the date of renewal (s24(4)).
1   The Channel Four Television Company.

4.52 Channel 4 is not expected to achieve total coverage of the United Kingdom because this would be disproportionately expensive [1]. Its provision is to be that which is 'reasonably practicable', as was the requirement in s2(1) of the Broadcasting Act 1981 that set up Channel 4.
1   House of Commons Committee, col 742.

Required Conditions in Channel 4 Licence (s25)

4.53   The licence granted to the Corporation by the ITC to provide Channel 4 for so much of England, Scotland and Northern Ireland as may be reasonably practicable must include such conditions as appear to the ITC to be appropriate for securing the requirements that (a) Channel 4 programmes [1] contain a suitable proportion of matter calculated to appeal to tastes and interests not generally catered for by Channel 3 and (b) innovation and experimentation in the form and content of those programmes is to be encouraged, and that generally Channel 4 is given a distinctive character of its own (sub-s(1)). The licence is also to contain such conditions as appear to the ITC to be appropriate for ensuring that Channel 4 complies with the requirements that (a) Channel 4 is provided as a public service for disseminating information, education and entertainment (b) Channel 4 programmes maintain (i) a high general standard in all respects (and, in particular, in respect of their content and quality) and (ii) a wide range in their subject matter, having regard both to the programmes as a whole but also to the days of the week on which, and the times of day at which, the programmes are broadcast (c) a suitable proportion of Channel 4 programmes are of an educational nature (d) a sufficient amount of time is given in Channel 4 programmes and current affairs programmes which are of high quality (e) a proper proportion of the matter included in Channel 4 programmes to news programmes is of European origin (when applying this requirement the ITC must have regard to the international obligations of the United Kingdom which may be notified to it by the Secretary of State (sub-s(3)) and (f) in each year not less than the 'prescribed percentage' of the total amount of time allocated to the broadcasting of 'qualifying programmes' on Channel 4 is allocated to the broadcasting of a range and diversity of 'independent productions' (sub-s(2)). The 'prescribed percentage' is not less that 25%. 'Qualifying programmes' and 'independent productions' have the same meaning as in s16(2)(h) [1] and the 'prescribed percentage' is the percentage for the time being specified in s16(2)(h). The reference to a range of independent productions is a reference to a range of those productions in terms of cost of acquisition as well as in terms of the types of programme involved (sub-s(4)). The licence granted by the ITC must also include conditions requiring the Corporation not to be involved in the making of programmes to be broadcast on Channel 4 except to the extent that the ITC may allow (sub-s(5)).

1   In s25 'programme' does not include an advertisement (sub-s(6)).
2   See para 4.13.

4.54   One of the reasons given for deregulating commercial television generally is that the public broadcasting service requirement is still imposed on BBC television and Channel 4 [1] and the government considers that education is still at the heart of the programming remit of Channel 4 [2]. Before the 1990 Act the Channel Four Television Company commissioned just over 25% of it programming from companies independent of a broadcaster [3], and the 25% requirement in the Act may be regarded as a means of catering for minority interests.

1   See s25(2)(a), para 4.53.
2   House of Commons Committee, col 755.
3   House of Commons Committee, col 751.

4.55   The 1990 Act does not require the ITC to set quotas on Channel 4 programmes to be made respectively in England, Scotland and Northern Ireland. It does provide the powers to implement the European Directive 'Television Without Frontiers' which must be achieved not later than 3 October 1991. Article 4 requires that member states ensure 'where practicable . . . broadcasters reserve for European works . . . a majority proportion of their transmission time' [1]. The requirement in the directive and the

European Convention on Transfrontier Television that there is to be a majority of European work where practicable is to be put into practice by the ITC and the Corporation. The directive requires that when a majority of European programming cannot be achieved, the average proportion of European work achieved by a state's broadcasters aggregated together should not fall below the 1988 level. The majority requirement, in fact, is achieved by the main television channels who have a record of 85% European production [2].

1   See para 1.21.
2   House of Commons Committee, col 752.

Corporation Deficits (s26(1) - (4))

4.56   Revenue deficits of the Corporation are to an extent funded by Channel 3 licensees. The ITC must, before 1 January 1993 and each subsequent year estimate [1] the (a) amount of the Corporation's qualifying revenue [2] for that year (b) amount of the total television revenues for that year (ie the aggregate of qualifying revenues of (i) all Channel 3 or Channel 5 licence holders (ii) the Welsh Authority and (iii) the Corporation itself and (c) Corporation's prescribed minimum income of 14% [3] of the total television revenues for that year (sub-s(1), (2)). If the aggregate of (a) the amount of the Corporation's qualifying revenue for that year as estimated by the ITC and (b) any amount which at the beginning of that year, is for the time being standing to the credit of the Corporation's reserve fund [4], is less than the amount of the Corporation's prescribed minimum income for that year as estimated by the ITC, the amount of the difference must be raised by the ITC by means of a levy imposed on all Channel 3 licence holders (sub-s(3)). The aggregate amount payable by virtue of any such levy must not exceed 2% [3] of the amount estimated by the ITC for the total television revenues. The amount to be paid by each of the Channel 3 licensees must be such proportion of that aggregate amount as is determined by the ITC in relation to him (and different proportions may be determined in relation to different persons) (sub-s(4)).

1   The ITC may, on one or more occasions, revise any estimate made by it (s26(1)).
2   Section 19(2) - (6) has effect, with any necessary modifications, for the purpose of enabling the ITC to estimate a person's qualifying revenue for any year for the purposes of s26 (s26(9)) - see paras 4.33, 4.34.
3   The Secretary of State may be order substitute a different percentage. No such order may be made before the end of 1997. An order requires approval by a resolution of each House of Parliament (s26(10), (11))
4   Mentioned in s27(3) - see para 4.61.

Channel 3 Licence Conditions (s26(5))

4.57   To secure payment of the levy every Channel 3 licence must include conditions (a) requiring the licence holder to pay to the ITC, by monthly instalments, the amount which he is liable to pay on the levy set by the ITC [1] (b) authorising the ITC to adjust the instalments payable by the licence holder to take account of any revised estimate it may make and (c) providing for the adjustment of any overpayment or underpayment (s26(5)).

1   Any amount received by the ITC must be transmitted by it to the Corporation (s26(6)).

Excess Repayments (s26(7), (8))

4.58   When in any year (a) the ITC have imposed a levy under s26 and (b) the aggregate amount forwarded by it to the Corporation exceeds the 'relevant amount' (ie when the aggregate of the Corporation's qualifying revenue for the year and the amount which, at the beginning of that year, stood to its credit in its reserve fund, mentioned

in s27(3) [1], is less than the Corporation's prescribed minimum income for that year), the ITC must notify the Corporation of that fact. The Corporation must, as soon as is reasonably practicable, repay to the ITC the excess (s26(7), (8)).
1   See para 4.61.

4.59   Section 26 seeks to ensure that the income of the Corporation can be reasonably predicted. The ITC must require Channel 3 licensees to fund a defecit of the Corporation's income below 14% of the total amount of terrestrial commercial television revenues (so far as the defecit cannot be met from the Corporation's reserves) up to a maximum of 2% of that amount. There is provision for a 'top up' (or clawback) if its income falls below (or is above) that 14%.

Application of Corporation's Excess Revenue (s27(1) - (3))

4.60   When the Corporation's qualifying revenue for a year exceeds the ITC's prescribed minimum income [1] for that year, the Corporation must (a) pay one half of the excess to the ITC and (b) carry one quarter to the credit of a reserve fund established by it under s27 and it may apply the remaining quarter towards meeting current expenditure incurred by it in the provision of Channel 4 to the extent that it is not carried to the credit of the reserve fund (sub-s(1), (3)). When the ITC receives one half of the excess it must distribute it ('the relevant amount') between Channel 3 licence holders in such a way that each receives such proportion of the relevant amount as corresponds to the proportion of the aggregate amount which he would in the ITC's opinion, have been required to pay had a levy been imposed under s26 (sub-s(2)).
1   The Corporation's prescribed minimum income for a year is construed in accordance with s26(2) - see para 4.56. Section 19(2) - (6) has effect for determining the Corporation's qualifying revenue for a year (s27(9)) - see paras 4.33, 4.34.

Management and Application of Reserve Fund (s27(3) - (5))

4.61   Although generally the Corporation may itself determine the management and application of the reserve fund, it can only be applied for Channel 4 purposes (sub-s(3), (4)). The Secretary of State, with Treasury approval, may give to the Corporation such directions as he thinks fit with respect to the management and application of the fund (including directions requiring the whole or part of it to be paid into the Consolidated Fund) and the Corporation must comply (sub-s(5)). However, no direction may be given by him with respect to the application of money standing to the credit of the fund which has been taken into account by the ITC for the purposes of determining the possibility of imposing a levy or in calculating the 'relevant amount' [1] in s26(4).
1   See para 4.56.

4.62   Section 27 provides that when Channel 4 income exceeds 14% of the total commercial revenues, the Corporation must pay half of any excess revenue to Channel 3 licensees and the remaining half is to be split between the Corporation's reserves and meeting current expenditure. This can be described as a 'swings and roundabouts' arrangement. The 50% that accrues to Channel 3 licensees is a quid pro quo for its liability to contribute up to 2% of the revenue if Channel 4 income falls below the 14% level. It can be justified because Channel 3 licensees must subsidise Channel 4 when required, even though they are competing for sales of advertising [1].
1   House of Commons Committee, cols 757, 758.

Channel 5

Channel 5 (s28)

4.63   The ITC must do all that it can to ensure the provision of a television broadcasting service for such minimum area of the United Kingdom as may be determined by it and this service is to be known as Channel 5 (s28(1)). In determining this area the ITC must have regard to the fact that the service should, so far as is reasonably practicable, make the most effective use of the frequencies on which it is to be provided (s28(2)). When the ITC have granted a licence to provide Channel 5 it may, if it appears to it to be appropriate to do so in view of any lack of facilities available for transmitting the service, dispense with the 'most effective use' requirement for such a period as it may determine (s28(4)). Also, if the ITC so determine, Channel 5 must be provided under a particular licence only between certain times of the day or on certain days of the week, or both (s28(3)).

4.64   In its White Paper 'Broadcasting in the 90's: Competition, Choice and Quality' (Cmnd 517) the government concluded that a national network covering 65-70% of the population could be made available at Ultra High Frequency (UHF) from the beginning of 1993, with perhaps some limited coverage earlier. The government was satisfied that aeronautical radar, one of the non-broadcasting users of Channels 35 and 37 could be moved without risk to aircraft safety (para 5.6). To go beyond 70% coverage entails the use of technologies other than the employment of terrestrial transmitters [1]. Use could be made of microwave or, where there is a cable system, a signal could be returned from a satellite to a satellite head distributory cable [2]. The 1990 Act adopts a flexible approach to coverage in that Channel 5 is likely to develop in stages with the ITC laying down the minimum required coverage area. Section 27(3) enables the ITC to take account of transmission problems in certain areas and stagger the commencement date. A phased introduction is likely because a Channel 5 licence holder must fund necessary changes such as arrangements for video [3] and set up distribution systems. Channel 5 is not anticipated to be a second version of Channel 4 or another complementary channel to Channel 3. In fact, Channel 5 is meant to be a direct competitor of Channel 3 and will almost certainly cater for the same tastes and interests catered to by that channel. Almost certainly Channel 5 will be a single national channel, perhaps having local programmes and consequently structurally different from the federal regional Channel 3 [4].

1   House of Commons Committee, col 776.
2   House of Commons Committee, col 773.
3   Section 30, see paras 4.67 to 4.70.
4   House of Lords Report, col 470.

Application to Channel 5 of Provisions Relating to Channel 3 (s29)

4.65   Sections 15 to 21 [1] generally apply in relation to a Channel 5 licence as they apply to a regional Channel 3 licence (s29(1)). However, s15(1)(b)(i) [2] is to be read so that the notice proposing to grant a Channel 5 licence must specify the minimum area of the United Kingdom determined by the ITC in accordance with s28(2) [3]. Also, s16(2) [4], which deals with certain requirements that are to be met by applicants for a Channel 3 licence, has effect with the omission of paragraphs (c) and (d) that relate to regional programming requirements (s29(2)). The ITC has a discretion though, when it has made a determination under s28(3) that Channel 5 is to be provided under a particular licence only between certain times of the day, or days of the week, to apply s16(2) to the extent that it considers appropriate having regard to the nature of the service being provided under that licence (s29(3)). Consequently, should the ITC advertise for two or more Channel 5 licensees, the remit for Channel 5 as a whole which is set out in s16(2) is to be shared between the licensees as the ITC determine. For example, there may be a Channel 5 breakfast licence. The holder of that licence may not have to fulfil the s16(2) requirements such as providing religious programmes and programmes for children. However, the service as a whole should meet all the requirements [5].

1   See paras 4.5 to 4.46.
2   See para 4.5.
3   See para 4.63.
4   See para 4.13.
5   House of Lords Committee, col 1045.

4.66   The remit for Channel 5 is much the same as for Channel 3 except for the regional commitment because it is intended to be a national and not a regional service. It may be anticipated that a regional commitment will be favoured by viewers and the ITC may require this commitment if, for example, a breakfast time service is provided. As with Channel 3, the ITC is to bear in mind the overarching provision in s2(2)(b) [1] to 'ensure the provision of such services which (taken as a whole) are of high quality and offer a range of programmes calculated to appeal to a variety of tastes and interests' and in particular, the requirement in s16(2)(f) [2] 'that (taken as a whole) the programmes . . . included are calculated to appeal to a wide variety of tastes and interests.' Applicants for a Channel 5 licence must cross the quality threshold in s16 before their cash bids are considered. It is within the discretion of the ITC whether to allot a Channel 5 franchise at the same time as allotting Channel 3 franchises or subsequently. Unsuccessful applications for a Channel 3 licence may be successful in an application to hold a Channel 5 licence. The government would like the headquarters of Channel 5 to be outside London [3]. One attraction of this is the lower costs incurred but the government did not wish to pre-empt the Channel 5 licence holder's decision as to becoming a production centre or commissioning house [4]. The Channel 5 licensee, like the Channel 3 licensee, is awarded a licence for 10 years with the option of applying for a semi-automatic renewal after six years. During the licence period he is committed to his cash bid and the net advertising revenue-related payments established from the beginning and only alterable when the licence is renewed.

1   See para 3.12.
2   See para 4.13.
3   House of Commons Committee, col 763.
4   House of Commons Committee, col 772.

Internal Channel 5 Licensee to Retune Equipment Susceptible to Interference (s30)

Arrangements to Modify Equipment (s30(1), (4), (6), (7)).

4.67   A Channel 5 licence which is in force at the 'commencement' of the provision of Channel 5 must include conditions (a) requiring the licence holder to make arrangements for any 'relevant equipment' to be retuned or otherwise modified (i) at the request of the person by whom the equipment is kept (being a request made before a date specified in the conditions) and (ii) without charge to the person, so far as is necessary to prevent the equipment from suffering interference caused by the transmission of Channel 5 (b) requiring the work (i) to be carried out in a proper manner and (ii) to be completed within a period specified in the conditions and (c) enabling the ITC to determine whether the work is carried out in a proper manner (s30(1)). The 'commencement' date is the date when Channel 5 began to be provided for reception in an area which includes the place where the equipment is kept when the request is made (s30(7)). Any dispute as to when the commencement date occurred is determined by the ITC (s30(4)). The 'relevant equipment' is any equipment capable of transmitting self-generated electro-magnetic signals for reception by a television set connected to it and liable, if used without being retuned or otherwise modified, to suffer interference caused by the transmission of Channel 5 (s30(7)). When the Channel 5 licence holder is required by virtue of the licence conditions to arrange for retuning or modification, those conditions are taken as requiring him also to make arrangements for any television set connected to the equipment to be retuned (a) at the request of the person by whom the equipment is kept and (b) without charge to that person, so far as is necessary to enable it to be used in conjunction with the equipment (as retuned or modified). Also the conditions are taken as requiring the work to be done properly within a specified period, enabling the ITC to scrutinise the work and requiring publicity of the arrangements (s30(6)). Consequently, when a home video recorder or computer is being retuned in accordance with s30 the licensee is responsible for retuning any television set which is used in conjunction with that equipment.

4.68   In the White Paper (Cmnd 517) the government acknowledged that 'most video cassette recorders (VCR) and some home computers' would need to be retuned in those areas where Channel 5 was receivable, irrespective of whether their owners choose to receive it (para 5.6). A study by the Department of Trade and Industry suggests the cost of retuning VCRs would be less that £20 million [1]. The licensee is also obliged to retune any television set used with those VCRs and home computers.
1   House of Commons Committee, col 772.

Publicity (s30(2), (5))

4.69   A Channel 5 licence must also include conditions requiring the licence holder to publicise, in a manner approved by the ITC, information with respect to (a) the likelihood of different kinds of equipment suffering interference caused by the transmission of Channel 5 (b) the arrangements which the licence holder is required to make because of the conditions imposed under s30 and (c) the kinds of equipment in relation to which those arrangements are to be made (s30(2)). When (a) in accordance with s28(3) [1] there is more than one Channel 5 licence in force at the same time and (b) each licence contains s30 conditions, the licence holder must comply with those conditions to the extent determined by the ITC (s30(5)).
1   See para 4.63.

Scope of Arrangement (s30(3))

4.70   The Channel 5 licence holder cannot be required by the s30 licence conditions to make arrangements for retuning or modification (a) unless the equipment (i) is, at the date of the request, kept wholly or mainly for domestic purposes and (ii) was so kept on the 'commencement' date (if this was before the request was made) or (b) if the equipment would not be liable to interference caused by the transmission of Channel 5 but for the installation at the place where it is kept of any apparatus for enabling Channel 5 to be received there (s30(3)). The licensee is exempt from liability to retune or modify equipment if the sole reason for interference is the installation of an aerial to receive Channel 5. On installation engineers are most likely to retune a VCR in order to obtain a clear reception of a Channel 5 signal [1]. When any 'relevant equipment' has been retuned or modified in accordance with the licence conditions, the licence holder cannot be required by the licence conditions to make subsequent arrangements for retuning or modifying the equipment (s30(3)).
1   House of Lords Committee, col 1046.

Provision of News Programmes

Provision of News on Channels 3 and 5 (s31)

4.71   A Channel 3 or Channel 5 licence must include conditions requiring the licence holder to (a) broadcast in the licensed service news programmes of high quality dealing with national and international matters and (b) broadcast such programmes in that service throughout the period for which the service is provided, in particular (except in the case of a national Channel 3 licence) at peak viewing times (sub-s(1)). In addition, a regional Channel 3 licence must include conditions requiring the news programmes broadcast by the licence holder, in compliance with the above conditions, to be programmes provided by a nominated news provider which are (a) presented live and (b) broadcast simultaneously with the broadcasts of news programmes by the same nominated news provider which are made by other holders of regional Channel 3 licences in compliance with those conditions (sub-s(2)). A 'nominated news provider' is a corporate body nominated for the above purposes under s32 [1] (sub-s(3)).
1   See para 4.73.

4.72   Section 31 requires a high quality news service as stipulated in s16(2)(a). In the case of regional Channel 3 there must be at least one news provider nominated by the ITC. However the 1990 Act does not require that all news must come from that source provided it is of high quality. Similarly, although there must be a national news programme shown in the regional Channel 3 network it may be supplemented at a different time by other programmes.

Nomination of Bodies to Provide News for Regional Channel 3 Services (s32(1) - (7), (12))

4.73   The ITC must invite corporate bodies that appear to it to be qualified to apply to be a nominated news provider. A corporate body so appears if it appears to the ITC to be both (a) effectively equipped and adequately financed to provide high quality news programmes for broadcasting in regional Channel 3 services and (b) not a disqualified person in relation to any ITC licence by virtue of any provision in Part II of Sch 2 [1] (sub-s(2)). The invitations must be issued when, in its opinion, it is appropriate for securing that there is at least one nominated news provider before it publishes the first notice that it proposes to grant a licence to provide a Channel 3 service under s15(1) [2] (sub-s(1)). When a corporate body (a) applies to the ITC (whether in pursuance of an invitation or not) to be a nominated news provider and (b) appears to the ITC to be qualified for nomination, the ITC must nominate it unless the ITC is satisfied that to do so would be likely, because of the number of bodies already nominated, to be prejudicial to the provision of high quality news programmes for broadcasting in regional Channel 3 services (taken as a whole) (sub-s(2)). Should the ITC refuse to nominate a body corporate on this ground, it must afterwards, at such intervals as it may determine, review the performance of the nominated news provider. If, on any review, the ITC is satisfied that another corporate body which (a) is not a nominated news provider but (b) appears to it to be qualified for nomination, would offer a better service than a nominated news provider as regards the provision of high quality news programme for broadcasting in regional Channel 3 services, it must by notice terminate that body's nomination and nominate the former body in its place (sub-s(4)). Likewise, if at any time, the ITC are (a) for any reason dissatisfied with a nominated news provider's performance and (b) satisfied that to terminate its nomination would not be prejudicial to the provision of high quality news programmes for broadcasting in regional Channel 3 services (taken as a whole), then the ITC must by notice terminate that body's nomination (sub-s(5)). In either case, the ITC must not terminate a body's nomination unless it has given the body a reasonable opportunity of making representations to it about the proposed termination (sub-s(6)). The ITC must, before terminating or nominating a body, consult with every regional Channel 3 licence holder (sub-s(7)). Any nomination made by the ITC is, subject to its powers of termination, for a 10 year period, at the end of which the ITC may renew the nomination for a further 10 year period (sub-s(3)).

1   See paras 10.13 to 10.23.
2   See para 4.5.

4.74   Channel 3 licence holders must contract for the national and international news that they are required to provide with one or more news providers nominated by the ITC. The price they pay is to be negotiated between the licensee and the news provider. Complaint about monopoly pricing may be made to the Office of Fair Trading[1]. A licensee may take additional news items from a non-nominated provider if it is of high quality. The ITC must nominate all news providers that it considers financially able and equipped to provide high quality news unless it considers that this would prejudice the supply of that news. It is likely to take into account the news provider's pricing policy when considering a nomination. The ITC must replace a nominated news provider if it believes that another is more able to provide the news. A review of a nominated news provider would probably take place after three years[2].

1   House of Commons Committee, col 799.
2   House of Lords Committee, col 1056.

Conditions in Instrument Nominating a Body (s32(8) - (11), (13))

4.75   Any instrument by which a body is nominated under s32 must include conditions (a) imposing limits on the extent to which persons of any specified class or description may be participants in the nominated news provider (b) requiring that body to provide the ITC with such information as it may reasonably require to determine whether any of those limits has been exceeded and (c) enabling the ITC to terminate that body's nomination if satisfied that any of those limits has been exceeded. The instrument may provide for any of those limits to apply only after the expiry of a specified period (s32(8)). Generally the limits may be such as the ITC determine. However, the limits must ensure that (a) no person is a participant with more than a 20% interest in the nominated news provider and (b) any participants in the nominated news provider who are holders of licences to provide regional Channel 3 services, when taken together (i) hold or are beneficially entitled to less than 50% of the shares in that body and (ii) possess less than 50% of the voting power in it (s32(9), (11)). Also, the limit imposed to ensure that no person is a participant with more than a 20% interest in the nominated news provider has effect in relation to a particular participant as if he and every person connected with him were one person. For this purpose the following persons are treated as connected with a particular participant - (a) a person who controls the participant (b) an associate of the participant or of a person who controls the participant and (c) a body which is controlled by the participant or by his associate (s32(10)). These provisions are to be construed in accordance with Part I of Sch 2[1] (s32(13).

1   See paras 10.2 to 10.12.

4.76   Section 32 seeks a balance between regional Channel 3 licensees actively contributing to the affairs of its news provider and the avoidance of too narrow an ownership base in the news provider. Four reasons may be given for providing that Channel 3 licensees are to only have a minority shareholding in the news provider[1]. It should encourage efficiency in the news provider. The wider share base gives scope for directors with relevant outside experience to be appointed. The advantage of diversification and expansion is the introduction of greater scope for risk capital for investment. It alleviates possible tensions because of the conflict of interests among Channel 3 licensees. The news provider (Independent Television News) before the 1990 Act was collectively owned by the 15 ITV regional companies. While s32 permits regional Channel 3 licensees to hold up to a 49% share in the news provider, no other single person or company can have more than a 20% shareholding. So, in theory the Channel 3 licensees do not have editorial and financial control of the news provider, which may be ITN in altered form. Majority control is exercised by people who do not hold Channel 3 licences.

1   House of Lords Committee, col 1055.

Miscellaneous Provisions Relating to Channels 3, 4 and 5

Conditions Requiring Holder of Channel 3 or Channel 5 Licence to Deliver Promised Service (s33)

4.77   A Channel 3 or Channel 5 licence must include conditions which appear to the ITC to be appropriate for ensuring (a) that the service provided accords with the proposals concerning programme and other requirements submitted under s15(3)(b) [1] and (b) the implementation of the proposals concerning the aurally and visually handicapped and training submitted under s15(3)(c) and (d) or [2] (as the case may be) the implementation of those proposals and those relating to regional commitments submitted under s15(3)(c) - (e) [3] (s33(1)). Any conditions imposed in pursuance of s33 may be varied by the ITC with the consent of the licence holder (s33(3)).

1   See para 4.6.
2   See para 4.6.

4.78   The ITC is required to insert conditions in Channel 3 and 5 licences to ensure that the service provided accords with the licensee's programme proposals and that they implement their proposals on the handicapped, training and on regional employment and facilities where appropriate. The ITC may, with the licensee's consent vary the conditions should this be deemed necessary in the light of changed circumstances.

Schools Programming (s34)

4.79   The ITC must do all it can to ensure that a suitable proportion of programmes included in Channel 3 services and Channel 4 and 5 (taken as a whole) are schools programmes (sub-s(1)). Accordingly, a Channel 3 licence or licence to provide Channel 4 or 5 may include conditions (a) requiring the licence holder to produce or finance the production of schools programmes (b) requiring the licence holder to acquire schools programmes provided by other persons (c) requiring the licence holder to ensure that schools programmes included in the licensed service (i) are of high quality and (ii) are suitable to meet the needs of schools in the area(s) in the United Kingdom for which the service is provided (d) specifying the minimum number of hours in term time or within normal school hours that are to be allocated to the broadcasting of schools programmes in the licensed service (e) requiring the licence holder to provide such material for use in connection with the schools programmes broadcast by him as may be necessary to ensure that effective use is made of those programmes in schools and (f) requiring the licence holder from time to time to consult with such bodies or other persons who are concerned with, or have an interest in schools or the production of schools programmes as the ITC thinks fit (sub-s(2)). The 1990 Act defines 'schools programmes' as programmes intended for use in schools (sub-s(3)).

4.80   Before the 1990 Act schools programmes were shown on Channel 4 and paid for by the 15 regional ITV companies. The ITC is to decide how best to provide schools programmes, having the opportunity of using Channels 3, 4 and 5 or a permutation of them. Different areas in the United Kingdom may have different educational requirements and s34 recognises this fact. Despite the increased use of video recorders by schools to re-schedule programmes, live broadcasting for schools is intended and an assurance was given that the government will maintain the pre-1990 Act service 'in all its material particulars' [1]. Adult education programmes are not prescribed in the 1990 Act.

1   Mr David Mellor, (minister of state, Home Office) House of Commons Committee, col 810.

Subtitling [1] for the Deaf (s35)

General Channel 3 and 5 Licence Conditions (s35(1) - (3), (7), (8))

4.81   A Channel 3 or Channel 5 licence must include (a) conditions (i) specifying the 'relevant minimum number of hours in a week' for s35 purposes and (ii) requiring programmes with subtitling to be broadcast in the licensed service during not less than that number of hours in a week and (b) conditions requiring the licence holder to attain such technical standards for the provision of subtitling as are specified in the conditions (sub-s(1)). The 'relevant minimum number of hours in a week' differs between Channel 3 and Channel 5. In relation to Channel 3 services taken as a whole (i) for the year including the commencement of s35 it is the number of weekly hours which the ITC determine so as to achieve an increase of at least 10% over the average number of weekly hours during which programmes with subtitling were in the preceding year broadcast on Independent Television (ITV) [2] and (ii) for each successive year, such number of weekly hours as the ITC determine being a number greater than in the previous year (sub-s(2)(a), (8)). The hours are to represent (i) in 1998, 50% of the average number of weekly hours during which programmes were, during 1997, broadcast on Channel 3 and (ii) for 1999 and each successive year, the greatest number of weekly hours that appears to the ITC to be reasonably practicable (sub-s3(a)). In relation to Channel 5 taken as a whole the 'relevant minimum number of hours in a week' is (i) for the year in which Channel 5 is first provided, such weekly hours as the ITC determine so as to ensure that the proportion of programmes broadcast on Channel 5 in a week which is represented by programmes with subtitling is the same as that achieved by Channel 3 services in their first year and (ii) for each successive year, such hours as the ITC determine, being a number greater than for the previous year (sub-s(2)(b), (8)). For the purposes of sub-s(2) when a week falls partly within two years to which s35 applies it is to be treated as falling within the earlier year (sub-s(6)). The hours are to represent (i) for the year which includes the fifth anniversary of the commencement of Channel 5's provision, 50% of the average weekly hours during which programmes were, during the preceding year, broadcast on Channel 5 and (ii) for subsequent years, the greatest number of weekly hours as appears to the ITC to be reasonably practicable (sub-s3(b)).

1   'Subtitling' means subtitling for the deaf; whether provided by means of a teletext service or otherwise (s35(8)).
2   As defined in s10(2) of the Broadcasting Act 1981.

4.82   Before the 1990 Act ITV broadcast 18 hours of subtitled programmes out of a total of 160 hours of television presentation a week, ie 11%. The IBA expected to have increased this to 19% of its total output by the end of its contract period in 1992 [1]. Under the 1990 Act 50% of all Channel 3 and 5 programmes should be subtitled within the first five years of the franchises being taken up. Clearly, the figures in s35 are minimum figures. It has been confirmed that the Welsh Authority intends to be bound up by the subtitling requirements for the deaf, as Channel 4 is [2]. The 1990 Act does not contain a sign language requirement. A licence holder cannot impose charges for providing subtitling (s35 (7)).

1   House of Commons Committee, col 824.
2   House of Commons Committee, col 881.

Particular Channel 3 and 5 Licence Conditions (s35(4))

4.83   In the case of (a) a Channel 3 service provided, as mentioned in s14(4) [1], for a particular area only between certain daily times or weekdays (or both) or, as mentioned in s14(5) [2], for two or more areas for which regional Channel 3 services are provided but only at certain times, or (b) a Channel 5 service provided, as mentioned in 28(3) [3] only between certain daily times or weekdays (or both), the relevant minimum hours in a week are for any year such as the ITC determine to be an appropriate proportion under s35(sub-s(4)).

1   See para 4.3.
2   See para 4.1.
3   See para 4.63.

Notification of Determination (s35(5))

4.84   As soon as the ITC have made a s35 determination other than for the year starting with the commencement of either s35 for Channel 3 or the provision of Channel 5 (a) it must notify every licence holder to which the determination relates of it and (b) every such licence has effect as if for the number in its conditions specifying the hours for s35 purposes there were the new hours substituted by the ITC (sub-s(5)).

Party Political Broadcasts (s36)

4.85   Any regional Channel 3 licence or licence to provide Channel 4 or 5 must include conditions requiring the licence holder to (a) include party political broadcasts in the licensed service and (b) observe such rules with respect to those broadcasts as the ITC may determine (s36(1)). These conditions may (but need not) be included in a licence to provide Channel 5 when any determination under s28(3) as to its provision being limited to certain times of the day or certain day(s) of the week is in force (s36(2)). For the purposes of s36, the ITC may determine (a) the political parties on whose behalf broadcasts may be made and (b) the length and frequency of these broadcasts (s36(3)). Any rules made by the ITC for the purposes of s36 may make provision for different cases or circumstances (s36(4)).

4.86   The ITC is empowered to determine the timing of any election, or party political, broadcast in the interests of equality of treatment of the different parties represented in Parliament [1]. As for parties not represented in Parliament, s36 appears to give the ITC a wide discretion as to if, and when, they broadcast. The ITC is given the option of not imposing requirements for party political broadcasts on a Channel 5 licensee who may be providing coverage for only certain weekly days or times of the day, for example providing a breakfast service.

1   House of Commons Committee, col 827.

Announcements of Programme Schedules (s37)

4.87   Any Channel 3 licence or licence to provide Channel 4 may include conditions requiring the licence holder to include in the licensed service such announcements concerning relevant programme schedules as the ITC may determine (s37(1)). In relation to a Channel 3 licence, 'relevant programme schedules' means schedules for programmes to be broadcast on Channel 4 and, where part of the area for which the licensed service is to be provided is in Wales, schedules for programmes to be broadcast on S4C (s37(2)(a)). In relation to the licence to provide Channel 4, they mean schedules for programmes to be included in any Channel 3 service (s37(2)(b)).

4.88   Section 37 provides for cross-announcements between Channel 3 and Channel 4 of their respective programme schedules. A Channel 3 licensee covering Wales must give announcements of S4C's programme schedules in the same way as Channel 3 as a whole will give Channel 4 announcements. Given the fact that Channels 3 and 4 compete for advertising sales, it would seem wrong to force them to disclose their commercially confidential schedules long in advance [1].
1   House of Commons Committee, col 832.

Promotion of Equal Opportunities (s38)

4.89   Any Channel 3 licence or licence to provide Channel 4 or Channel 5 must include conditions requiring the licence holder to (a) make arrangements for promoting, in relation to employment by him, equality of opportunity between men and women and between persons of different racial groups [1] and (b) review those arrangements from time to time (s38(1)).
1   'Racial group' has the same meaning as in the Race Relations Act 1976 (s38(1)).

4.90   A similar duty to impose equal opportunity conditions in domestic satellite service licences is placed on the ITC and in national radio licences on the Radio Authority. These provisions may work in practice by the ITC and Radio Authority inviting applicants for licences to explain their proposed arrangements for equal opportunities and then judging their adequacy. Although the ITC and Radio Authority have no locus in monitoring the outcome of the equal opportunities policies, they may consider that it be part of the licence condition that the licensee publish such information in his company annual report [1].
1   House of Lords Committee, col 1081.

Networking Arrangements Between Holders of Regional Channel 3 Licences (s39)

Scope of Networking Arrangements (s39(1), (10))

4.91   Section 39 is concerned with the making of 'networking arrangements' which (a) apply to all regional Channel 3 licence holders and (b) provide for programmes made, commissioned or acquired by or on behalf of one or more such licence holders to be available for broadcasting on all regional Channel 3 services, being arrangements made to enable regional Channel 3 services (taken as a whole) to be a nationwide system of such services which is able to compete effectively with other television programme services provided in the United Kingdom (sub-s(1)). The arrangements are essentially concerned with the commissioning and acquisition of programmes to be shown on the network. The scheduling of programmes is a matter for the licensees [1]. The ITC must refuse to approve an arrangement or its modification if it is not satisfied that this would be appropriate for the above purpose (sub-s(10)).
1   House of Lords Committee, col 1087.

Regional Channel 3 Applications Networking Proposals (s39(2))

4.92   An application for a regional Channel 3 licence must be accompanied by the proposals mentioned in s15(3)(b) - (e) [1] and proposals for participation in networking arrangements made under s39. Then, (a) when a person has duly made an application, the ITC (i) must, as soon as reasonably practicable after the closing date for applications send details of his networking proposals to the Director General of Fair Trading and (ii) (without prejudice to the operation of s16(1)) [2] not proceed to consider whether to award him the licence mentioned in s16 unless it appears to the ITC that the proposals are satisfactory and (b) the miscellaneous provisions relating to Channels 3, 4 and 5 contained in s33 [3] apply to the proposals as it applies to the proposals submitted under s15(3)(c) - (e) [4] (s39(2)).

1   See para 4.6.
2   See para 4.11.
3   See para 4.77.
4   See para 4.6.

Guidance for Applications (s39(3))

4.93   The ITC may publish, in the manner it considers appropriate, general guidance to applicants for a regional Channel 3 licence as to the kinds of proposals it would consider satisfactory for the purposes of sending them to the Director General of Fair Trading. Before doing so the ITC (a) must consult the Director and (b) if he requests it make any change in the guidance (s39(3)).

Networking Licence Conditions (s39(4) - (9), (13))

4.94   Each regional Channel 3 licence must include conditions requiring the licence holder to do all that he can to ensure (a) (in the case of a licence granted before the relevant date ie the date which the ITC determine to be that by which arrangements made under this provision would need to have been made by licence holders so that they are fully operational when the licensed service begins) that, by that date, there are networking arrangements (i) entered into by all the licence holders and (ii) approved by the ITC and (b) (in any case) that, so long as he provides his service, there are in force networking arrangements which have been entered into and approved (unless there is in force an arrangement made by the ITC) (s39(4), (13)). If (a) no arrangement is made before the relevant date or (b) such an arrangement is made but ceases to be in force before 1 January 1995, the ITC may draw up such networking arrangements as it considers appropriate. If it does so (i) it must notify all regional Channel 3 licence holders of those arrangements and (ii) those arrangements must generally come into force on a date determined by the ITC. Each regional Channel 3 licence must include conditions requiring the licence holder to give effect to this arrangement (s39(5)). However, no arrangement made by the ITC can come into force after 31 December 1994 (s39(6)). When any arrangements have been made by the ITC, it may (whether before or after 31 December 1994) modify them as it considers appropriate. If it does so (a) it must notify all the holders of regional Channel 3 licences of the modification and (b) the modification comes into force on a date determined by the ITC (s39(9)). When (a) ITC arrangements are in force but (b) networking arrangements are subsequently (i) entered into by all holders of regional Channel 3 licences and (ii) approved by the ITC, the latter arrangements come into force (s39(7)). When arrangements have been approved by the ITC no modification of them can be made by regional Channel 3 licence holders, unless it too has been approved (s39(8)).

4.95   There is the time limit on the ITC's power to impose networking arrangements in the absence of voluntary agreement between the licensees because voluntary agreement is less likely if the ITC could impose an alternative network at any time during the licence period [1].

1   House of Lords Committee, col 1088.

Publication of Approval or Notification (s39(11), (12))

4.96   When the ITC have (a) approved any arrangements or modification under s39 or (b) given with respect to any arrangements or modification the notification required by s39, it must, as soon as reasonably practicable after giving its approval or (as the case may be) that notification (i) publish details of the arrangements or modification in the manner that it considers appropriate and (ii) comply with the 'appropriate requirement' (s39(11)). The 'appropriate requirement' is in the case of (a) the arrangements, to refer them to the Director General of Fair Trading and (b) any modification, to inform him of it. Sch 4 [1] has effect with respect to any reference of arrangements and any matters arising out of it, including the subsequent modification of the arrangements to which it relates (s39(12)).
1   See paras 4.98 to 4.106.

4.97   Section 39 requires regional Channel 3 licensees to participate in networking arrangements agreed between themselves to provide programmes for broadcasting in all regional Channel 3 services. The ITC may impose a networking scheme, which would last for a maximum period of two years, in the absence of voluntary arrangements. The government felt that it is particularly important that networking arrangements, whether agreed voluntarily or imposed by the ITC, do not continue the pre-1990 Act practices involving production quotas for certain contractors or enabling larger companies to abuse their dominant position [1]. Section 39(3) requires the ITC to consult the Director General of Fair Trading before publishing guidance on networking. This enables him to assess the implication for competition of any networking arrangements, whether voluntarily agreed between the licensees or imposed by the ITC. The ITC is required, by s2(2)(a)(ii) [2] to ensure fair and effective competition and given the federal structure of regional Channel 3 it may be anticipated that networked programmes will be provided from a range of Channel 3 regions. Section 193 [3] enables the Secretary of State by order to modify networking arrangements in certain circumstances and s194 [4] provides that the Restrictive Trade Practices Act 1976 does not apply to those arrangements. The ITC is required, when it has approved any networking arrangements or imposed its own arrangements, to publish details of the arrangements and to refer them to the Director General of Fair Trading. Sch 4 sets out the Director's role when such a reference is made.
1   House of Lords Committee, col 1087..
2   See para 3.10.
3   See paras 4.107, 4.108.
4   See paras 4.109, 4.110.

References with Respect to Networking Arrangements (Sch 4) - in Outline

Report by Director (para 1)

4.98   When a reference is made to the Director General of Fair Trading (the Director) under s39(12)(a) [1] he must (a) publish a notice of the reference and the arrangements so as to bring it to the attention of persons affected by it (b) consider whether the arrangements satisfy the competition test in para 2 and (c) report within six months of the notice's publication his conclusions on whether the arrangements satisfy the competition test and, if not, any necessary modifications to them (para 1(1), (3), (4)). A copy of his report is sent to the ITC and every regional Channel 3 licence holder (para 1(6)).
1   See para 4.96.

The Competition Test (para 2)

4.99   Arrangements satisfy the competition test if (a) they do not have, and are not intended or likely to have, the effect of restricting, distorting or preventing competition in connection with any business activity in the United Kingdom or (b) they do have or are intended or likely to have, such an effect but they would satisfy the criteria in para 3 of Art 85 of the EEC Treaty (agreement contributing to improving the production or distribution of goods or to promoting technical or economical progress) if that paragraph were to be construed as relating only to the effects within the United Kingdom of agreements between undertakings (para 2(1)).

Duty to Modify Arrangement (para 3)

4.100   When the Director specifies modifications to arrangements made by (a) regional Channel 3 licence holders, the ITC must notify them by when the modifications must be incorporated in the arrangements (b) the ITC, the ITC must incorporate the modifications in the arrangements and notify all licence holders of the modified arrangements (para 3(1)). However, if a reference relating to the Director's report is made to the Monopolies and Mergers Commission (MMC), the modifications are not to be incorporated into the arrangements (a) if the reference is in respect of the arrangements as a whole or (b) (in any other case) to the extent that the modifications are referred to the MMC (para 3(2)).

Appeal to MMC (para 4)

4.101   When the Director's report contains modifications to arrangements as mentioned in para 1(4) [1], the ITC or a regional Channel 3 licence holder may refer to the MMC within four weeks of the report the questions whether (a) the arrangements satisfy the competition test and/or (b) the modifications specified in the report ought to be incorporated in the arrangements to satisfy the competition test (para 4(1), (2)). The MMC must (a) publish a notice of the reference to bring it to the attention of people affected by it and (b) report on it within three months of the notice's publications (para 4(3)). Certain provisions of the Fair Trading Act 1973 and the Competition Act 1980 are applied in relation to the reference to the MMC (para 4(7)).
1   See para 4.98.

Report by MMC (para 5)

4.102   The MMC's report gives its conclusions to the questions contained in the reference (para 5(1)). Any modifications necessary to satisfy the competition test must be specified in the report (para 5(2)). A copy of the report is to be sent to the Director, the ITC and every regional Channel 3 licence holder (para 5(4)(b)).

Duty to Modify Arrangements (para 6)

4.103   When the MMC's report specifies modifications to arrangements made by (a) regional Channel 3 licence holders, the ITC must notify them by when the modifications must be incorporated in the arrangements (b) the ITC, the ITC must incorporate the modifications in the arrangements and notify all licence holders of the modified arrangements (para 6(1)).

Director's Power to Review Decisions (para 7)

4.104   The Director may, after making a report under paragraph 1 [1] (a) consider afresh whether the arrangements satisfy the competition test and (b) make a further report (para 7(1)). He must send a copy of the report to the ITC and every regional Channel 3 licence holder (para 7(3)). Paragraphs 2 - 6 [2] have effect in relation to the report (para 7(4)).

1   See para 4.98.
2   See paras 4.99 to 4.103.

Power to Obtain Information (para 8)

4.105   The Director may serve a notice on any person requiring him to (a) produce to the Director documents in his custody or control or (b) furnish him with the estimates, returns or other information specified in the notice, as the Director may require to make a report under Sch 4 (para 8(1)). A person cannot be compelled to (a) produce any document which he could not be compelled to produce in civil proceedings before the High Court (or in Scotland) the court of Session (b) in complying with the requirement for furnishing evidence, to give information which he could not be compelled to give in evidence in such proceedings (para 8(2)). Certain provisions of the Fair Trading Act 1973 as amended by the Companies Act 1989 are applied to the Director's powers in para 8 (para 8(4)).

Duty of Director to Assist MMC (para 9)

4.106   The Director must assist the MMC in its investigation of a reference made under para 4 [1] by giving it any information in his possession and relating to matters being investigated which is either (i) requested by the MMC or (ii) information which he considers appropriate to assist the MMC without it making a request. The MMC must take account of any information given (para 9(1)).

1   See para 4.101.

Modification of Networking Arrangements Because of Reports under Competition Legislation (s193)

4.107   The Secretary of State may, in certain circumstances, by order provide for any networking arrangement specified in the order to have effect with such modifications as appear to him to be appropriate (s193(1)). Networking arrangements are those arrangements mentioned in s39(1) [1] (s193(4)). An order made under s193 is subject to annulment in pursuance of a resolution of either House of Parliament (s193(3)). The circumstances are those as mentioned in (a) s56(1) of the Fair Trading Act 1973 (order on report on monopoly reference) and the monopoly situation exists in connection with the provision of programmes for broadcasting on regional Channel 3 services (b) s73(1) of the same Act (order on report on merger reference) and one or more of the enterprises which ceased to be distinct enterprises was engaged in the provision of such programmes and (c) s10(1) of the Competition Act 1980 (order on report on competition reference) and the anti-competitive practice was pursued in connection with the provision of such programmes (s193(2)). Expressions used in s193 which are also used in the Fair Trading Act 1973 or the Competition Act 1980 have the same meaning as in that Act (s193(4)).

1   See para 4.91.

4.108   Section 193 enables the Secretary of State to make an order requiring the modification of networking arrangements should any general investigation into broadcasting, which is unconnected with the provisions of the 1990 Act, and which is conducted by the Office of Fair Trading, reveal that changes in the networking arrangements were necessary on competition grounds [1].

1   House of Lords Report, col 492.

Restrictive Trade Practices Act 1976 not to Apply to Networking Arrangements (s194)

4.109 The Restrictive Trade Practices Act 1976 does not apply, and is deemed never to have applied, to any relevant networking arrangements which are specified, or are of a description specified, in an order made by the Secretary of State (whether before or after the making of those arrangements) and which satisfy any specified conditions (s194(1)). 'Relevant networking arrangements' are (a) s39 arrangements [1] or (b) other arrangements made for the purpose mentioned in s39(1) [2] (s194(2)). Before making an order the Secretary of State must consult the ITC and the Director General of Fair Trading. The order is subject to annulment in pursuance of a resolution of either House of Parliament (s194(3)).

1   See para 4.94 (s 39(4), (7) (b)).
2   See para 4.91.

4.110 Schedule 4 provides a competition test for the network arrangements. Consequently it is not necessary for the arrangements to be subject to the Restrictive Trade Practices Act 1976. Section 194 provides that the 1976 Act does not apply and is deemed never to have applied to any relevant network arrangements specified in an order by the Secretary of State.

Enforcement of Licences

Direction to Broadcast Correction or Apology or not to Repeat Programme (s40)

4.111 If the ITC are satisfied that (a) the holder of a Channel 3 or Channel 5 licence has failed to comply with any condition of the licence and (b) that failure can be appropriately remedied by the inclusion in the licensed service of a correction or apology (or both), it may direct the licence holder to include in the licensed service a correction or apology (or both) in the form and at the time(s) that it may determine (sub-s(1)). The ITC must not give such a direction unless it has given the licence holder a reasonable opportunity of making representations to it about the matters complained of (sub-s(2)). When the licence holder includes a correction or apology in the licensed service he may announce that he is doing so in pursuance of a direction (sub-s(3)). If the ITC are satisfied that the inclusion by the holder of a Channel 3 or Channel 5 licence of a programme in the service involved a failure by him to comply with a licence condition, it may direct him not to include that programme in the service on any future occasion (s40(4)). Section 40 applies in relation to a Channel 4 as if any reference to a Channel 3 licence is a reference to the licence to provide Channel 4 (s40(5)).

Imposition of Financial Penalty or Shortened Licence Period (s41)

4.112 If the ITC is satisfied that the holder of a Channel 3 or Channel 5 has failed to comply with any condition of the licence or with any proper direction given by it, then the ITC may serve on him a notice (a) requiring him to pay, within a specified period, a specified penalty to it or (b) reducing the period for which the licence is to be in force by a specified period not exceeding two years (sub-s(1)). In relation to breach of a licence condition these s41 powers are in addition to s40 powers (s40(5)). The ITC must not serve on any person such a notice unless it has given him a reasonable opportunity of making representations to it about the matters complained of (sub-s(3)). The maximum amount of any financial penalty imposed depends on whether or not such a penalty has previously be imposed on the licence holder during any period for which his licence has been in force ('the relevant period'). If it has not been imposed, the maximum penalty is 3% of his qualifying revenue for his last complete accounting period ¹ (sub-s(2)(a)). If it has, the maximum is increased to 5% (sub-s(2)(b)). The ITC can estimate the qualifying revenue of any person whose first complete accounting period falling within the relevant period has not yet ended (sub-s(2)). When the ITC serve a notice on any person under s41 reducing the licence period, and consequently the licence expires on a particular date, it may, on his application, revoke that notice if satisfied that his conduct in relation to the operation of the licensed service has been such as to justify the revocation (sub-s(4)). Section 41 applies in relation to Channel 4 as if (a) any reference to a Channel 3 licence is a reference to the licence to provide Channel 4 and (b) the power to shorten the licence period in s41(1)(b) was omitted (s41(6)).

1   This is determined in accordance with s19(2) - (6) (s41(2)(b)) - see para 4.33

Power to Revoke Channel 3 or 5 Licence (s42)

Breach of Licence Condition or Direction (s42(1) - (3))

4.113 If the ITC is satisfied that (a) the holder of a Channel 3 or 5 licence is failing to comply with any licence condition or with any proper direction given by it and (b) the failure is such that, if not remedied, it would justify the revocation of the licence, it must serve on the licence holder a notice (s42(1)). The notice must (a) state that the ITC is satisfied that there is the above failure (b) specify the respects in which, in its opinion, the licence holder is failing to comply with any mentioned condition or direction and (c) state that, unless the licence holder takes, within the period specified in the notice, specified steps to remedy the failure, the ITC will revoke his licence (s42(2)). If at the end of the period specified in the notice the ITC is satisfied that (a) the person on whom the notice was served has failed to take the steps specified in it and (b) it is necessary in the public interest to revoke his licence, it must serve on him a notice revoking his licence (s42(3)).

Failure to Provide Licence Service (s42(4))

4.114 If the ITC is satisfied in the case of any Channel 3 or Channel 5 licence that (a) the licence holder has ceased to provide the licensed service before the end of the period for which the licence is to continue in force and (b) it is appropriate for it to do so, it must serve on him a notice revoking his licence (s42(4)).

Misleading Information (s42(5))

4.115 If the ITC is satisfied that (a) a holder of a Channel 3 or Channel 5 licence provided it, in connection with the application for the licence, with information which was false in a material particular or (b) in connection with his application for the licence, he withheld any material information with the intention of causing the ITC to be mislead, it may serve on him a notice revoking his licence (s42(5)).

The Notice (s42(6) to (8))

4.116 A notice served under s42 takes effect as from the time when it is served on the licence holder (s42(6)). If it appears to the ITC to be appropriate to do so for the purpose of preserving continuity in the provision of the service, it may provide in the notice for it to take effect as from a specified date (s42(7)). The ITC must not serve a notice on a person unless it has given him a reasonable opportunity of making representation to it about the matters complained of (s42(8)).

4.117 Sections 40 - 42 permit the ITC to deal in a measured way with difficulties as they arise. This graduation of enforcement powers was not enjoyed by the IBA, which unlike the ITC, as a broadcaster had the power to preview programmes. The role of the ITC is seen by the Government as basically to act on the receipt of complaints [1]. The licence conditions include those imposed by the 1990 Act and others agreed upon between the ITC and the individual licence holder. Should a licence be revoked, the replacement service for the transitional period would probably be a licensee of an adjoining region. Employees of a company whose licence had been revoked would enjoy employment law rights against their employer if they were made redundant or were constructively dismissed.

1   House of Commons Committee, col 841.

Satellite Services

Introduction

High Power Direct Broadcasting By Satellite
4.118 Satellite technology enables the spectrum to be used efficiently and economically. Positioned in a geostationary orbit, a satellite can transmit a signal in a 'foot-print' pattern sufficient to cover a large area and broadcast a service to a great many homes. In 1977 the World Administrative Radio Conference allocated the United Kingdom frequencies for Direct Broadcasting by Satellite (DBS) sufficient for providing five television channels as well as a number of associated sound and data channels. The Cable and Broadcasting Act 1984 gave the IBA the power to award franchises for, and regulate the provision of, a DBS service.

Other Satellite Services
4.119 Other satellite systems were regulated by the Cable Authority if they were taken by United Kingdom cable systems. However, since 1985 direct reception of low and medium power satellite services has been permitted in the United Kingdom and, if not taken by cable, only became subject to United Kingdom regulation under the 1990 Act. These services employ capacity on telecommunications satellites using frequencies and facilities which are the same as those used for international telephone and data links [1]. Services may be uplinked from the United Kingdom or made available here from other countries. The commercial providers of these services may finance their operations by making a direct charge to cable operators who take their services, inserting advertising in their services or selling their services to individual subscribers who are equipped with the necessary receiving equipment. The satellite 'Astra' with a capacity for 16 channels is an example of a medium powered satellite capable of direct reception by viewers.

1   White Paper (Cmnd 517, 1988), paras 4.23 to 4.26.

Domestic Satellite Services (s44)

Licensing Authority (s44(1))
4.120 The ITC may grant licences to provide domestic satellite services.

Meaning of Domestic Satellite Service (s43(1), (4))
4.121 A 'domestic satellite service' is a television broadcasting service where the television programmes included in the service are transmitted by satellite from a place in the United Kingdom (a) on an 'allocated frequency' and (b) for general reception in the United Kingdom (s43(1)). An 'allocated frequency' is a frequency allocated to the United Kingdom for broadcasting by satellite (s43(4)).

4.122 For the foreseeable future the United Kingdom is restricted by international agreement to a maximum of five DBS channels [1]. All five were originally allocated to the British Satellite Broadcasting (BSB) by the IBA, thereby giving it a monopoly of what are now known as domestic satellite services.
1   House of Lords Report, col 209.

Scope of Licence (s44(2))
4.123 While a licence may be granted for the provision of a service specified, or a service of such a description as is specified, in the licence, a licence to provide a domestic satellite service may authorise the provision of a service which to any extent consists in the simultaneous transmission of different programmes on different frequencies (s44(2)). The ITC may consequently awarded a single licence to cover programming on all five DBS channels. This reflects the pre-1990 Act position when the five BSB channels were provided under one IBA contract.

Relevant Provisions (s44(3), (4))
4.124 The following provisions apply in relation to a licence to provide a domestic satellite service as they apply in relation to a licence to provide a Channel 3 service, namely: s15 [1] (applications for licences), save that s15(1) has effect with the omission of para (b) [2], s16 [3] has effect as if the licence were a licence to provide a regional Channel 3 licence but with the omission of paras (a) - (f) of sub-s(2) [4], s17 [5] (award of licence); s18 [6] (failure to begin providing the licensed service and financial penalties on revocation of licence) has effect with the omission of sub-ss (3) - (5) [7]; s19 [8] (additional payments) and s20 [9] (duration and renewal of licence) has effect but with the substitution in sub-s(1) of 'fifteen years' for ten years in both places where those words occur and with the omission of sub-s(4)(b) [10]. Other provisions that apply to a domestic satellite service licence are ss33 [11] (conditions to deliver promised service), 38 [12] (promotion of equal employment opportunities), 40 [13] (direction to broadcast correction or apology or not to repeat programme), 41 [14] (power to impose financial penalty or shorten licence period) and 42 [14] (power to revoke licence).
1   See paras 4.5 to 4.9.
2   See para 4.5.
3   See paras 4.11 to 4.19.
4   See para 4.13.
5   See paras 4.20 to 4.25.
6   See paras 4.28 to 4.30.
7   See para 4.30.
8   See paras 4.31 to 4.35.
9   See paras 4.36 to 4.42.
10   See paras 4.36 and 4.40.
11   See para 4.77.
12   See para 4.89.
13   See para 4.111.
14   See para 4.112.
15   See paras 4.i13 to 4.116.

Non-Domestic Satellite Service

Licensing of Non-Domestic Satellite Service (s45(1))
4.125 An application for a licence to provide a non-domestic satellite service must be (a) made in the manner determined by the ITC and (b) accompanied by such fee (if any) as it may determine (s45(1)). Certain satellite services [1] are regulated for the first time because of the 1990 Act and to this extent at least, the 1990 Act is not a deregulating statute.
1   See para 4.119.

Meaning of Non-Domestic Satellite Services (s43(2), (3), (4))
4.126 A 'non-domestic satellite service' has two meanings. It is (a) a service which consists in the transmission of television programmes by satellite (i) otherwise than on an allocated frequency [1] and (ii) for general reception in the United Kingdom or in a 'prescribed country' (or both), where the programmes are transmitted from a place in the United Kingdom (s43(2)(a)). A 'prescribed country' is any country specified in an order made by the Secretary of State for these purposes (s43(4)) [2]. To the extent that the programmes included in it consist of material provided by a person in the United Kingdom who is in a position to determine what is to be included in the service (so far as it consists of programme material provided by him), the service is regarded as provided by him (whether the programmes are transmitted by him or not). Otherwise, the service is regarded as provided by the person by whom the programmes are transmitted (s43(3)(a)). A non-domestic satellite service is also a service which consists in the transmission of television programmes by satellite (i) from a place which is neither in the United Kingdom nor in a 'prescribed country' but (ii) for general reception in the United Kingdom or in a 'prescribed' country (or both) to the extent that the programme included in it consists of material provided by a person in the United Kingdom who is in a position to determine what is to be included in the service (so far as it consists of programme material provided by him (s43(2)(b)). The service is to be regarded as provided by him (s43(3)(b)).
1 See para 4.121.
2 Mr Mellor, (minister of state, Home Office), considered 'prescribed country' would be a country covered by the European Convention on Transfrontier Television: House of Commons Committee, col 846.

4.127 An example of non-domestic satellite services are the satellite Astra channel services. Its frequencies are not allocated by a United Kingdom regulatory body but can be received here. There are 16 channels available on Astra. Eventually there may be 48 or more channels from Astra satellites and one estimate is that by 1992 there will be at least 160 transponders capable of carrying satellite television channels in Europe [1]. A satellite may have a number of transponders (radio transmitter-receivers) each capable of effectively providing a separate television channel. The nature and size of the potential market for non-domestic satellite services is unknown [2].
1 House of Lords Report, col 209.
2 House of Commons Committee, col 845.

Consideration of Application (s45(2))
4.128 When an application for a non-domestic satellite licence is duly made to the ITC, it may only refuse to grant the licence if it appears to it that the service which would be provided under the licence would not comply with the requirements in s6(1)) [1].
1 See para 3.37.

Scope of Licence (s45(3))
4.129 Section 44(2) [1] applies to a licence to provide a non-domestic satellite service as it applies to a licence to provide a domestic satellite service.
1 See para 4.123.

Duration of Licence (s45(4))
4.130 A licence granted by the ITC to provide a non-domestic satellite service continues in force for a period of 10 years, subject to the powers of the ITC to shorten or revoke the licence.

Power to Direct Licensee to Broadcast Correction or Apology or Not to Repeat Programme (s45(5))
4.131   Section 40 [1] applies in relation to a licence to provide a non-domestic satellite service as it applies in relation to a licence to provide a Channel 3 service.
1   See para 4.111.

Power to Impose Financial Penalty or Shorten Licence Period (s45(6), (8), (9))
4.132   Section 41 [1] applies in relation to a licence to provide a non-domestic satellite service as it applies in relation to a licence to provide a Channel 3 service, save with the omission of sub-s(2) and the maximum financial penalty imposed in pursuance of sub-s(1)(a) is £50,000. The Secretary of State may by order substitute a different sum. The order is subject to annulment in pursuance of a resolution of either House of Parliament.
1   See para 4.112.

Power to Revoke Non Domestic Satellite Licence (s45(7))
4.133   Section 42 [1] applies to such a licence with the omission of sub-s(7).
1   See paras 4.113 to 4.116.

4.134   Section 45 provides the framework for the enforcement of the European Convention on Transfrontier Television. Its purpose is to ensure that unacceptable programme content of non-domestic satellite services can be dealt with by the ITC. The government anticipates that countries covered by the convention for example, Italy and France, will take similar action under the convention should the United Kingdom receive unacceptable satellite television services from those countries [1].
1   House of Commons Committee, col 847.

4.135   The European directive 'Television Without Frontiers' provides that states may implement its provisions by law, regulation or administrative means. The Government envisages that in relation to non-domestic satellite services implementation of the directive's provisions on programming will be done administratively [1]. The power given in s188 [2] to the Secretary of State to give directions relating to international obligations could be used in relation to the provisions in the directive and the European Convention on Transfrontier Television.
1   House of Lords Committee, col 1107.
2   See para 5.36.

Licensable Programme Services

4.136   Section 46 defines the expression 'licensable programme service' (LPS), which may consist of the provision of television programmes for delivery by local delivery operators. Service provision (ie making or acquiring programmes and packaging them into channels) is to be distinguished from retailing (ie arranging for channels to be offered to viewers in return for viewer subscription payments or advertising revenue) and delivery of services. The Home Secretary acknowledged in a 1989 ministerial announcement [1] that while there should be a 'new, flexible technology-neutral framework for local services' that left operators free to decide upon the best mix of technologies; in practice this presently means cable or Multi-Point Video Distribution Service (MVDS), or a mixture of the two. Cable was used as a television delivery system in the 1950s in parts of the country where off-air reception was poor. Known as 'narrowband' systems, they were capable of carrying only the terrestrial television channels, perhaps together with one or two sound channels, and were simply an adjunct of the terrestrial transmission system. Technological advances in coaxial and fibre optic cable and electronic switches has enabled the newer 'broadband' systems to have a more independent function in the broadcasting environment. They have the capacity to carry many television and sound channels, text and data services as well as 'return' signals which make possible 'interactive' services like home-banking and home-shopping. Broadband cable systems therefore have the technical potential to offer a fully comprehensive range of telecommunications services[2]. The Home Secretary noted that many applicants for cable franchises plan to provide telecommunications as well as television services over their networks. MVDS is a technology which uses microwave frequencies to transmit television and sound channels from terrestrial transmitters to aerials on individual buildings and is used in the United States as a system for the delivery of multi-channel television services to the viewer[3].

1   House of Commons, 27 April 1989, Vol 151, col 637 w.
2   See White Paper (Cmnd 517, 1988), paras 4.11, 4.12. Also see para 8.13.
3   See White Paper (Cmnd 517, 1988), para 5.3. Also see para 8.13.

Comparative Features [1]

4.137 Compared with MVDS, broadband cable offers greater channel capacity, interactivity without the use of the Public Switched Telephone Network (PSTN) and perhaps better future picture and sound quality. However, the capital costs of setting up an MVDS system are potentially lower. Whether the delivery of programmes is by MVDS, cable or satellite the viewer must pay for the receiving equipment and all delivery systems, except cable, have a cost in spectrum terms. The most efficient use of the spectrum is made by satellite broadcasting. A single transmitter in space can achieve national or international coverage when a comparable terrestrial service would require many transmitters and a number of frequencies.

1   See White Paper (Cmnd 517, 1988), para 5.12, 5.13. Also see para 8.13.

Meaning of Licensable Programme Service (s46(1), (5))

4.138 A 'licensable programme service' (LPS) is a service consisting in the provision by any person of 'relevant programmes' with a view to their being conveyed by means of a telecommunication system (a) for reception in two or more dwelling-houses in the United Kingdom otherwise than for the purpose of being received there by persons who have a 'business interest' in receiving them or (b) for reception at any place, or for simultaneous reception at two or more places, in the United Kingdom for the purpose of being presented there either to members of the public or to a group(s) of persons some or all of whom do not have a business interest in receiving them. It is irrelevant whether the telecommunication system is run by the person providing the programmes or by some other person, and whether the programmes are to be conveyed as mentioned in (a) above for simultaneous reception or for reception at different times in response to requests made by different users of the service (s46(1)). A 'relevant programme' is a television programme other than one consisting wholly or mainly of non-representational images (within the meaning of s2(6) [1] (s46(5)). A person has a 'business interest' in receiving programmes if he has an interest in receiving them for the purpose of his business, trade, profession or employment (s46(5)).

1   See para 3.8.

Scope of LPS (s46(3), (4))

4.139 Section 46 declares that a person who (a) uses a telecommunication system for conveying relevant programmes as mentioned in s46(1) [1] and/or (b) runs a telecommunication system which is so used, is not to be regarded as providing a LPS in respect of the programmes except to the extent that they are provided by him with a view to their being so conveyed by means of that system (s46(3)). Also, where (a) any service constitutes a service as is mentioned in s46(1) [1] and (b) the relevant programmes in respect of which the service is provided, are provided for transmission in the course of the provision of any additional service [2], that service is licensable under s47 [3].

1   See para 4.138.
2   See para 4.152.
3   See paras 4.141 to 4.146.

Non-Licensable Programme Services (s46(2))

4.140   A service is not a licensable programme service if there is (a) a service where the programmes are provided for transmission in the course of the provision of a television broadcasting service or a non-domestic satellite service (b) a service where the running of the telecommunication system does not require to be licensed under Part II of the Telecommunications Act 1984 or (c) a two-way service, that is to say a service of which it is an essential feature that while visual images or sounds (or both) are being conveyed by the service provider there will or may be sent from each place of reception, by means of the same telecommunication system or (as the case may be) the part of it by means of which they are conveyed, visual images or sounds (or both) for reception by the service provider or other persons receiving it (other than signals sent for the operation or control of the service) (s46(2)).

Licensing Authority (s47(1))

4.141   An application for a licence to provide a licensable programme service must be (a) made in the manner that the ITC determines and (b) be accompanied by such fee (if any) as it may determine.

Duration of Licence (s47(3))

4.142   A licence to provide a LPS continues in force for such period not exceeding 10 years as may be specified in the licence (s47(3)).

Presumption of Grant of LPS Licence (s47(2))

4.143   When an application for a licence to provide a LPS is duly made to the ITC, it may only refuse to grant it if it appears to it that the service which would be provided would not comply with the requirements of s6(1) [1] (whether the ITC make a s47 determination or not) [2] (s47(2)). Consequently, the presumption that a LPS licence will be granted is only displaced if the proposed programme standards are unacceptable to the ITC.

1   See para 3.27.
2   See para 4.144.

ITC Determination to Modify s6 Requirements (s47(4), (5) - (7))

4.144   If the ITC (a) are satisfied that a particular LPS is to be provided with a view to its programmes being conveyed for reception only in a particular area or locality in the United Kingdom and (b) consider that it is appropriate to do so, it may, when licensing the service, determine that s6 [1] shall, in its application in relation to the service, have effect subject to certain modifications (s47(4)). The modifications are listed in s47(5)). Substituted for s6(1)(c) [2] is the paragraph: '(c) that undue prominence is not given in its programmes to the views and and opinions of particular persons or bodies on matters of political or industrial controversy or relating to current public policy'.

Substituted for s6(2) [2] is the sub-s: '(2) in applying sub-s(1)(c) to any licensed service, the programmes included in that service shall be taken as a whole'. Section 6(3) [2] and (5) - (7) [3] are omitted. In s6(4) [4] the words from the beginning to 'sub-s(1)' are omitted (s47(5)). When a s47 determination is in force, the ITC must draw up, and from time to time review, a code giving guidance as to the rules to be observed in connection with the application of the modified s6(1)(c) in relation to the service and do all that it can to ensure that the provisions of the code are met (s47(6)). The ITC must publish the code, and every revision of it, in the manner that it considers appropriate (s47(7)).

1   See paras 3.27 to 3.30.
2   See para 3.27.
3   See paras 3.29, 3.30.
4   See para 3.28.

4.145   Should the ITC so determine, the 'no undue prominence' requirement will apply to a local channel. Less rigourous than the 'due impartiality' requirement which applies to the satellite and main terrestrial channels of BBC1, BBC2, and Channel 3, it will be considered in the context of that local channel. This is because each licensed channel may be owned by a different individual [1].

1   House of Commons Committee, col 852.

Enforcement of LPS Licences (s47(8) - (12))

4.146   Generally ss40 - 42 [1] apply in relation to a licence to provide a LPS as they apply in relation to a licence to provide a Channel 3 service (s47(8)). However, in its application, s41 has effect with the omission of sub-s(2) [2] and the maximum financial penalty is £50,000 (s47(9)). The Secretary of State may be order substitute a different sum and his order is subject to annulment in pursuance of a resolution of either House of Parliament (s47(11), (12)). Section 42 applies in relation to a licence with the omission of sub-s(7) [3] (s47(10)).

1   See paras 4.111 to 4.117.
2   See para 4.112.
3   See para 4.116.

Satellite Master Antenna Television (SMATV) Systems

4.147   SMATV systems are systems whereby a large dish is used to receive satellite signals which are then distributed by cable to individual homes. For example, SKY and BSB worked with SMATV operators and landlords, such as local authorities and housing associations, to provide their services to many thousands of flat dwellers. Before the 1990 Act any cable system serving two or more households required a licence from the Cable Authority under the Cable and Broadcasting Act 1984 unless it carried only BBC services or channels regulated by the IBA. The reason for the exemption was that the 1984 Act's purpose was to ensure acceptable standards of taste and decency in programmes and systems carrying only BBC and IBA services carried programmes subject to separate regulation. In a 1989 ministerial statement [1] the Home Secretary proposed to relax the regulation of SMATV. Under his proposals, systems covering up to 1,000 homes do not need to be licensed under the 1990 Act, although they continue to need to be licensed under the Telecommunications Act 1984. Systems covering single buildings of whatever size or adjacent semi-detached or pairs of houses in a terrace will be covered by a class licence under the Telecommunications Act 1984. The Government has indicated that it is prepared to consider extending this class licence to cover groups of up to five terraced houses [2]. Larger SMATV systems would need individual Telecommunications Act licences. Where the proposed system is in a franchise area, the cable or local delivery operator would be given a right of first refusal. A reason for this partial liberalisation of SMATV systems is that, unlike the Cable Authority, the ITC has no statutory duty to exercise its licensing powers in a way which promotes broadband cable systems [3].

1   House of Commons, 27 April 1989, Vol 151, cols 638, 640 W. See also paras 2.27 to 2.29.
2   House of Lords Committee, col 1104.
3   See para 4.136.

Retailing Programme Services

4.148   To allow for more competition in the retailing of programme services, the 1988 White Paper [1] suggested that local delivery operators should not, except at the ITC's discretion, be permitted to retail them. In his 1989 ministerial announcement [2] the Home Secretary conceded that this could inhibit investment in local delivery services and he therefore proposed that local operators be able to retail programme services without restriction and without the need for permission from the ITC.

1   Cmnd 517, para 6.36.
2   House of Commons, 27 April 1989, Vol 151, 638 W. See also para 2.27.

Transitional Arrangement

4.149   In 1990 there were over 50 channels approved by the Cable Authority and while recognising the licensing of LPS was at the discretion of the ITC, it was seen as being 'excessive' if established bodies which the Cable Authority regarded as satisfactory and who had carried out the undertakings given on being granted their licence were required to undergo an onerous licensing process [1].

1   Mr Mellor, (minister of state, Home Office), House of Commons Committee, col 848.

Additional Services Provided on Television Broadcasting Frequencies

4.150   Section 48 essentially defines the expression 'additional services' as a telecommunication service provided on part of the signal used for carrying a television broadcasting service. Additional services can include teletext (Ceefax for the BBC, Oracle for commercial television), subtitling for the deaf, data broadcasting and transmission text and control signals and noise tests. In the future, spare capacity in signals could be used for enhanced definition television. Section 35 [1] requires Channel 3 and 5 licensees to achieve subtitling of 50% of their programming within five years and thereafter such subtitling as the ITC may consider it reasonable to require. The policy of the 1990 Act is not to make specific provision for services as yet not fully developed but, as possibilities for services emerge, to enable licensees to consider how best to exploit the potential that they offer [2].

1   See paras 4.81 to 4.84.
2   House of Lords Committee, col 1343.

Licensing Authority (s49(1))

4.151   Subject to its s49 duty as regards teletext [1] the ITC must do all that it can to ensure that in the case of (a) any frequencies falling within s48(1)(a) [2] on which television broadcasting services are provided and (b) any frequencies notified to the ITC under s48(1)(b) [2], all of the spare capacity available for the provision of additional services on that frequency is used for the provision of those services under additional services licences granted by the ITC (s49(1)).

1   See para 4.154.
2   See para 4.152.

Meaning of Additional Services (s48)

4.152 'Additional service' is any service which consists in the sending of 'telecommunication signals' for transmission by wireless telegraphy by using the 'spare capacity' within the signals carrying any television broadcasting service provided (a) on any frequency assigned under s65(1) by the Secretary of State to the ITC (other than a frequency which is assigned by the ITC to a local delivery service under s73(2)) or (b) on any other allocated frequency in the United Kingdom notified to the ITC by the Secretary of State (s48(1)). 'Telecommunication signals' means anything within s4(1)(a) - (d) of the Telecommunications Act 1984 (s48(6)) [1] The meaning of 'spare capacity' within signals carrying a television broadcasting service depends on the category of frequency. When the service is provided on a frequency notified to the ITC by the Secretary of State, it is such part of those signals as the Secretary of State may specify when making the notification (s48(2)(b)). The notification may specify a date beyond which the frequency is not to be used for the provision of additional services (s48(5)). When the service is provided on a frequency assigned under s 65(1), it is any part of those signals which is not required for providing that service and is determined by the ITC to be available for the provision of additional services (s48(2)(a)). The ITC must, when making this determination have regard to three facts. If it is a frequency (a) on which a Channel 3 service or Channel 5 is provided, the obligations of the service provider as respects subtitling for the deaf by means of a teletext service in accordance with s35 conditions [2] (b) on which Channel 4 is provided, the need for subtitling to be provided with Channel 4 programmes and (c) falling within the previous two categories, the need of the service provider to be able to use part of the signals carrying it for providing services (other than subtitling) which are ancillary to the service's programmes and directly related to their content [3] (s48(3)(6)). A person holding a licence to provide a Channel 3 service or Channel 4 or 5 is taken to be authorised by his licence to provide the above subtitling and services (s48(4)).

1   See para 8.13.
2   See paras 4.81 to 4.84. In s48 'subtitling'means subtitling for the deaf provided by means of a teletext service (sub-s(6)).
3   See para 4.8.

4.153 Section 48 enables the Secretary of State to notify the ITC that BBC frequencies are available for allocation for additional services. An assurance was given that the government would allow the BBC to retain sufficient spare capacity to continue to provide its Ceefax and Datacast service at pre-1990 Act levels and to continue to provide subtitling for the deaf after there has been full consultation with the BBC to safeguard its public broadcasting service requirements [1].

1   House of Commons Committee, col 858.

Single Teletext Service on Channels 3 and 4 (s49(2), (3))

4.154 The ITC must do all it can to ensure, in relation to the combined spare capacity available for the provision of additional services on frequencies on which Channel 3 services and Channel 4 are respectively provided, that a single teletext service is provided on that spare capacity. The service is to be provided only on so much of the spare capacity as the Secretary of State may approve (sub-s(2)). In so far as the service is provided for reception wholly or mainly in Wales, the spare capacity is that available for the provision of additional services on frequencies on which S4C is provided. The Secretary of State must exercise his powers under s48(1)(b) and (2)(b) [1] in allocating frequencies and specifying the spare capacity in the manner he considers appropriate to take account of the Welsh position (sub-s(3)).

1   See para 4.152.

4.155 A public teletext service on Channel 3 is protected, the intention being the continuation of a service with the same general characteristics of the pre-1990 Act Oracle service, though not necessarily provided by Oracle [1]. Sch 5 requires that the service include high quality news including international news (para 3(2)(a)) and other information services, including regional information (para 3(2)(b)) and cater for a wide variety of interests (para 3(2)(c)). The operation of this quality threshold before consideration of the cash bids is similar to that for Channel 3 and 5 (para 3(3)) and the winning applicant's proposals will be written into his licence (para 4(1)).

1   House of Lords Committee, col 1349.

4.156 The provisions of ss50 [1], 51 [2] and 53 [3], in relation to the teletext service referred to in s49(2), have effect subject to the provisions of Sch 5 (s50(7)). Those Sch 5 provisions relate to a public teletext service and are concerned with licence applications, their consideration and award of licence, conditions requiring the licence holder to deliver the promised service, failure to begin providing the licensed service and financial penalties on revocation of licence, licence renewal and additional methods of enforcement of licence to provide the service.

1   See paras 4.159 to 4.161.
2   See paras 4.162 to 4.164.
3   See paras 4.167 to 4.172.

Scope of Licence (s49(4))

4.157 An additional services licence may relate to the use of spare capacity within more than one frequency. Two or more additional services licences may relate to the use of spare capacity within the same frequency where it is to be used at different times, or in different areas, in the case of each of those licences.

Authorisation By Licence Holder of Another to Provide Local Delivery Services (s49(5) - (9))

4.158 An additional services licence may include provisions enabling the licence holder, subject to and in accordance with such conditions as the ITC may impose, to authorise any person who is not a 'disqualified person' in relation to an additional services licence by virtue of Part II of Sch 2 [1] to provide any additional service on the spare capacity allocated by the licence (sub-ss(5), (6)). This seeks to ensure that anyone disqualified from holding an ITC licence cannot be authorised by the licensee to provide a service as a sub licensee. Any conditions included in an additional services licence apply in relation to the provision of additional services by a duly authorised person as they apply in relation to the provision of the service by the licence holder. Any failure by such a person to comply with the conditions is treated as a failure by the licence holder to comply with those conditions (sub-s(7)). Every licence to provide a television broadcasting service must include conditions that appear to the ITC to be appropriate for ensuring that the licence holder grants (a) to any person holding a licence to provide additional services on the frequency on which that broadcasting service is provided and (b) to any person who is duly authorised by the additional services licence holder to provide additional services on that frequency, access to facilities reasonably required by that person for the purposes of, or in connection with, the provision of the additional services (sub-s(8)). Any person who grants to another access to facilities in accordance with these conditions may require the other person to pay a reasonable charge. Disputes as to the amount of the charge are determined by the ITC (sub-s(9)).

1   See paras 10.13 to 10.23.

Proposal Notice (s50(1), (2))

4.159   When the ITC propose to grant a licence to provide additional services it must publish, in the manner it considers appropriate, a notice (a) stating that it proposes to grant such a licence (b) specifying (i) the television broadcasting service(s) on whose frequency or frequencies the services are to be provided and (ii) (subject to the approval of the Secretary of State) the extent and nature of the spare capacity which is to be allocated by the licence (c) inviting applications for the licence and specifying the closing date for applications and (d) specifying (i) the application fee and (ii) the percentage of qualifying revenue for each accounting period payable by an applicant under s52(1)(c) [1] if he were granted the licence (sub-s(1)). The ITC may, if it thinks fit, specify (a) different percentages for different accounting periods falling within the licence period (b) a nil percentage for any accounting period so falling (sub-s(2)).

1   See para 4.165.

Application (s50(3) - (5))

4.160   The application is to be in writing and accompanied by (a) the application fee (b) [1] a technical plan indicating (i) the nature of any additional services which the applicant proposes to provide and (ii) so far as is known to the applicant, the nature of any additional services which any other person proposes to provide in accordance with s49(5) [2]; (c) the applicant's cash bid for the licence and (d) [1] such information as the ITC may reasonably require as to the applicant's present financial position and projected financial position for the licence period (sub-s(3)).

1   Before determining the application the ITC may require additional information, in the form or verified in the manner that it specifies, about this part of the application (sub-ss(4), (5)).
2   See para 4.158.

Publication of Applications (s50(6))

4.161   The ITC must, as soon as is reasonably practicable after the closing date for applications, publish in the manner it considers appropriate (a) the name of every applicant (b) particulars of the technical plans submitted by the applicants and (c) such other information connected with the application as the ITC consider appropriate.

Consideration of Applications (s51(1), (2), (7))

4.162   The ITC must not proceed to consider whether to award an applicant the licence on the basis of his cash bid unless it appears to it that (a) the technical plan submitted with his application is, so far as it involves the use of any telecommunication system, acceptable to the 'relevant licensing authorities', and (b) that the services proposed to be provided under the licence would be capable of being maintained throughout the licence period (sub-s(1)). Before deciding whether the first requirement is met, the ITC must consult the 'relevant licensing authorities' which means the Secretary of State and Director General of Telecommunications (sub-ss(2), (7)).

Award of Licence to Person Submitting Highest Cash Bid (s51(3), (4))

4.163   The provisions of s17 [1] concerning the award of a licence to the person submitting the highest cash bid apply in relation to an additional services licence as it applies in relation to a Channel 3 licence, save that (a) the provisions of sub-s(4) down to the end of para (b) [2] regarding exceptional circumstances are omitted (b) in sub-s(7)(a) [3] the reference to s19(1) is taken as a reference to s52(1) which provides for additional payments for licences and (c) sub-s12(b) [4] is to be read '(b) the name of every other applicant in whose case it appeared to the [ITC] that the requirement specified in s51(1)(a) [5] was satisfied' (sub-ss(3), (4)). The requirement is that the technical plan appears, to the ITC, acceptable with the relevant licensing authorities.

1   See para 4.20 to 4.25.
2   See para 4.20.
3   See para 4.23.
4   See para 4.25.
5   See para 4.162.

Refusal to Begin Additional Services (s51(5), (6))

4.164 If at any time after an additional services licence has been granted to any person but before the licence has come into force (a) that person indicates to the ITC that no services will be provided once the licence has come into force or (b) the ITC for any other reason have reasonable grounds for believing that none of the services will be provided, then (i) the ITC must serve on him a notice revoking the licence as from the time the notice is served on him and s17 as applied by s52 [1] shall, subject to s17(14) [2] have effect as if he had not made an application for the licence (sub-s(5)). When the ITC have a reasonable belief that the service will not be provided, it must serve on the person granted the licence a notice stating its grounds for believing that he will not provide the service. It must not serve such a notice unless it has given him a reasonable opportunity of making representations to it about the matters complained of (sub-s(6)).

1   See para 4.163.
2   See para 4.23.

Additional Payments (s52(1), (2), (5))

4.165 An additional services licence must include conditions requiring the licence holder to pay to the ITC (in addition to any fees required to be paid under s4(1)(b) [1] to the ITC towards its expenses) three categories of payment in respect of (a) the first complete calendar year falling within the licence period, the amount specified in his cash bid (b) each subsequent year falling wholly or partly within that period, a specified amount as increased by the appropriate percentage and (c) each accounting period of his falling within the licence period, an amount representing such percentage of the qualifying revenue for that accounting period as was specified in the ITC's proposal notice to grant the licence under s50(1)(d)(ii)(sub-s(1)). For the purposes of the third category of additional payments the qualifying revenue for any accounting period of the licence holder consists of all payments which are received or to be received by him or by any connected person and are referable to the right under the licence to use, or authorise any other person to use, in that period the spare capacity allocated by the licence (sub-s(2)). When (a) the first complete accounting period of his falling within the licence period does not end at the same time as that period or (b) the last complete accounting period of his falling within the licence period does not end at the same time as that period, the reference to an accounting period in the third category of additional payments includes a reference to that part of the accounting period preceding that first complete accounting period or (as the case may be) following that last complete accounting period, as falls within the licence period (sub-s(5)).

1   See para 3.17.

Additional Payment Licence Conditions (s52(3), (4))

4.166 An additional services licence may include conditions (a) enabling the ITC to estimate, in relation to the third category of additional payments, before the beginning of an accounting period the amount due for that period and (b) requiring the licence holder to pay the estimated amount by monthly instalment throughout that period (sub-s(3)). A licence may, in particular, include conditions (a) authorising the ITC to revise any estimate on one or more occasions, and to adjust the instalments payable by the licence holder to take account of the revised estimate (b) providing for the adjustment of any overpayment or underpayment (sub-s(4)).

Duration of Licence (s53(1), (3), (4))

4.167   A licence for the provision of additional services on a frequency notified to the ITC by the Secretary of State under s48(1)(b) must not continue in force beyond the date specified by him in relation to that frequency under s48(5) [1]. A licence for the provision of additional services on a frequency assigned by the Secretary of State under s65(1) [1] continues in force for 10 years and may be renewed on one or more occasions for a period of 10 years beginning with the date of renewal (sub-s(1)). Both periods of time are extended to 15 years when the additional services are on a frequency used for the broadcasting of a domestic satellite service (sub-s(3)(a)).

1   See para 4.152.

Renewal of Licence (s53(2)(3b)(11))

4.168   An application for the renewal of a licence may be made by the licence holder not earlier than four years (five years when the additional services are on a frequency used for the broadcasting of a domestic satellite service) before the date on which it would otherwise cease to be in force and not later than the 'relevant date' (sub-ss(2), (3)(b)). The 'relevant date' is the date which the ITC determine to be that by which it would need to publish a proposal notice under s50 if it were to grant, as from the date on which the licence would expire if not renewed, a fresh licence to provide the additional services formerly provided under that licence (sub-s(11)).

Refusal to Renew Licence (s53(5), (6))

4.169   When an application for the renewal of an additional services licence has been duly made to the ITC, it may only refuse the application if (a) it is not satisfied that any additional service specified in the technical plan submitted with the application under s50(3)(b) would, if the licence were renewed, be provided as proposed in that plan or (b) it proposes to grant a fresh additional services licence for the provision of an additional service that would differ in 'any material aspect' from the service authorised to be provided under the applicant's licence or (c) it proposes to determine that all or part of the spare capacity allocated by the licence is to cease to be available for the provision of additional services so that it may be used by a 'relevant person' to enhance the technical quality of his television broadcasting service. A 'relevant person' is a person providing a television broadcasting service on whose frequency the licensed service has been provided (sub-s(5)). The provisions safeguarding the public interest if there is a suspicion that any 'relevant source of funds' may be used by the applicant and found in s17(5) - (7) [1] apply in relation to an applicant for the renewal of an additional services licence save that (a) any reference to the awarding of a Channel 3 licence to the applicant is as if it is a reference to the renewal of an applicant's additional services licence under s53 and (b) in s17(7), the reference to s19(1) is a reference to s52(1) [2] which provides for additional payments (sub-s(6)).

1   See para 4.23.
2   See para 4.165.

Determination of Post Grant Payments (s53(7), (8))

4.170 On the grant of an application for licence renewal the ITC (a) must determine an amount which is to be payable to the ITC by the licence holder in respect of the first complete calendar year falling within the period for which the licence is to be renewed and (b) may specify a different percentage from that specified in the notice proposing to grant the licence under s50(1)(d)(ii) [1] as the percentage of qualifying revenue for each accounting period of his that will be payable by the applicant as the third category of additional payment in pursuance of s52(1)(c) [2] during the period for which the licence is to be renewed. The ITC may specify (a) different percentages for different accounting periods falling with the licence period or (b) a nil percentage for any accounting period so falling (sub-s(7)). The amount determined by the ITC above must be such amount as would, in its opinion, be payable to it under s52(1)(a) as if it were granting a fresh licence to provide the additional services (sub-s(8)).

1   See para 4.159.
2   See para 4.165.

Formal Renewal (s53(3), (9), (11))

4.171 When the ITC have granted a person's application it must formally renew his licence not later than the 'relevant date' or, if that is not reasonably practicable, as soon after that date as is reasonably practicable. The ITC must not renew his licence unless it has notified him of (a) the amount determined and (b) any percentage specified under sub-s(7) [1] and he has, within the period specified in the notification, notified it that he consents to the licence being renewed on these terms (sub-s(9)). Provided the application is made before the 'relevant date', the ITC may postpone consideration of it for as long as it thinks appropriate having regard to sub-s(9) (sub-s(4)). The 'relevant date' is the date which the ITC determine to be that by which it would need to publish a notice under s50 if it were to grant, as from the date on which that licence would expire if not renewed, a fresh licence to provide the additional service formerly provided under that licence (sub-s(11)).

1   See para 4.170.

Renewed Licence Conditions (s53(10))

4.172 When an additional services licence is renewed any conditions included in it in pursuance of s52 [1] must have effect during the renewed licence period (i) as if the amount determined by the ITC under sub-s(7)(a) [2] were an amount specified in a cash bid submitted by the licence holder and (ii) subject to any determination made under sub-s(7)(b) [3]. Subject to this, s52 has effect for the renewed licence period as it has for the original licence period (sub-s(10)).

1   See paras 4.165, 4.166.
2   See para 4.170.

No Interference Conditions (s54)

4.173 An additional services licence may include such conditions as the ITC consider appropriate for ensuring that the provision of an additional service under the licence does not cause any interference with (a) the television broadcasting service(s) on whose frequency or frequencies it is provided or (b) any other wireless telegraphy transmissions (sub-s(1)). Before imposing conditions the ITC must consult the relevant licensing authorities (the Secretary of State and the Director General of Telecommunications) (sub-s(2)).

Enforcement of Additional Services Licences (s55)

Power to Impose Financial Penalty (sub-ss(1), (2), (3))

4.174 If the ITC is satisfied that the holder of an additional services licence has failed to comply with a licence condition or with any direction given by the ITC under or by virtue of the 1990 Act, it may serve on him a notice requiring him to pay, within a specified period a specified financial penalty to the ITC (sub- s(1)). The amount of the penalty (a) must, if such a penalty has not been previously imposed on him during the period for which his licence has been in force (the 'relevant period') not exceed 3% of the qualifying revenue for his last complete accounting period falling within the relevant period (as determined under s52(2) [1]) and (b) must, in any other case, not exceed 5% of the qualifying revenue for that accounting period (as so determined). In relation to a person whose first complete accounting period falling within the relevant period has not yet ended, it is 3% or (as the case may be) 5% of the amount which the ITC estimate to be the qualifying revenue for that accounting period (as so determined) (sub-s(2)). The ITC must not serve on a person a financial penalty notice unless it has given him a reasonable opportunity of making representations to it about the matters complained of (sub-s(3)).
1   See para 4.165.

Power to Revoke Licence (s55(4))

4.175 The powers of the ITC to revoke a licence under s42 [1] apply in relation to an additional service licence as they apply in relation to a licence to provide a Channel 3 service save with the omission of sub-s(7) [2] (s55(4)).
1   See paras 4.113 to 4.116.
2   See para 4.116.

Television Broadcasting by the Welsh Authority

Welsh Authority to Continue as Sianel Pedwar Cymru (s56)

4.176 The Welsh Fourth Channel Authority continues in existence as a body corporate but it is (a) known as Sianel Pedwar Cymru (or S4C) and (b) constituted in accordance with, and have the functions conferred by, the 1990 Act. References to the Welsh Authority in the 1990 Act are references to that Authority. (s56(1)). The Welsh Authority consists of a chairman appointed as such, and between four and eight other members. All appointments are made by the Secretary of State (s56(2)). Further provisions for the Welsh Authority's constitution and procedure are found in Sch 6 (s56(3)). Some of the more relevant ones are mentioned here. It is within the Welsh Authority's capacity to do such things and enter into such transactions as are 'incidental or conducive' to the discharge of its functions under the 1990 Act (para 1(2)). A person is disqualified from being a member if he is a member or employee of the Radio Authority, Broadcasting Complaints Commission or Broadcasting Standards Council (para 2(1)). The members must not at any time include more than one person who is either a governor or an employee of the BBC or more than one person who is either a member or an employee of the ITC (para 2(2)). Appointments are made for a maximum period of five years (para 3(2)). Members are disqualified from sitting in the House of Commons (para 5). The public accountability of the Welsh Authority is demonstrated by the fact that at the end of each financial year, it must prepare a general report of its proceedings during that year and transmit it to the Secretary of State who must lay copies of it before Parliament (para 13(1)). The report must have attached to it the statement of accounts for the year, any report by the auditors on that statement and include such information as the Secretary of State may from time to time direct (para 13(2)). There is no statutory guarantee this will be debated in Parliament. The Welsh Authority may appoint advisory committees to give it advice on those matters relating to its functions as it may determine (para 14).

4.177 In 1981 the Welsh Fourth Channel Authority was created and primarily concerned itself as a commissioning, purchasing and editing body rather than a programme-making organisation. Funded out of subscriptions raised from ITV companies, it provided a mixture of Welsh language programmes and Channel 4 material in Wales. The programming remit remains.

Assignment of Frequencies by the Secretary of State (s65(3), (4))

4.178 The Secretary of State may by notice assign to the Welsh Authority for the purpose of the provision of the S4C service such frequencies as he may determine. Any such frequencies must be taken to be assigned only for the purpose of being used for the provision of the S4C service and any ancillary programme services which it is authorised to provide by virtue of s57(4). Section 57(4) provides that the Welsh Authority may use part of the signals carrying S4C to provide (a) subtitling (provided by means of a teletext service) in connection with programming on S4C and (b) other services which are ancillary to such programmes and directly related to their content. The Secretary of State may by notice revoke the assignment under s65 of any frequency specified in the notice (s65(4)).

Function of the Welsh Authority (s57(1))

4.179 The function of the Welsh Authority is to provide a television broadcasting service of high quality for reception wholly or mainly in Wales to be known as Sianel Pedwar Cymru (or S4C). References to S4C in the 1990 Act are references to that service (s57(1)).

The Duty of the Welsh Authority (s57(2))

4.180 It is the duty of the Welsh Authority to (a) provide S4C as a public service for disseminating information, education and entertainment (b) ensure that a substantial proportion of the programmes [1] broadcast on S4C are in Welsh and that the programmes broadcast on S4C between 6.30 pm and 10 pm consist mainly of programmes in Welsh and (c) ensure that the programmes in Welsh which are broadcast on S4C maintain a (i) high general standard in all respects (and, in particular, in respect of their content and quality) and (ii) wide range in their subject matter, having regard both to the programmes as a whole and also to the days of the week on which, and the times of the day at which, the programmes are broadcast (s57(2)).

1   In ss57 and 58 'programme' does not include an advertisement (s57(5)).

4.181 The Welsh Authority is established to provide public service broadcasting. The nature and content of its programmes is a matter to be decided by it: 'it is a matter of principle that such content should not be defined in statute' [1]. Clearly, the Authority is committed to the Welsh culture and language.

1   Mr David Mellor, (minister of state, Home Office), House of Commons Committee, col 881.

Sources of Programmes for S4C (s58)

Provision by BBC (s58(1))

4.182 For the purpose of enabling the Welsh Authority to comply with its duty to ensure Welsh programmes under s57(2)(b) [1] the BBC must provide it (free of charge) with sufficient television programmes in Welsh to occupy not less than 10 hours' transmission time per week, and to do so in a way which meets the reasonable requirements of the Authority (s58(1)).
1   See para 4.180.

4.183 When the Welsh Authority was set up in 1981 a set percentage of the licence fee was to be paid to the BBC for it to produce programmes for it but there was no reference to the number of hours per week. The reference in s58 is to 10 hours. The form of the BBC's obligations is unchanged in that the programming is to be as the Welsh Authority reasonably require.

Provision By Channel Four Television Corporation (s58(2)(4))

4.184 It is the duty of the Channel Four Television Corporation to (a) provide the Welsh Authority with programme schedules for the programmes broadcast on Channel 4, including information as to the periods available for the broadcasting of advertisements, far enough in advance to enable the Authority to comply with the s57(3) [1] duty of normally broadcasting Channel 4 programmes and (b) provide the Authority (free of charge) with any programmes which are required by it for complying with s57(3) [1] (s58(2)). Where any programmes provided by the Corporation each form part of a series of programmes, the Welsh Authority must ensure that the intervals between those programmes when broadcast on S4C normally correspond to the intervals between them when broadcast on Channel 4 (s58(4)). Consequently, viewers in Wales should be able to follow a series of Channel 4 programmes in the same sequence as they were originally shown elsewhere in the United Kingdom.
1   See para 4.185.

4.185 The Welsh Authority must ensure that, during any period allocated by it to the broadcasting of a programme not in Welsh, the programme broadcast by it on S4C is normally a programme which is being, has been or is to be broadcast on Channel 4 (s57(3)). This provision allows the Welsh Authority to show Channel 4 programmes which are not necessarily being broadcast at the same time to the rest of the country and consequently draw up a programme schedule that is special for Wales.

Other Provision (s58(3), (5))

4.186 The programmes broadcast on S4C may, to the extent that they are not provided by the BBC or Channel Four Television Corporation under s58, be obtained by the Welsh Authority from such persons as it thinks fit (s58(3)). The Welsh Authority must publish, in the manner that it considers appropriate, advance notice of the programme schedules for the programmes to be broadcast on S4C (s58(5)).

Requirements as to S4C Programmes (s59(1), (2))

4.187 The Welsh Authority must ensure that the following requirements are complied with in relation to S4C, namely that (a) nothing is included in its programmes which offends against good taste or decency or is likely to encourage or incite to crime or to lead to disorder or to be offensive to public feeling (b) any news given (in whatever form) in its programmes is presented with due accuracy and impartiality (c) due impartiality is preserved on the part of the Authority as respects matters of political or industrial controversy or relating to current public policy [1] (d) due responsibility is exercised with respect to the content of any of its programmes which are religious programmes, and that in particular any such programmes do not involve (i) any improper exploitation of any susceptibilities of viewers or (ii) any abusive treatment of the religious views and beliefs of those belonging to a particular religion or religious denomination and (e) its programmes do not include any technical device which, by using images of very brief duration or by any other means, exploits the possibility of conveying a message to, or otherwise influencing the minds of, viewers without their being aware, or fully aware, of what has occurred (s59(1)). These requirements are identical to those imposed on the ITC as respects its licensed services and were discussed earlier [2].

1   In applying this requirement a series of programmes may be considered as a whole (s59(2)).
2   See para 3.27.

Editorialising (s59(3))

4.188   The Welsh Authority must ensure that there are excluded from the programmes broadcast on S4C all expressions of the views and opinions of the Authority on matters (other than broadcasting) which are of political or industrial controversy or relate to current public policy (s59(3)). There is a similar duty imposed on the ITC as regards the views and opinions of the providers of its licensed services [1]. The Welsh Authority is not to present an equivalent of a newspaper editorial column.

1   See para 3.28.

Impartiality and General Codes (s59(4), (5))

4.189   The impartiality code referred to in s6(3) [1] has effect in relation to the application of the requirement for due impartiality by the Welsh Authority as respects matters of political or industrial controversy or current public policy found in s59(1)(c) [2] to S4C as it has effect in relation to the application of the identical requirement in s6(1)(c) [3] to a licensed service. The General Code for Programmes referred to in s7 [4] has effect in relation to S4C as it has to a licensed service (s59(4)). The Authority must observe the requirements of these codes in the provision of S4C (s59(5)).

1   See paras 3.29 to 3.31.
2   See para 4.187.
3   See para 3.27.
4   See para 3.32.

Advertising on S4C (s60(1), (6))

4.190   The Welsh Authority [1] must ensure that the following rules are complied with in relation to S4C: (a) S4C must not include (i) any advertisement which is inserted by or on behalf of any body whose objects are wholly or mainly of a political nature (ii) any advertisement which is directed towards any political end or (iii) any advertisement which has any relation to any industrial dispute (other than an advertisement of a public service nature inserted by, or on behalf of, a government department) (b) in the acceptance of advertisements for inclusion in S4C there must be no unreasonable discrimination either against or in favour of a particular advertiser and (c) (except in the case of any programme to which the Welsh Authority may determine this provision is not to apply) S4C must not include a programme which is sponsored by any person whose business consists, wholly or mainly, in the manufacture or supply of a product, or in the provision of a service, which the Welsh Authority are prohibited from advertising by virtue of the application of s9 of the Advertisements and Sponsorship Code [2] or directions from the Secretary of State under s60(4) [3] (s60(1)). After consultation with the Welsh Authority the Secretary of State may make regulations amending, responding or adding to the rules in s60. Such regulations can only be made after a draft of them has been approved by a resolution of each House of Parliament (s60(6)). These provisions mirror the general provisions in s8 [4] concerning advertisements included in services licensed by the ITC.

1   The Welsh Authority is not to act as an advertising agent (s60(5)). See para 10.3, footnote 1.
2   See paras 3.36, 3.37.
3   See para 4.192.
4   See paras 3.33, 3.34.

Advertisements and Sponsorship Code (s60(2), (3))

4.191   The code under s9 [1] has effect in relation to advertisements broadcast on S4C as it has effect in relation to advertisements on Channel 4, and the Welsh Authority must observe the provisions of that code (as it so has effect) in the provision of S4C (s60(2)). When the ITC give any directions under s9(7) [2] as to the times of advertisements to the Channel Four Television Corporation, it must send a copy of those directions to the Welsh Authority. So long as they remain in force, the Welsh Authority must, in broadcasting advertisements on S4C, give effect to the provision of the directions as if they were provisions regulating the times when advertisements are to be allowed on S4C (s60(3)).

1   See paras 3.36 to 3.38.
2   See para 3.38.

Directions on Advertising from the Secretary of State (s60(4))

4.192   The Welsh Authority must (a) from time to time consult the Secretary of State as to the classes and descriptions of advertisements which must not be broadcast on S4C and the methods of advertising or sponsorship which must not be employed in, or in connection with, the provision of S4C and (b) carry out any directions which he may give to it in respect of those matters (s60(4)).

Funding of Welsh Authority (s61)

Funding by the Secretary of State (s61(1), (5), (6))

4.193   The Secretary of State must, for the year 1993 and each subsequent year pay to the Welsh Authority an amount representing 3.2% of the total television revenues for the preceding year (s61(1)). The 'total television revenues' has two meanings. In relation to the year 1992 it means the aggregate of the qualifying revenues for that year of (i) the TV programme contractors which s10(2) of the Broadcasting Act 1981 defines as persons whose contracts as programme contractors gives them the right and the duty to provide programmes or parts of programmes for broadcasting on ITV and (ii) the body corporate referred to in s12(2) of the Broadcasting Act 1981 as a subsidiary of the IBA for the provision of programmes (other than advertisements) for the Fourth Channel [1] (s61(5)(a)). In relation to any year subsequent to 1992 'total television revenues' means the aggregate of the qualifying revenues for that year of (i) all holders of Channel 3 or Channel 5 licences (ii) the Welsh Authority and (iii) the Channel Four Television Corporation (s61(5)(b)). Section 19(2) - (6) [2], which deals with the computation of additional payments, has effect, with any necessary modifications, for enabling the ITC to estimate or determine a person's qualifying revenue for any year for the purposes of s61 (s61(5)). Any sums required by the Secretary of State under s61 must be paid out of money provided by Parliament (s61(6)).

1   The Channel Four Television Company
2   See paras 4.33, 4.34.

Duty of the ITC (s61(2), (3), (4))

4.194 The ITC must, before the beginning of 1993 and each subsequent year (the 'relevant year') (a) estimate the amount of the 'total television revenues' [1] for the preceding year and (b) notify the Secretary of State of that estimated amount. He must at the beginning of the relevant year pay to the Welsh Authority by way of interim payment for that year, an amount representing 3.2% of that estimated amount (s61(2)). Once the ITC has finally determined the amount of the total television revenues for a particular year, it must notify the Secretary of State of the amount. On receiving this notification the Secretary of State must, in respect of the year following that year (a) pay to the Welsh Authority the amount payable by him by virtue of s61(1) [2] after taking into account the interim payment made for that year under s61(2) above. Alternatively, he must notify the Welsh Authority of the amount of any overpayment made by him by means of the interim payment (s61(3)). The Welsh Authority must, as soon as reasonably practicable after receiving notification of an overpayment, pay to the Secretary of State the amount specified in the notification (s61(4)).

1   For meaning, see para 4.193.
2   See para 4.193.

Amending of Funding (s61(7), (8))

4.195 The Secretary of State may, after consulting the ITC and the Welsh Authority, by order substitute a different percentage for the percentage of the total television revenues for the time being specified in s61(1) [1] and (2) [2]. No order may be made before the end of 1997 unless the Secretary of State is satisfied that it is necessary to make the order having regard to the cost to the Authority of transmitting S4C (s61(7)). An order can only be made after a draft of it has been approved by a resolution of each House of Parliament (s61(8)).

1   See para 4.193.
2   See para 4.194.

4.196 Before the 1990 Act the Welsh Authority received from the IBA a payment equivalent to 3.4% of net advertising revenue and did not pay the costs of transmission. Section 61 provides that it is 3.2% of total television revenues and paid by the Secretary of State. This guaranteed income may be contrasted with Channel 4's income which is not guaranteed and has the possibility of a 2% subsidy if it falls below a certain amount [1]. Section 61(7) provides the Secretary of State with the opportunity to revise the figure of 3.2% before 1997. The Government estimated that the extra transmission costs will be about 0.11% of net advertising revenue and that the real and hidden costs of the Welsh Authority will be 3.51% of net advertising revenue [2]. The Welsh Authority is expected to earn the difference by, for example, selling advertising space, sponsorship and subscription.

1   See para 4.56.
2   House of Commons Committee, col 893.

Information to be Supplied to the ITC by the Welsh Authority (s62)

4.197 The Welsh Authority must provide the ITC with such forecasts, estimates, information and documents as the ITC may reasonably require for the purpose of enabling it to perform its functions concerning both the funding of revenue deficits of the Channel Four Television Corporation by Channel 3 licensees under s26 [1] and the funding of the Welsh Authority under s61 [2] (s62).

1   See paras 4.56 to 4.59.
2   See paras 4.193 to 4.195.

Government Control over S4C (s63)

4.198   If it appears to him to be necessary or expedient to do so in connection with his functions, the Secretary of State or any other Crown Minister may at any time by notice require the Welsh Authority to broadcast, at times specified in the notice a specified announcement, with or without visual images of any picture, scene or object mentioned in the announcement (s63(1)). The Welsh Authority must comply with the notice and when it broadcasts the announcement it may announce that it is doing so in pursuance of the notice (s63(1), (2)). Such announcements can be used in cases of civil emergency. The Welsh Authority may be required to exclude specified material from S4C. The Secretary of State may at any time by notice require the Welsh Authority to refrain from broadcasting any matter or classes of matter specified in the notice (s63(3)). The Authority must comply with the notice and may broadcast an announcement of the giving, revocation or expiration of the notice when this happens (s63(3), (4)). The powers conferred by s63 are in addition to any power specifically conferred on the Secretary of State by any other provision in the 1990 Act (s63(5)). These provisions mirror the provisions concerning government control under s10 over services licensed by the ITC [1] and discussed earlier [2].

1   See para 3.39.
2   See para 3.40.

Audience Research By Welsh Authority (s64)

4.199   The Welsh Authority must make arrangements for ascertaining (a) the state of public opinion concerning programmes broadcast on S4C (b) any effects of these programmes on the attitudes or behaviour of viewers and (c) the types of programme that members of the public would like to be broadcast on S4C (s64(1)). These arrangements must (a) ensure that, so far as is reasonably practicable, any research undertaken in pursuance of the arrangements is undertaken by people who are neither members nor employees of the Welsh Authority and (b) include provision for full consideration by the Authority of the results of any research (s64(2)). This provision is modelled on s12 [1] which imposes a similar requirement on the ITC.

1   See para 3.42.

Chapter 5

COPYRIGHT AND MISCELLANEOUS MATTERS

Copyright and Related Matters

5.1   Section 175 inserts seven sections (135A - 135G) after s135 of the Copyright, Designs and Patents Act 1988 under the heading 'Use as of right of sound recordings in broadcasts and cable programme services'. They relate to needletime. In 1988 the Monopolies and Mergers Commission (MMC) reported on a dispute between Phonographic Performance Ltd (PPL), which administers the public performing right in sound recordings on behalf of record companies, and independent local radio stations, over fees and needletime limits. These are the number of hours that sound recordings can be used in a given period and what could legitimately be charged for that right. The MMC concluded that collective licensing bodies are the best available mechanism for licensing sound recording provided they can be restrained from using this monopoly unfairly. Some of the MMC recommendations were implemented, with minor modifications in the 1988 Act and s175 makes further legislative change. It provides for a system of statutory copyright licensing in respect of collectively administered sound recordings included in a broadcast or cable programme service as a check on the unfair use of monopoly. Should a user not reach an agreement with a collective licensing body like PPL for the use of its repertory of sound recordings he can rely on a statutory licence pending a Copyright Tribunal order on the level of payment. During this interim period the user must pay the royalty that he considers reasonable and comply with any reasonable conditions notified to him by the collective licensing body. The Copyright Tribunal can award costs against either party under powers given to it by s151 of the 1988 Act. The scheme represents a fresh start and the Copyright Tribunal is not to be guided by orders made under the old legislation as to setting terms of payment. Its order as to the appropriate level of remuneration is back-dated to when the user started to broadcast under a statutory licence. He cannot be prevented from playing records while awaiting the Tribunal's adjudication on the terms of the licence because whether any condition is reasonable may be referred to the Tribunal by the user. Before the 1990 Act the PPL abandoned the practice of limiting the number of hours for which recordings from its repertoire and the statutory licence procedure seeks to prevent the reimposition of needletime restrictions [1]. The new sections are considered immediately below.
1   House of Commons Committee, col 1458.

Circumstances in which Right Available (s135A)

5.2   Section 135C [1] applies to the inclusion in a broadcast or cable programme service of any sound recordings [2] if (a) a licence to include them could be granted or procured by a licensing body (b) the condition in s 135(2) or (3) applied and (c) the includer had complied with s 135B [1] (sub-s(1)). If the includer does not hold a licence to do so, the condition is that the licensing body refuses to grant or procure the grant of a licence [3] (a) whose terms as to payment for inclusion would be acceptable to him or comply with an order of the Copyright Tribunal under s 135D and (b) allowing unlimited, or such needletime [4], as he demanded (sub-s(2)). If the includer holds a licence to do so, the condition is that the terms of the licence limit needletime and the licensing body refuses to substitute or procure the substitution of terms [3] allowing unlimited or such needletime as he demanded or refuses to do so on terms that fall within s 135A(2)(a) sub-s(3)).

1   See para 5.4.
2   'Sound recording' does not include a film sound track when accompanying a film (sub-s(5)).
3   This includes failing to do so within a reasonable time of being asked (sub-s(4)).
4   'Needletime' is the time in any period (whether determined as a number of hours in the period or a proportion of the period or otherwise) in which recordings may be included in a broadcast or cable programme service (sub-s(5)).

Notice of Intention to Exercise Right (s135B)

5.3   A person intending to avail himself of the right conferred by s 135C [1] must (a) give notice to the licensing body of his intention, asking it to propose terms of payment and (b) after receiving the proposal or on the expiry of a reasonable period, give reasonable notice to the body of the date when he proposes to begin exercising that right and the terms of payment [2] in accordance with which he intends to do so (sub-s(1)). When he has a licence to include the recordings, the date specified must not be sooner than the licence's expiry date except in a case falling with s 135A(3) (sub-s(2)) [3]. Before exercising the right, he must (a) give reasonable notice to the Copyright Tribunal of his intention to do so and when he proposes to do so and (b) apply to it under s 135D [4] to settle the terms of the payment (sub-s(3)).

1   See para 5.4.
2   In ss135B - 135G 'terms of payment' means terms as to payment for including sound recordings in a broadcast or cable programme service (s135A(6)).
3   See para 5.2.
4   See para 5.5.

Conditions for Exercise of Right (s135C)

5.4   A person who, on or after the date specified in a notice under s135 B (1)(b), [1] includes in a broadcast or cable programme service sound recordings in circumstances in which s135 C applies and who (a) complies with any reasonable condition notified to him by the licensing body as to their inclusion (b) provides that body with such information about their inclusion as it may reasonably require and (c) makes payments to it as required by s135C, is in the same position as regards infringement of copyright as if he had at all material times held a licence granted by the owner of the copyright in question (sub-s(1)). Payments must be made at not less than quarterly intervals in arrears (sub-s(2)). The amount of payment is determined in accordance with an order of the Copyright Tribunal under s135D [2]. If no order has been made the amount is determined (a) in accordance with any proposal for terms of payment made by the licensing body pursuant to a s135B request or (b) where there is no such proposal or the proposed amount is unreasonably high, in accordance with the terms of payment notified to the licensing body under s135B(1)(b) [1] (sub-s(3)). When s135 C applies to the inclusion of sound recordings, it does so in place of a licence (sub-s(4)).

1   See para 5.3.
2   See para 5.5.

Applications to Settle Payments (s135D)

5.5   On an application to settle the terms of payment, the Copyright Tribunal must consider it and make the order that it determines reasonable in the circumstances (sub-s(1)). Any order has effect from the date the applicant began exercising the s135C[1] right and any necessary repayments or further payments are to be made (sub-s(2)).
1   See para 5.4.

References etc about Conditions, Information and other Terms (s135E)

5.6   A person exercising the s135C[1] right or who has given notice to the Copyright Tribunal of his intention to do so, may refer to it any question whether (a) any condition as to the inclusion of sound recordings notified to him by the licensing body, is a reasonable condition or (b) any information is information which the licensing body can reasonably require him to provide (sub-s(1)). On a reference, the Tribunal must consider it and make the order that it determines reasonable in the circumstances (sub-s(2)).
1   See para 5.4.

Application for Review of Order (s135F)

5.7   A person exercising the s135C[1] right or the licensing body may apply to the Copyright Tribunal to review a s135D[2] or 135E[3] order (sub-s(1)). Application can not be made, except with the special leave of the Tribunal (a) within 12 months from the date of the order, or of the decision of a previous application under s135F or (b) if the order was made so as to be in force for 15 months or less, or as a result of a decision of a previous application is due to expire within 15 months of that decision, until the last three months before the expiry date (sub-s(2)). On an application, the Tribunal must consider it and make the order that it determines reasonable in the circumstances (sub-s(3)). The order takes effect from the date on which it is made or a later date specified by the Tribunal (sub-s(4)).
1   See para 5.4.
2   See para 5.5.
3   See para 5.6.

Factors to be Taken into Account (s135G)

5.8   In determining what is reasonable on an application or reference under s135D[1] or 135E[2], or on reviewing an order under s135F[3], the Copyright Tribunal must (a) have regard to the terms of any orders which it has made in the case of persons in similar circumstances exercising the right conferred by s135C[4] and (b) exercise its powers so as to secure that there is no unreasonable discrimination between persons exercising that right against the same licensing body (sub-s(1)). In settling the terms of payment under s135D[1] the Tribunal is not to be guided by an order made under other legislation (sub-s(2)). Section 134 (factors to be taken into account: retransmissions) applies on an application or reference under sections 135D - 135F[5] as it applies on an application or reference relating to a licence (sub-s(3)).
1   See para 5.5.
2   See para 5.6.
3   See para 5.7.
4   See para 5.4.
5   See paras 5.5 to 5.7.

5.9   Consequential amendments to the 1988 Act are provided. These relate to s149 (jurisdiction of the Copyright Tribunal) and s179 (index of defined expressions) (s175(2)(3)).

Duty to Provide Advance Information about Programmes (s176)

5.10   The provider of a programme service to which s176 applies must make available information relating to programmes [1] to be included in the service to any person ('the publisher') wishing to publish it in the United Kingdom (sub-s(1)). The information as to the titles of programmes which are to be, or may be, included in a service on any date, and the time of their inclusion, is to be made available to a publisher who asks for this and reasonably requires it (sub-s(2)). It is to be made available as soon after its preparation as is reasonably practicable but, in any event, (a) not later than when it is made available to another publisher and (b) when information relates to all the service's programmes in a period of seven days, not later than the beginning of the preceding 14 day period, or such other number of days as may be prescribed by the Secretary of State by order (sub-s(3)). His order is subject to annulment in pursuance of a resolution of either House of Parliament (sub-s(4)). This duty is not satisfied by providing the information on terms, other than as to copyright, prohibiting or restricting publication in the United Kingdom by the publisher (sub-s(5)). Sch 17 applies to the information or future information to be made available (sub-s(6)). For example, it contains provisions as to the circumstances in which the use of information as of right is available (para 2), notice of intention to exercise the right and the conditions for its exercise (paras 3 and 4). The following table shows the programme services to which s176 and Sch 17 applies and the persons who provide them or are to be treated as providing them (sub-s(7)).

Programme service	Provider of Service
Services other than services under the 1990 Act	
Television and national radio services provided by the BBC for reception in the United Kingdom	The BBC
Services under the 1990 Act	
Television programme services subject to ITC regulation	The person licensed to provide the service
The television broadcasting service provided by the Welsh Authority	The Authority
Any national service (see s84(2)(a)(i)) [2] subject to regulation by the Radio Authority	The person licensed to provide the service
Services provided during interim period only	
Television broadcasting services provided by the ITC in accordance with Sch 11 other than Channel 4	The programme contractor
Channel 4, as so provided	The body corporate referred to in s12(2) of the Broadcasting Act 1981.

1   Section 176 does not require information to be given about any advertisement (sub-s(8)).
2   See para 8.8.
3   Channel Four Television Co Ltd.

5.11   Section 176 ends the programmes listings duopoly and the new licensing scheme was introduced on 1 March 1991. The information that broadcasters must make available is limited to the date, time and title of programmes. The copyright in this information is not reserved by s176 which ends the monopoly of its use and requires that copyright holders should license others to use it. The requirement that a complete schedule for any one week period is to be available 14 days before the first day of that week strikes a balance between the broadcaster's need not to release commercially sensitive information too soon and the publishers's need to have time to prepare their listings. In cases of dispute, the 1990 Act does not lay down guidelines for the Copyright Tribunal when it must consider the amount that it is reasonable for a publisher to pay the copyright owner. It may be expected that it will establish a reasonable market value for the particular licence. As a transitional measure, the government has decided that Reed, the copyright assignees of the ITV and Channel 4 listings, may negotiate licence fees with publishers until the end of 1992, when that assignment expires [1].

1   House of Lords Committee, col 1715.

Foreign Satellite Services

Orders Proscribing Unacceptable Foreign Satellited Services (s177)

5.12   Subject to the provisions of s177, the Secretary of State may make an order proscribing a foreign satellite service for the purposes of s178 which provides for the offence of supporting such a service (sub-s(1)). A 'foreign satellite service' is a service consisting wholly or mainly in satellite transmission from a place outside the United Kingdom of television or sound programmes receivable there (sub-s(6)) [1]. If the ITC (or Radio Authority) consider that the quality of a relevant foreign service is unacceptable, they must notify to the Secretary of State details of the service and their reasons why the order should be made (sub-s(2)). A 'relevant foreign satellite service' is a service consisting wholly or mainly in the transmission of television (or sound) programmes (sub-s(6)) [1]. The ITC (or Radio Authority) must be satisfied that there is repeatedly transmitted matter which offends against good taste or decency or is likely to encourage or incite crime or to lead to disorder or to be offensive to public feeling (sub-s(3)). The Secretary of State must be satisfied that the making of the order is (i) in the public interest and (ii) compatible with any international obligations of the United Kingdom (sub-s(4)). A s177 order (a) may make such provision for the purpose of identifying a particular foreign service as is thought fit and (b) is subject to annulment in pursuance of a resolution of either House of Parliament (sub-s(5)).

1   The definition applies also to s178.

Offence of Supporting Proscribed Foreign Satellite Service (s178)

5.13   Section 178 applies to any foreign satellite service which is proscribed for its purposes by virtue of a s177 order [1] (a 'proscribed service') (sub-s(1)). A person is guilty of an offence if, in the United Kingdom, he (a) supplies [2] any equipment or other goods for use in connection with the operation or day-to-day running of a proscribed service (b) supplies or offers to supply, programme material [3] to be included in any programme transmitted in the provision of a proscribed service (c) arranges for, or invites, any other person to supply programme material to be so included (d) advertises, by means of programmes transmitted in the provision of a proscribed service, goods supplied, or services provided, by him (e) publishes the times or other details of any programmes which are to be transmitted in the provision of a proscribed service or (otherwise than by publishing those details) publishes an advertisement of matter calculated to promoted a proscribed service (directly or indirectly) (f) supplies or offers to supply [4] any decoding equipment which is designed or adapted to be used primarily to enable the reception of programmes transmitted in the provision of a proscribed service (sub-s(2), (3)). The accused has a defence if he proves that he did not know, and had no reasonable cause to suspect, that the service in connection with which the act was done was a proscribed service (sub-s(4)). The maximum penalty (a) on summary conviction, is six months imprisonment and/or a fine not exceeding the statutory maximum (b) on indictment, is two years imprisonment and/or a fine (sub-s(5)).

1   See para 5.12.
2   Section 46 of the Consumer Protection Act 1987 has effect for construing references in s178 to the supply of any thing as it has in that Act to the supply of any goods (s178(7)).
3   'Programme material' includes (a) a film (within the meaning of Part 1 of the Copyright, Designs and Patents Act 1988)(b) any other recording and (c) an advertisement or other advertising material (s178(8)).
4   A person exposing decoding equipment for supply or having such equipment in his possession for supply is deemed to offer to supply it (s178(6)).

5.14   Section 178 provides for the offence of supporting a satellite service uplinked from abroad and proscribed in an order made by the Secretary of State under s177 after notification by the monitoring body (the ITC (or Radio Authority)) of its unacceptable quality. The defendant must, in the United Kingdom, cease the forbidden support. The offence was anticipated in the White Paper (Cmnd 517) [1].
1   See para 7.14.

Unauthorised Decoders

Unauthorised Decoders for Encrypted Services etc (s179)

5.15   A new s(297A) is inserted after s297 of the Copyright, Designs and Patents Act 1988 (sub-s(1)). It provides that a person who makes, imports, sells or lets for hire an unauthorised decoder is guilty of an offence and liable on summary conviction to a fine not exceeding level 5 on the standard scale (s297A(1)). It is a defence for the defendant to prove that he did not know, and had no reasonable ground for knowing, that the decoder was an unauthorised decoder (s297A(2)). In that section 'apparatus' includes any device, component or electronic data, 'decoder' means any apparatus which is designed or adapted to enable (whether on its own or with any other apparatus) an encrypted transmission to be decoded, 'transmission' means any programme included in a broadcasting or cable programme service which is provided from a place in the United Kingdom and 'unauthorised', in relation to a decoder, means a decoder which will enable encrypted transmissions to be viewed in decoded form without payment of the fee (however imposed) which the person making the transmission, or on whose behalf it is made charges for viewing them or any services of which they form part (s297A(3)). In s299 of the 1988 Act (fraudulent reception of programmes broadcast from countries or territories outside the United Kingdom (a) sub-s(2) ceases to have effect and (b) in sub-s(5) after '297' there is inserted '297A' (s179(2))

5.16   The provision seeks to deal with the mischief of unauthorised decoding of encrypted programmes without payment to those charging for the broadcast. It creates the criminal offence of making, importing, selling or letting for hire unauthorised decoders. The amendment of s299 of the 1988 Act seeks to deter the piracy of foreign satellite television services. It means that, by order, any person who dishonestly receives a programme included in a broadcasting or cable programme service provided from a place outside the United Kingdom with intent to avoid payment of a charge applicable to the programmes' reception also commits an offence. This extends the protection already offered to United Kingdom television services under the 1988 Act to services from abroad, regardless of whether the country of origin offers reciprocal protection for United Kingdom broadcasters, when it appears to the Secretary of State that the reception of those services here is materially affecting United Kingdom broadcasters.

5.17   At the time of the House of Lords Report stage of the Broadcasting Bill an appeal to the House of Lords in its judicial capacity was pending in the case of *BBC Enterprises Ltd v Hi-Tech Xtravision Ltd* [1990] 2 WLR 1123. An electronics company manufactured decoders which were adapted to decode BBC TV Europe, a satellite service which sends coded transmission of BBC transmissions to other European countries. Civil proceedings were brought under s298 of the Copyright, Designs and Patents Act 1988. The Court of Appeal reversed the High Court decision and held that the effect of s298 was that a person who charged for programmes or sent encrypted transmissions had the right not to have others making apparatus designed to be used by persons not authorised by him to receive the programmes. The government considered that it would be premature to try to revise ss297 - 299 of the 1988 Act to cover this kind of situation [1].

1   House of Lords Report, col 836.

Television Licensing

Transfer to BBC of Functions Connected with Television Licences (s180)

5.18   The Wireless Telegraphy Act 1949 (the '1949 Act') has effect subject to the amendments specified in Part I of Sch 18 which transfers functions of the Secretary of State as respects the issue and renewal of television licences to the BBC (sub-s(1)). Section 1 of the 1949 Act (licensing of wireless telegraphy) is amended so that s1(1) provides that the grant of a television licence is made by the BBC (para 1(1)(2)). In s1(2)(b) a television licence may be issued subject to such terms, provisions and limitations as the Secretary of State may direct or (subject to any such direction) the BBC may think fit (para 1(3)). In s1(3) a television licence, unless revoked by the BBC, continues in force for the period specified in the licence (para 1(4)). Section 1(4) provides that a television licence may be revoked, or the terms, provisions or limitations of it varied, by the BBC (either of their own motion or to give effect to any direction of the Secretary of State under s1(2)(b) by (a) notice in writing served on the licence holder or (b) general notice (para 1(5)). A new s1(7) provides that 'television licence' means a wireless telegraphy licence authorising the installation and use of a television receiver and 'television receiver' means television receiving apparatus of any class or description specified in regulations made by the Secretary of State under s2 of the 1949 Act (para 1(6)). Section 2 (fees and charges for wireless telegraphy licences) is amended so that in s 2(1)(b) payment, in the case of a television licence, is to the BBC (para 2(1)(2)). Section 2(2) provides, in its first paragraph, that notwithstanding anything in s2(1), where (a) an application for the issue or renewal of a television licence is made to the BBC by a person ordinarily resident in the United Kingdom and (b) the BBC are satisfied, by means of a certificate issued by the local authority and produced to them by the applicant, that the applicant is a blind person not resident in a public or charitable institution or in a school, the BBC must, to the extent determined by the Secretary of State, dispense with the payment of any sum which would otherwise be payable on the issue or renewal of a licence (para 2(3)). In s 15(1) (entry and search of premises etc) a search warrant may be granted authorising, where the offence under the 1949 Act relates to the installation or use of a television receiver, any person(s) authorised in that behalf by the BBC (or the Secretary of State (para 3)). When sums are paid to the BBC under the above amended s 2(1) of the 1949 Act, s 3(3) of the Post Office Act 1969 (refunds in respect of wireless telegraphy licences) does not apply. However, refunds may be made by the BBC out of sums received by it under s2(1) in such cases or classes of cases as it may determine (sub-s(2)). The balance of sums received is paid into the Consolidated Fund (sub-s(3)). Part I of the Wireless Telegraphy Act 1967 (obtaining of information as to the sale and hire of television sets) has effect subject to the amendments specified in Part II of Sch 18 which provides that all the Secretary of State's functions under Part I of the 1967 Act, apart from his power to make regulations under ss2(7) or 6(1) are transferred to the BBC (sub-s(4)).

Certain Apparatus Deemed to be for Wireless Telegraphy (s181)

5.19   Any apparatus which is (a) connected [1] to the telecommunications system by means of which a relevant cable service is provided and (b) is so connected to enable any person to receive programmes included in that service by means of reception and immediate re-transmission of programmes included in a television broadcasting service [2], is deemed for the purposes of the Wireless Telegraphy Act 1949 to be apparatus for wireless telegraphy (sub-s(1)). It is also deemed, for the purpose of (a) the amended s1(7) of the 1949 Act [1] and (b) any regulation made by the Secretary of State for that provision's purposes under s2 of the 1949 Act, to be television receiving apparatus (sub-s(2)). 'Relevant cable service' means a service provided by any person that consists in the use of a telecommunications system (whether run by him or someone else) to deliver, otherwise than by wireless telegraphy, programmes included in one or more television broadcasting services, where they are delivered for (a) simultaneous reception at two or more places in the United Kingdom or (b) reception at any place in the United Kingdom for presentation there either to members of the public or to any group of persons (sub-s(3)).

1   'Connected' has the same meaning as in the Telecommunications Act 1984 (sub-s(4)).
2   'Television broadcasting service' means a television broadcasting service within the meaning of the 1990 Act, whether provided by a licence holder of a licence granted by the ITC, or by the BBC or the Welsh Authority or in accordance with the transitional provisions of Part II of Sch 11) (sub-s(4)).
3   See para 5.18.

5.20   Schedule 21 repeals the Cable and Broadcasting Act 1984. Section 31 of the 1984 Act provided that those who received their television programmes via cable, rather than via an aerial, still required a television licence. Section 181's purpose is to continue the effect of s31 [1].

1   House of Lords Committee, cols 1740, 1741.

Listed Events

Certain Events Not to be Shown on Pay-per-View Terms (s182)

5.21   The ITC must do all that it can to ensure that a programme which consists of or includes the whole or part of a listed event is not included on pay-per-view terms in a service provided by the holder of a licence granted by it for the provision of television programme services and additional services (s182(1)). Also, such programmes are not to be included on those terms in a television broadcasting service provided by the BBC or Welsh Authority (s182(2)). A 'listed event' is a sporting or other event of national interest which is included in a list drawn up by the Secretary of State for the purposes of s182 (s182(3)(a)). 'National interest' includes interest within England, Scotland, Wales or Northern Ireland (s182(7)). A programme is included in a service on pay-per-view terms if any payments falling to be made by subscribers to the service will or may vary according to whether that programme is or is not actually received by them (s182(3)(b)). The s182 prohibition does not apply to a recording of the whole or part of a listed event in a programme more than 48 hours after the original recording was made (s182(6)). Before drawing up, revising or ceasing to maintain the listed events, the Secretary of State must first consult (a) the BBC (b) the Welsh Authority (c) the ITC and (d) in relation to a particular sporting or other event of national interest which the Secretary of State proposes to include in, or omit from, the list, the person from whom the rights to televise that event may be acquired (s182(4)). The list is to be published in the manner the Secretary of State considers appropriate for bringing it to the attention of (a) the above persons and (b) every holder of a licence granted by the ITC for the provision of television programme services and additional services (s182(5)).

5.22   The access of viewers to listed events was protected by s14 of the Cable and Broadcasting Act 1984 in two ways. First, it provided that listed events could not be shown on cable television on a pay-per-view basis. Pay-per-view is where viewers pay an additional sum for viewing a particular event. The 1990 Act extends the prohibition on the showing of listed events on pay-per-view terms to television services licensed by the ITC and provided by the BBC and Welsh Authority. The 1990 Act removes the second protection afforded by the 1984 Act whereby when a cable channel proposed to show a listed event, ITV and BBC had to be given the opportunity of acquiring the rights to show the event on comparable terms. A practical reason for removing the matching-bid safeguard is that in an increasingly complex and competitive broadcasting industry it would be increasingly difficult for the ITC to enforce it [1].
1   House of Lords Committee, col 1704.

Gaelic [1] Television Programmes

Financing of Programmes in Gaelic out of Gaelic Television Fund (s183)

5.23   The Secretary of State (a) may, for the financial year beginning 1 April 1991 and (b) must, for each subsequent year, pay to the ITC the amount that he determines appropriate for the purposes of s183. The approval of the Treasury is required and Parliament provides the money (s183(1), (8)). The money received by the ITC must be carried by it to the credit of a fund established by it under s183 and known as the Gaelic Television Fund (s183(2)). The fund is to be managed by Comataidh Telebhisein Gaidhlig (the Gaelic Television Committee). It consists of a chairman, appointed as such, and between four and eight other members. All appointments are made by the ITC who must ensure that a majority of members are persons who appear to it to represent the Gaelic-speaking community. Sch 19 contains supplementary provisions for the Committee (s183(3), (7)). The Fund may be applied by the Committee (a) in the making of grants for (i) financing the making of television programmes in Gaelic primarily with a view to their being broadcast for reception in Scotland [2] (ii) financing the training of persons employed or to be employed in connection with the making of those programmes and (iii) other purposes connected with or related to the making of the programmes and (b) in financing research into the types of television programmes in Gaelic that members of the Gaelic-speaking community would like to be broadcast (s183(4)). When making a grant the Committee may impose such conditions as it thinks fit, including conditions requiring the grant to be repaid in specified circumstances (s183(5)). The Committee is to make grants in the manner that it considers will ensure that a wide range of high quality television programmes in Gaelic are broadcast for

reception in Scotland. However s183 does not authorise programmes to be commissioned by the Committee (s183(6)).
1   Gaelic, in ss183 and 184, means the Gaelic language as spoken in Scotland (s183(9)).
2   'For reception in Scotland' in ss183 and 184 means for reception wholly or mainly in Scotland (s183(9)).

5.24   The Gaelic Television Committee, although appointed by, and subject to the oversight of, the ITC, is an independent statutory body whose status is given effect to by the provisions of Sch 19. Its fund is not regarded as forming part of the ITC's revenues. The Committee's making of grants for television programmes in Gaelic, training and other purposes connected with them is a prominent part of the scheme. The Government saw it as important that the regulatory functions of the ITC should not be blurred by a grant-making function [1]. The Committee's power to finance research into the types of programmes that the Gaelic-speaking community would like broadcast is similar to the ITC power, under s12(1)(b) [2], to arrange for audience research to discover the types of programmes that the public would like to see included in licensed services.
1   House of Lords Committee, col 1746.
2   See para 3.42.

Broadcasting of Programmes in Gaelic on Channel 3 in Scotland (s184)

5.25   Provision is made for programmes in Gaelic (a) in any regional Channel 3 service that is to be provided for an area the whole of which is in Scotland and (b) if the ITC so determine, any regional Channel 3 service that is to be provided for an area the greater part of which is in Scotland (s184(4)). The procedure to be followed by the ITC in connection with consideration of applications for licences under s16 applies to that service as if certain further requirements were included among those specified in s16(2) [1]. They are that (a) a suitable proportion of programmes included in the service are programmes in Gaelic other than funded Gaelic productions [2] (b) the service includes funded Gaelic productions of which (i) a suitable proportion are of high quality and (ii) a suitable proportion are shown at peak viewing times and (c) that (taking the programmes included in the service in accordance with (a) and (b) above as a whole) the service includes a wide range of programmes in Gaelic (s18(1)). The conditions which are, by virtue of s33(1) [3], to be included in the appropriate regional Channel 3 licence accordingly include conditions to ensure the requirements specified in s184 are complied with in relation to the service (s184(3)).
1   See para 4.13.
2   These are programmes in Gaelic the making of which has been wholly or partly financed out of grants made by the Gaelic Television Committee in pursuance of s183(4) to the service provider (s184(2)).
3   See para 4.77.

5.26   The 1990 Act does not provide for either government funding of Irish language broadcasting in Northern Ireland by means of the Gaelic Television Fund or a requirement to provide a wide range of programmes in the Irish language be imposed in Channel 3 licences in Northern Ireland. The government did not consider that a case for its support for Irish language broadcasting in the 1990 Act had been made out [1]. Government funding for the Scottish Gaelic broadcasting is anticipated to provide 200 hours of Gaelic programming per year in addition to the 100 hours provided by the BBC, STVB and Grampian before the 1990 Act. Irish language programming in Northern Ireland before the 1990 Act amounted to three hours per week on BBC radio and some schools' programming. A requirement for Irish language programmes in a

Channel 3 licence to cover the province was seen as possibly so onerous as to put its viability in doubt.
1   See House of Lords Committee, col 1748.

National Television Archive

Contributions towards Maintenance of National Television Archive (s185)

5.27   The ITC must, for the financial year which includes the commencement of s185 and each subsequent financial year, determine an aggregate amount which it considers it would be appropriate for the holders of Channel 3 and Channel 5 licences to contribute, in accordance with s185, towards the expense incurred by its nominated body in maintaining a national television archive (s185(1)). The body nominated by the ITC must be (a) a designated body for the purposes of s75 of the Copyright, Designs and Patents Act 1988 (recordings for archival purposes) and (b) appear to the ITC to be in a position to maintain a national television archive (s185(2)). A Channel 3 or Channel 5 licence must include conditions requiring the licence holder to pay to the ITC, in each financial year, the amount notified by it to him for the purposes of s185. The amount is a proportion of the aggregate amount determined as the ITC considers appropriate. Different proportions may be determined in relation to different people (s185(3)). The amount received by the ITC is transmitted by it to the nominated body (s185(4)).

5.28   Section 185 enables the ITC to require Channel 3 and 5 licensees to contribute towards the cost of a body nominated by it to maintain a national television archive. The body is to be a designated body for the purposes of the Copyright, Designs and Patents Act 1988 so as to avoid any breach of copyright. It will almost certainly be the National Television Archive which is maintained by the British Film Institute and it is intended that the funding required should not exceed, in real terms, the pre 1990 Act voluntary ITV contribution to the then archive arrangements. It is envisaged that the BBC will continue to be responsible for the archiving of its own material [1].
1   House of Lords Committee, cols 1752, 1754.

Duties of BBC as respects Independent Productions

Duty of BBC to Include Independent Productions in their Television Services (s186(1), (2), (9))

5.29   It is the duty of the BBC to ensure that, in each of relevant period, not less than the prescribed percentage of the total amount of time allocated to the broadcasting of qualifying programmes in the television broadcasting services provided by it is allocated to the broadcasting of a range and diversity of independent productions (s186(1)). The 'relevant periods' are (a) the period beginning with 1 January 1993 and ending with 31 March 1994 (b) the financial year beginning with 1 April 1994 and (c) each subsequent financial year (s186(9)). 'Qualifying programmes' and 'independent productions' have the same meanings as in s16(2)(b) [1] and are, in each case, programmes of such description as the Secretary of State may by order specify for the purpose. The 'prescribed percentage' is the percentage for the time being specified in s16(2)(h) and is 25% in the 1990 Act (s186(2)(a)). The reference to a range of independent productions is a reference to a range of such productions in terms of cost and acquisition as well as in terms of the types of programme involved (s186(2)(b)). Before making an order under s16(5) specifying the meaning of 'qualifying programme' and 'independent production' or s16(6) substituting a different prescribed percentage, the Secretary of

State must (in addition to consulting the ITC in accordance with s16(7) consult the BBC (s186(2)).
1   See para 4.13.

5.30   The purpose of s186 is to impose on the BBC the same statutory independent production requirement as is imposed on ITC licensees of Channels 3 [1], 4 [2] and 5 [3]. Their licence conditions must include a requirement each year that at least 25% of the total amount of time allocated to the broadcasting of qualifying programmes in the service is allocated to the broadcasting of a range and diversity of independent productions. The Secretary of State is enabled to define by order the terms 'qualifying programmes' and 'independent productions'. The contents of these orders apply equally to the BBC as to ITC licensees and consequently the same independent productions quota applies equally to all major broadcasters in the United Kingdom. The government regards this as a 'major and permanent feature of our broadcasting system in the future' [4].
1   Section 16(2)(h). See para 4.13.
2   Section 25(2)(f). See para 4.53.
3   Section 29(1). See para 4.65.
4   Mr Mellor, (minister of state, Home Office), House of Commons Committee, col 1472.

Director General of Fair Trading's Report (s186(3), (4), (5), (8))

5.31   The Director General of Fair Trading (the Director), in respect of each relevant period, must make a report to the Secretary of State on his conclusions as to the extent to which the BBC has, in his opinion, performed its s186 duty in that period (s186(3)). The report may also contain (a) his reasons for those conclusions which, in his opinion, facilitate their proper understanding and (b) his observations, in the light of those conclusions and his reasons for them, with regard to (i) competition in connection with the production of television programmes for broadcasting by the BBC or (ii) matters appearing to him to arise out of, or to be conducive to, such competition (s186(4)). In any proceedings relating to the BBC's performance of its s186 duty, the Director's report is evidence of any facts stated in it and any conclusions are evidence of the extent to which the BBC has performed that duty in the particular relevant period. There is a rebuttable presumption that a document purporting to be a copy of the report is such a copy (s186(8)).

5.32   The Director may at any time make a report to the Secretary of State on any matter related to or connected with the BBC's performance of its s186 duty. The report may include his observations on any matter falling within s186(4)(b) [1] and pertinent to the report's subject matter (s186(5)).
1   See para 5.31.

Publication of Report (s186(6), (7))

5.33   When he makes a report the Director must have regard to the need for excluding from it, so far as it is practicable to do so, two matters: any matter that relates to an individual's private affairs where, in the Director's opinion, its publication would, or might, seriously prejudice his interests; also, any matter which relates specifically to a body's affairs where, in the Director's opinion (i) its publication would, or might seriously prejudice its interests and (ii) it is unnecessary for the report's purposes to include the matter as specifically relating to that body. The Director must publish any report in the manner that he considers appropriate and absolute privilege attaches to that report for the purposes of the law of defamation (s186(6), (7)).

Information to be Furnished by BBC for s186 Reports (s187)

5.34 The Director may serve on the BBC a notice requiring it, at a time and place specified in the notice to (a) produce to him specified or described documents in its custody or control or (b) furnish him, in a specified form, with specified or described estimates, returns or other information, as he may require to make a s186 report (s187(1)). The BBC cannot be compelled by this provision to produce any document (or give any information) which it could not be compelled to produce (or give in evidence) before the High Court or, in Scotland, the Court of Session (s187(2)).

5.35 The broadcaster's compliance with the 25% production requirement is monitored externally. The ITC monitors its licensees as it is a regulatory and not a broadcasting body. The governors of the BBC, although they have supervisory powers under its charter are charged with the responsibility of being broadcasters. Therefore the Government concluded that it is only proper that an outside body also monitor it. The 25% requirement is concerned to ensure fair competition between the two sectors of the programme production industry, one of which is in competition with the BBC itself. The Director General of Fair Trading's monitoring and reports are intended to examine the policy issues, such as competition, efficiency and innovation that arise from the 25% requirement. When carrying out his duties the Director has absolute privilege against defamation under s16 of the Competition Act 1980. Section 186(7) [1] extends that to his report.
1   See para 5.33.

Power to give Broadcasting Bodies etc Directions Relating to International Obligations (s188)

5.36 Section 188 provides that the BBC, ITC, Welsh Authority, Radio Authority and Broadcasting Standards Council must carry out any functions which the Secretary of State may by order direct it to carry out to enable the government to give effect to any international obligations of the United Kingdom (sub-s(1), (2)). An order is subject to annulment in pursuance of a resolution of either House of Parliament (sub-s(3)). Implementation of the EC Directive 'Television without Frontiers' and the Council of Europe Convention on Transfrontier Television could be the subject matter of an order which is subject to the negative resolution procedure.

Matters Relating to Telecommunications Systems

Sharing of Apparatus by Operators of Telecommunications Systems (s189)

5.37 Where (a) the telecommunications code in Sch 2 to the Telecommunications Act 1984 expressly or impliedly imposes any limitation on the use to which any telecommunications apparatus [1] installed by a person (the operator) may be put and (b) the operator is a party to a relevant agreement, that limitation is not to preclude the doing of anything to that apparatus in pursuance of that agreement. Anything which is done must be disregarded in determining, for the purposes of the telecommunications code as it applies to the operator, the purposes for which the apparatus is used (sub-s(1)). 'Relevant agreement', in relation to telecommunications apparatus, means a written agreement (a) to which the parties are either (i) two or more persons to whom s189 applies or (ii) one or more persons to whom s189 applies and one or more telecommunications operators [2] who are not such persons and (b) which relates to the sharing by them of the use of that apparatus (sub-s(2)). Section 189 applies to (a) the holder of a licence to provide a local delivery service granted by the ITC (b) the holder of any licence to provide a prescribed diffusion service continued in force, or granted under, the transitional provisions of Part II of Sch 12 (c) a telecommunications operator in his capacity as a person providing the means of delivery for the service provided under his licence by a person falling within (a) or (b) above and (d) the company nominated for the purposes of s127(1)(sub-s(3)) [3]. Section 189, in relation to a person authorised by a relevant agreement to share the use of apparatus installed by another party to the agreement, does not affect any requirement on him (whether imposed by a statutory provision [4] or otherwise) to obtain any consent or permission in connection with the installation by him of any apparatus, or the doing by him of any other thing, in pursuance of the agreement (sub-s(3)).

1   'Telecommunication apparatus' has the same meaning as in the Telecommunications Act 1984 (sub-s(5)).
2   'Telecommunications operator' is a person who runs a telecommunications system the running of which is, or is not required to be, licensed under Part II of the 1984 Act (sub-s(5)). See para 5.42 on the application of the Fair Trading Act 1973 to s189(2) agreements.
3   See para 2.3.
4   'Statutory provision' means any provision of an enactment or of an instrument having effect under an enactment (sub-s(5)).

5.38   In explaining the purpose of the introduction of s189 at the House of Lords' committee stage of the Broadcasting Bill it was revealed that some operators were uncertain whether ducts and other apparatus which were installed by use of the powers in Sch 2 to the Telecommunications Act 1984 could legally be shared with other operators [1]. The Government supported the principle of such sharing which would have the possible environmental benefit of there being less digging up of streets.

1   House of Lords Committee, col 1764.

Modification of Certain References in Telecommunications Act Licences (s190)

5.39   Section 190 applies to licences granted under s7 of the Telecommunications Act 1984 (licensing of telecommunication systems) before the transfer date appointed under s127(1) [1] and which continue in force on or after that date (a 'telecommunications licence') (sub-s(1), (3), (5)). In such a licence, any reference to a cable programme service sent under a licence granted under s4 of the Cable and Broadcasting Act 1984 (the 'Cable Act') [2] is to be construed, as from the transfer date, as a reference to a licensable service within the meaning of Part I of that Act (other than an exempt service) [3], whether sent (a) under a diffusion licence [4] which is continued in force by, or granted under, the transitional provisions of Part II of Sch 12 or (b) under a local delivery licence granted under the 1990 Act, or otherwise (sub-s(2), (5)). When a telecommunications licence authorises the Secretary of State to revoke it, should a licence granted under s4 of the Cable Act in respect of the licensed systems [5] (the 'cable licence') be revoked, he may similarly revoke the telecommunications licence should a licence granted in respect of the licensed systems, in succession to the cable licence, under or in pursuance of any of paras 2 - 4 in Part II of Sch 12, be revoked (sub-s(3)). When a telecommunications licence provides for it to remain in force so long as there remains in force in respect of the licensed systems a cable licence, then if a local delivery licence is granted in respect of the licensed system, in succession to the cable licence, in pursuance of para 6 in Part II of Sch 12, the telecommunications licence will (subject to its terms) remain in force so long as does the local delivery licence (sub-s(4)).

1   See para 2.3.
2   A reference to a licence granted under s4 of the Cable Act includes, in relation to a licence to which s190 applies (the relevant licence), a reference to a licence granted under s58 of the Telecommunications Act 1984 (whether described in the relevant licence in those terms or in any other way) (sub-s(5)).

3   An 'exempt service' is a service falling within any description of services exempted from licensing under Part I of the Cable Act by virtue of an order in force under s3 of that Act immediately before the transfer date (sub-s(5)).
4   'Diffusion licence' is a licence to provide a prescribed diffusion service or other diffusion service within the meaning of Part I of the Cable Act (sub-s(5)).
5   'Licensed systems', in relation to a licence to which s190 applies, are the telecommunications systems the running of which is authorised by the licence (sub-s(5)).

5.40   Section 190 seeks to preserve the intent of licences granted under the Telecommunications Act 1984 which made reference to the Cable and Broadcasting Act or concepts from it [1]. The latter statute is repealed by the 1990 Act (Sch 21). A number of Telecommunications Act licences prohibit their holders from carrying cable entertainment services ('licensable cable programme services') on their network. Examples of licences imposing the prohibition are British Telecommunication plc's main licence and those granted to Mercury and the cellular radio operators. Section 190(2) maintains the prohibition. Similarly s190(3) and (4) relate to certain cable systems where Cable and Broadcasting Act 1984 licences are exchanged for follow-on licences granted under the transitional provisions in Sch 12. A parallel licence under the Telecommunications Act 1984 contained provisions whereby they could be revoked if the parallel Cable and Broadcasting Act licence was revoked or they remained in force only for so long as the Cable and Broadcasting Act licence remained in force. These parallel provisions are applied in the same way in respect of the new follow-on licences.
1   House of Lords Committee, cols 1760, 1761.

Revocation of Class Licence to Run Broadcast Relay Systems (s191)

5.41   The licence entitled 'Class licence to run broadcast relay systems', which was granted by the Secretary of State on 25 November 1986 under s7 of the Telecommunications Act 1984, is revoked. Such a class licence purportedly authorised the running of cable relay systems. These were systems which only carried broadcasts from the BBC or the IBA, including BSB. At the House of Lords committee stage of the Broadcasting Bill it was admitted by the Government that such licences were defective and did not provide the intended authorisation [1].
1   House of Lords Committee, col 1763.

Application of Competition Legislation

Application of Fair Trading Act 1973 Provisions to Broadcasting and Telecommunications Services (s192(1))

5.42   Paragraph (f) is inserted in s137(3) of the Fair Trading Act 1973 (definition of 'supply of services') to include the making of arrangements, by means of such an agreement as is mentioned in s189 (2) [1] for the sharing of the use of any telecommunications apparatus (within the meaning of Sch 2 to the Telecommunications Act 1984 (sub-s(1)). Consequently, the provisions of the Fair Trading Act 1973 (and thereby also the provisions of the Competition Act 1980) are extended to the arrangements for the sharing of telecommunications apparatus referred to in s189. Should operators act in an anti-competitive or monopolistic way by charging an unfair rental or refusing to enter into sharing arrangements, reference can be made under the competition legislation to the Monopolies and Mergers Commission.
1   See para 5.37.

5.43   Section 192 declares, for the avoidance of doubt, that the provision of a broadcasting service is not a service falling within para 7 of Sch 5 to the Fair Trading Act 1973 (restriction on making references under ss14, 50, or 51 of the Act in connection with telecommunications services) by reason of the fact that the broadcasting service is provided by means of the running of a system mentioned in para 7 (sub-s(2)). A 'broadcasting service' is a programme service or a local delivery service (sub-s(3)). The Director General of Fair Trading has no power to refer a monopoly of goods or services listed in Schs 5 and 7 to the Fair Trading Act 1973 to the Monopolies and Mergers Commission. This power is reserved to the Secretary of State. Before the 1990 Act the provision by IBA programme contractors of programmes for transmission and the provision of cable programme services licensed under the Cable and Broadcasting Act 1984 were excluded from monopoly reference by the Director. This exclusion is not continued in the 1990 Act and does not apply to the provision of the equivalent programme services and delivery services. Their provision is not the same as running a telecommunications system which remains excluded from the Director's reference powers.

5.44   Section 192 provides that in Part 1 of Sch 7 to the Fair Trading Act 1973, paras 8 and 9 (provision of programmes for transmission by IBA, or of licensed cable programme services, wholly excluded from references under ss50 or 51 of the Act) cease to have effect (sub-s(4)). Consequently the pre-1990 Act exclusion of the provision of programmes by IBA programme contractors for broadcasting and the provision of licensed cable programme services from the Director General of Fair Trading's monopoly reference powers is removed. This accords with the government's intention, as far as possible, to bring the provision of all goods and services under a common competition regime and, in particular, reduce the number of exclusions in the Fair Trading Act 1973 [1].

1   House of Lords Committee, col 1762.

Chapter 6

PROVISIONS RELATING TO WIRELESS TELEGRAPHY

6.1   Part VIII of the 1990 Act strengthens the provisions dealing with unlicensed broadcasting. The Wireless Telegraphy Act 1949 is amended to create the offences of keeping wireless telegraphy apparatus for unauthorised use [1], allowing premises to be used for the purpose of unlawful broadcasting [2] and facilitating unauthorised broadcasting [3]. The 1949 Act is also amended in respect of penalties and forfeiture [4] and with the Telecommunications Act 1984 is amended so as to extend the search and seizure powers in relation to unlawful broadcasting [5]. The Marine, &c, Broadcasting (Offences) Act is subject to amendments in Sch 16 [6]. Section 174 makes provision for extending Part VIII to the Isle of Man and the Channel Islands.

1   See para 6.2.
2   See para 6.3.
3   See para 6.4.
4   See para 6.10.
5   See para 6.11.
6   See paras 6.6 to 6.9.

Offence of Keeping Wireless Telegraphy Station or Apparatus Available for Unauthorised Use (s168)

6.2   Section 168 inserts a new s1A after s1 of the Wireless Telegraphy Act 1949 (the '1949 Act'). It provides that any person who has a station for wireless telegraphy or apparatus for wireless telegraphy in his possession or under his control and either (a) intends to use it in contravention of s1 of the 1949 Act [1] or (b) knows, or has reasonable cause to believe, that another person intends to use it in contravention of s1 is guilty of an offence.

1   Section 1 provides for the licensing of wireless telegraphy.

Offence of Allowing Premises to be Used for Purpose of Unlawful Broadcasting (s169)

6.3   Section 169 inserts a new s1B in the 1949 Act. Section 1B provides that a person who is in charge of premises [1] used for making an unlawful broadcast [2], or for sending signals for the operation or control of any apparatus used for the purpose of making an unlawful broadcast from another place, is guilty of an offence if (a) he knowingly causes or permits the premises to be so used or (b) having reasonable cause to believe that the premises are being so used, he fails to take such steps as are reasonable in the circumstances to prevent the premises from being so used (sub-s(1)). A person is in charge of premises if he (a) is the owner or occupier of the premises or (b) has, or acts or assists in, in the management or control of the premises (sub-s(2)). A broadcast is unlawful if (a) it is made by means of the use of any station for wireless telegraphy or

109

apparatus for wireless telegraphy in contravention of s1 of the 1949 Act or (b) the making of the broadcast contravenes any provision of the Marine &c, Broadcasting (Offences) Act 1967 (sub-s(3)).

1   'Premises' includes any place and, in particular, includes (a) any vehicle, vessel or aircraft and (b) any structure or other object (whether moveable or otherwise and whether on land or otherwise) (s1A (4)).
2   'Broadcast' has the same meaning as in the Marine, &c, Broadcasting Offences Act 1967)(s1A(4)).

Prohibition of Acts Facilitating Unauthorised Broadcasting (s170)

6.4   Section 170 inserts a new s1C in the 1949 Act. Section 1C provides that if a person (a) does any act mentioned in s1C(2) in relation to a broadcasting station [1] by which unauthorised broadcasts [2] are made and (b) if any knowledge or belief or any circumstances is or are specified in relation to the act, does it with that knowledge or belief or in these circumstances, he is guilty of an offence (s1C(1)). These acts are (a) participating in the management, financing, operation or day-to-day running of the station knowing, or having reasonable cause to believe, that unauthorised broadcasts are made by the station (b) supplying [3], installing, repairing or maintaining wireless telegraphy apparatus or any other item knowing or having reasonable cause to believe that it is to be, or is, used to facilitate the operation or day-to-day running of the station and that unauthorised broadcasts are made by the station (c) rendering any other service to any person, knowing, or having reasonable cause to believe that this would facilitate the operation or day-to-day running of the station and that unauthorised broadcasts are so made (d) supplying a film or sound recording [4] knowing or having reasonable cause to believe that an unauthorised broadcast of it is to be so made (e) making a literary, dramatic or musical work [4], knowing or having reasonable cause to believe that an unauthorised broadcast of the work is to be so made (f) making an artistic work [4] knowing or having reasonable cause to believe that an unauthorised broadcast including that work is to be so made (g) doing any of the following acts — (i) participating in an unauthorised broadcast made by the station, being actually present as an announcer, as a performer or one of the performers concerned in an entertainment given or as the deliverer of a speech [5] (ii) advertising or inviting another to advertise, by means of an unauthorised broadcast made by the station or (iii) publishing the times or other details of any unauthorised broadcasts made by the station or (otherwise than by publishing such details) publishing an advertisement of matter calculated to promote the station (whether directly or indirectly), knowing or having reasonable cause to believe that unauthorised broadcasts are made by the station (s1C(2)). If, by means of an unauthorised broadcast made by a broadcasting station, it is stated, suggested or implied that any entertainment of which broadcast has been made has been supplied by, or given at the expense of a person, then for the purposes of s1C he must, unless he proves that it was not so supplied or given, be deemed thereby to have advertised (s1C(4)).

1   'Broadcasting Station' means any business or other operation (whether or not in the nature of a commercial venture) which is engaged in the making of broadcasts (s1C(6)).
2   'Broadcast' has the same meaning as in the Marine, &c, Broadcasting (Offences) Act 1967. 'Unauthorised broadcast' means a broadcast made by means of the use of a station for wireless telegraphy or wireless telegraphy apparatus in contravention of s1 of the 1949 Act (s1C(6)).
3   Section 46 of the Consumer Protection Act 1987 has effect for the purpose of construing references in s1C to the supply of any thing as it does for construing references in that Act to the supply of goods (s1C(5)).
4   'Film', 'sound recording', 'literary, dramatic or musical work' and 'artistic work' have the same meaning as in Part I of the Copyright, Designs and Patents Act 1988 (s1(6)).
5   'Speech' includes lecture, address and sermon (s1C(6)).

Section 1C defence

6.5 In proceedings against a person for an offence under s1C consisting in the supplying of any thing or the rendering of any service, it is a defence for him to prove that he was obliged, under or by virtue of any legislation, to supply or render it (s1C(3)).

Amendments of 1967 Act (s171)

6.6 Section 171 provides that the Marine, &c., Broadcasting (Offences) Act 1967 has effect subject to the amendments specified in Sch 16 (which include amendments that impose further restrictions on broadcasting at sea and on acts facilitating such broadcasting). For example, s2 (prohibition of broadcasting from marine structures) applies to tidal waters in the United Kingdom, external waters and waters in a designated area within the meaning of the Continental Shelf Act 1964 (para 1). A new s2A is inserted providing for unlawful broadcasting from within prescribed areas of the high seas (para 2). Section 2A states that it is not lawful to make a broadcast which is (a) made from a ship (other than one registered in the United Kingdom, the Isle of Man or any of the Channel Islands) while the ship is within an area of the high seas prescribed for the purposes of s2A by an order made by the Secretary of State and (b) is capable of being received in, or causes interference with any wireless telegraphy in the United Kingdom (s2A(1)). An order is made by statutory instrument subject to annulment by resolution of either House of Parliament (s2A(5)). If a broadcast is made from a ship in contravention of s2A, the owner of the ship, its master and every person who operates, or participates in the operation of, the apparatus by means of which the broadcast is made is guilty of an offence (s2A(2)). A person who procures the making of such a broadcast is guilty of an offence (s2A(3)). The making of a broadcast does not contravene s2A if it is shown to have been authorised under the law of any country or territory outside the United Kingdom (s2A(4)).

6.7 Criticism of this provision centres on the principle of territoriality, namely that no state may pass a law creating an offence committed outside its jurisdiction. The Hijacking Act 1971 and the Suppression of Terrorism Act 1978 are exceptions to the principle. Section 2A is modelled on Arts 109 and 110 of the United Nations Convention on the Law of the Sea [1]. They cover interference and reception. Unauthorised transmissions from pirate radio stations are capable of interfering with aeronautical radio navigation beacons which assist helicopters as well as ship-to-shore communications channels. Arts 109 and 110 provide for a state to take action against broadcasters on ships in the high seas if their broadcasts contravene international regulations and can be received in the state's territory or cause interference there. The Government does not anticipate objection from other states in relation to its new s7A powers of enforcement [2], although it would normally consult the state where the ship is registered.

1   House of Lords Committee, col 1606.
2   See para 6.9.

6.8 Schedule 16 inserts a new s3A in the 1967 Act providing for the prohibition of management of stations broadcasting from ships, aircraft etc (para 4). Proceedings for an offence under the 1967 Act may only be instituted by or with the consent of the secretary of State or the Director of Public Prosecutions in England and Wales, or the Secretary of State or the Attorney General for Northern Ireland in Northern Ireland. A person on summary conviction can be sentenced to six months' imprisonment (para 7, which amends s6 of the 1967 Act).

6.9   A new s7A is inserted in the 1967 Act by Sch 16 (para 8). It provides for powers of enforcement in relation to marine offences under the 1967 Act. These are wide ranging. For example, if an enforcement officer has reasonable grounds for suspecting that an offence under s2A of the 1967 Act [1] has been or is being committed and the Secretary of State has issued a written authorisation for the exercise of the powers conferred by s7A in relation to that ship then the officer may exercise those powers (s7A(2)). The powers include ones to (a) board and search the ship (b) seize and detain it (c) arrest and search any person on board the ship reasonably suspected of committing a 1967 Act offence (d) arrest any person who assaults, or intentionally obstructs, him in the exercise of his powers (e) require any person on the ship to produce any items in his custody or possession which may be evidence of the commission of any offence under the 1967 Act (f) require such a person to do anything to facilitate the exercise of the powers conferred by s7A and (g) use reasonable force, if necessary, in exercising those powers (s7A(5)). These powers may generally be exercised only in tidal waters in the United Kingdom or in external waters (s7A(6)). However, in relation to a suspected offence under s2A of the 1967 Act committed in a ship in an area of the high seas prescribed for the purposes of s2A by an order made by the Secretary of State, the powers may also be exercised in that area (s7A(7)(c)). An enforcement officer is not liable in any civil or criminal proceedings for anything done in purported exercise of the powers if the court is satisfied that the act was done in good faith and that there was reasonable grounds for doing it (s7A(9)).

1   See para 6.6.

Amendment of 1949 Act's Provisions Relating to Penalties and Forfeiture (s172)

6.10   Section 172 amends s14 of the Wireless Telegraphy Act 1949 in a number of ways. It provides for the penalties available for an offence under the new ss1A, 1B and 1C inserted by ss168 [1], 169 [2] and 170 [3] respectively (sub-s(2), (3)). A new sub-s(3) replaces the previous sub-s(3) and provides that where a person is convicted of an offence under (a) Part I of the 1949 Act in relation to a station for wireless telegraphy or any wireless telegraphy apparatus (including an offence under ss1B [2] or 1C [3]) or in the use of apparatus for the purpose of interfering with any wireless telegraphy [4] (b) s12A of the 1949 Act (regulations with respect to resistance to interference) (c) the Marine, &c, Broadcasting (Offences) Act 1967 or (d) the 1949 Act which is an offence under s7 of the Wireless Telegraphy Act 1967, the court has powers additional to any other penalty provided in the respective statute. It may order any of the following things to be forfeit to the Secretary of State as it considers appropriate (i) any vehicle, vessel or aircraft, or any structure or other object, used in connection with the commission of the offence (ii) any wireless telegraphy apparatus or other apparatus [5] in relation to which the offence was committed or which was used in its commission (iii) any wireless telegraphy apparatus or other apparatus [5] not within (ii) above which was, at the time of the offence, in the possession or control of the person convicted of the offence and was intended to be used (whether or not by that person) in connection with the making of any broadcast or other transmission that would contravene s1 of the 1949 Act or any provision of the Marine, &c., Broadcasting (Offences) Act 1967) (sub-s(4)).

1   See para 6.2.
2   See para 6.3.
3   See para 6.4.
4   This power does not apply to an offence mentioned in s141A(a) or (aa) of the 1949 Act (s14(3AA)).
5   Reference to apparatus other than wireless telegraphy apparatus includes references to (a) recordings (b) equipment designed or adapted for use in (i) making recordings or (ii) in

reproducing from recordings any sounds or visual images and (c) equipment not falling within (a) or (b) above but connected, directly or indirectly, to wireless telegraphy apparatus (s14(3AB)).

Extension of Search and Seizure Powers in Relation to Unlawful Broadcasting etc (s173)

6.11   Section 173 amends s15(1) of the Wireless Telegraphy Act 1949 (entry and search of premises) so that its provisions on search warrants extend to offences reasonably suspected of being committed under the Marine, &c, Broadcasting (Offences) Act 1967. The warrant need not name the person(s) authorised by it (sub-s(1)). A person authorised to enter under s15(2) need not be named (sub-s(2)). A new sub-s(2A) is inserted into s15 which provides that, without prejudice to any power exercisable by him apart from s15(2), a person authorised by the Secretary of State or (as the case may be) by the BBC to exercise any s15 power may use reasonable force, if necessary in the exercise of that power (sub-s(3)). Section 79(1)(b) of the Telecommunications Act 1984 (seizure of apparatus and other property in committing certain offences connected with wireless telegraphy) is amended so that the section applies to an offence under s5(b) of the 1949 Act and any offence under the Marine, &c, Broadcasting (Offences) Act 1967 (sub-s(4)). Section 79(2) of the 1984 Act is amended so that the search warrant may authorise any person authorised by the Secretary of State to exercise the power conferred by s79(2) (sub-s(4)). A new s79(4A) is inserted providing that without prejudice to any power exercisable by him apart from s79(4A), a person authorised by the Secretary of State to exercise any power conferred by s79 may use reasonable force, if necessary, in the exercise of that power.

Chapter 7

LOCAL DELIVERY SERVICES

Licensing and Regulatory Authority

7.1   The Independent Television Commission (ITC) may grant licences to provide local delivery services (s73(1)). It must regulate the provision of those services which are provided from places in the United Kingdom (s2(1)).

Meaning of Local Delivery Services (s72)

7.2   A 'local delivery service' is a service provided by any person which (a) consists in the use of a telecommunication system [1] (whether run by that or any other person for the purpose of the delivery of one or more 'services' for simultaneous reception in two or more dwelling-houses in the United Kingdom and (b) is of a class or description specified in an order made by the Secretary of State (sub-s(1)). The 'services' are (a) television broadcasting services [2] whether provided by the holder of a licence under the 1990 Act, the BBC or the Welsh Authority (b) non-domestic satellite services [3] (c) licensable programme services [4] (d) sound broadcasting services to which s84 applies [5] or which is provided by the BBC and (e) licensable sound programme services [6] (sub-s(2)). Any class or description of service specified in an order made by the Secretary of State may be framed by reference to (a) the nature of the telecommunications system by means of which the service is to be provided or (b) the nature of the programmes, or any of the programmes, delivered by the service (sub-s(3)). An order is subject to annulment in pursuance of a resolution of either House of Parliament (sub-s(4)). In the House of Commons Committee the Minister of State said that the government intends to make such an order taking systems covering 1000 homes or fewer outside the local delivery licensing arrangements. The measure is intended to meet public demand for direct to home satellite broadcasting and inject competition in to the local delivery services.

1   'Telecommunication System' has the same meaning as in the Telecommunications Act 1984 (s202).
2   See para 3.8.
3   See para 4.126.
4   See para 4.138.
5   See para 8.8.
6   See paras 8.13, 8.88.

7.3   The regulatory framework for cable proposed in the 1983 White Paper 'The Development of Cable Systems and Services' (Cmnd 8866) was enacted in the Cable and Broadcasting Act 1984. The 1984 Act set up the Cable Authority. Its function was to promote the development of broadband cable and supervise the content of programme services carried on cable systems. In its 1988 White Paper 'Broadcasting in the 90s: Competition, Choice and Quality' (Cmnd 517) the Government acknowledged that it was keen to facilitate the development of broadband cable, at a market led pace, as a means of providing additional programme services, developing new interactive services and, in the longer term, as a possible way to increasing competition in telecommunications (para 4.13).

7.4   The delivery of television and radio services to the home has been facilitated in new ways by the development of satellite technology. Positioned in a geostationary orbit, a satellite can transmit a signal that will cover a large area (its "foot-print"). This efficient use of the spectrum means a single frequency can be used to broadcast a service to many homes. In 1977, frequencies for Direct Broadcasting by Satellite (DBS) were allocated by the World Administrative Radio Conference. The United Kingdom was allocated an orbital position for a direct broadcasting satellite(s) with frequencies sufficient for providing five television channels and a number of associated sound and data channels. The IBA was empowered by the Cable and Broadcasting Act 1984 to award franchises for the provision of DBS services and they were awarded to British Satellite Broadcasting. Parliament decided, because of the high cost of satellite technology, that DBS should have a 15-year contract period rather than the 8-year franchises awarded to terrestrial contractors. In the 1990 Act a local delivery licence lasts for 15 years (s78(1)) [1]. Separate sound and data services, as well as television channels, can be delivered by DBS. The content of these satellite services were regulated before the 1990 Act.
1   See para 7.30.

7.5   The providers of other services financed their enterprise by making a direct charge to cable operators who took their services. They inserted advertising (their own or others) in their services. Section 79(4) regulates advertisements inserted by a local delivery licence holder in the local delivery service. They sold their services to individual subscribers equipped with suitable receiving equipment. In May 1985 the government announced that it was ready to allow individuals to receive television signals from telecommunications satellites provided permission was obtained for the receiving dish. Later, a medium-powered satellite ('Astra') was launched with a capacity for 16 channels capable of direct reception by United Kingdom viewers.
1   See para 7.40.

7.6   A technology suited to the delivery of services is Multipoint Video Distribution System (MVDS) which uses microwave frequencies to transmit television and sound channels from terrestrial transmitters to ariels on individual buildings. The amount of spectrum made available for MVDS determines the number of channels and the coverage achieved by MVDS. In the 1988 White Paper it was recognised that most broadband cable systems offered at least 16 or more television channels in addition to the BBC and IBA channels, text and data services as well as the capability to carry return signals. Compared with MVDS, broadband cable offered greater channel capacity, interactivity with the use of the Public Switched Telephone Network (PSTN) and perhaps better future picture and sound quality. This was to be balanced against the potentially lower capital costs of setting up an MVDS system (para 5.12).

7.7   In a statement the Home Secretary said the Government believed in a new, flexible technology-neutral framework for local services, leaving operators free to decide upon the best mix of technologies and in practice this would mean cable or MVDS, or a mixture of the two for the foreseeable future [1]. He recognised that the restrictions on the development of satellite master antenna television (SMATV) had been due to the Cable Authority's statutory duty to exercise its licensing powers in such a way as to promote broadband cable systems. The 1990 Act imposes no such duty on the ITC. SMATV is a system whereby a large dish is used to receive satellite signals which are then distributed by cable to individual homes. The Home Secretary said that SMATV would be licensed in areas where a cable franchise was already established, provided that the cable operator was given the right of first refusal to provide a service within a reasonable timescale. Mr Mellor, minister of state, confirmed in the House of Commons Committee that this proviso will be policed by the Department of Trade and Industry using its licensing power under the Telecommunications Act 1984 [2].

1   HC Vol 151, 27 April 1989, cols 638 - 640w.
2   House of Commons Committee, col 910.

7.8   The framework provided in the 1990 Act for local delivery services is designed to permit operators to choose the nature and level of service they wish to offer the public. The importance of local delivery systems to met certain standards relating to safety, interference and compatibility between systems is provided for in the 1990 Act, eg ss75(1), (2) [1] and 81 [2]. Franchises are awarded under a competitive tender mechanism (s76) [3]. Licences are for 15 years (s78(1)) [4] and the content of foreign programmes regulated (ss79 [5] and 80 [6]). It may be anticipated that local delivery operators will offer viewers a convenient method of receiving a wide range of channels rather than distinctive programming that is unavailable from other sources [7].

1   See para 7.18.
2   See paras 7.37, 7.38.
3   See paras 7.19 to 7.24.
4   See para 7.30.
5   See para 7.40.
6   See para 7.41.
7   House of Commons Committee, col 932.

Scope of Licence (s73(2)).

7.9   Local delivery licences authorise the provision of local delivery services for such areas in the United Kingdom as the ITC may determine. When licences authorise the provision of such services to any extent by wireless telegraphy, they must be provided on frequencies assigned to those services by the ITC (s73(2)). In order to make a local delivery service a saleable proposition it will generally carry the main terrestrial broadcasting channels as well as other local and satellite channels. However, the 1990 Act contains no 'must carry' provisions. Those cable operators who continue to operate after the 1990 Act came into effect because of a licence granted under the Cable and Broadcasting Act 1984 will continue to have 'must carry' obligations as they were included in the original licence and continue until the licence expires. Consequently, the 1990 Act distinguishes between the service provider, that is the local delivery operator, and the person who provides the programmes. This is an implied recognition that a local delivery operator does not generally have editorial control over the programmes that he delivers. Mainly, he simply retails programmes which others provide.

General Provisions about Local Delivery Licences (s73(3), (4))

7.10   The general provisions applying to licences granted by the ITC under s3 [1] apply to local delivery licences, save that s3(5) [2] has effect as if the first reference to s19(1) included a reference to s77(1) [3] which also is concerned with additional payments.

1   See paras 3.14, 3.15.
2   See para 3.15.
3   See para 7.27.

General Licence Conditions (s73(3), (4))

7.11   The general licence conditions that apply to licences granted by the ITC under s4 [1] apply to local delivery licences.
1   See paras 3.16 to 3.18.

Restrictions on the Holding of Licences (s73(3), (4)).

7.12   The restrictions on the holding of licences granted by the ITC under s5 [1] apply to local delivery licences.
1   See paras 3.20 to 3.26.

Authorisation By Licence Holder of Another to Provide Local Delivery Services (s73(5), (6), (7))

7.13   A local delivery licence may include provisions enabling the licence holder, subject to and in accordance with such conditions as the ITC may impose, to authorise any person who is not a 'disqualified person' in relation to a local delivery licence by virtue of Part II of Sch 2 [1] to undertake to any extent the provision of the licensed service on the licence holder's behalf (sub-s(5), (6)). Any conditions included in a local delivery licence apply in relation to the provision of the licensed service by a duly authorised person as they apply in relation to the provision of the service by the licence holder. Any failure by such a person to comply with the conditions is treated as a failure by the licence holder to comply with those conditions (sub-s(7)). Consequently, a person disqualified from holding a local delivery licence by virtue of Part II of Sch 2 cannot be authorised by the licensee to provide a service as a sub-licensee.
1   See paras 10.13 to 10.23.

Proposal Notice (s74(1), (2))

7.14   When the ITC propose to grant a licence to provide a local delivery service it must publish in the manner that it considers appropriate a notice (a) stating that it proposes to grant a licence (b) specifying (i) the area in the United Kingdom for which the service is to be provided, and (ii) any frequencies that would be available for it to be provided by wireless telegraphy should it be desired so to provide it (c) inviting applications and specifying the closing date and (d) specifying (i) the application fee and (ii) the percentage of qualifying revenue for each accounting period payable by an applicant under s77(1)(c) [1] if he were granted the licence (sub-s(1)). The ITC may, if it thinks fit, specify (a) different percentages for different accounting periods within the licence period (b) a nil percentage for any such accounting periods (sub-s(2)). By ensuring, on occasions, that local delivery operators are not obliged to pay for a specified period a percentage of their revenues, perhaps before they start to make a profit, the attractions of making an application are enhanced. Should an applicant be unambitious and not propose to cover a viable area, he takes the risk of failing in his application if others are more ambitious. Doubtless the ITC will be aware of the industry's views on what is a viable local delivery service proposition in different sets of circumstances and tailor its proposal notice so as to attract realistic applications. The minimum licence price is set at the point at which the franchise is advertised, and if set unrealistically will not attract applications.
1   See para 7.27.

Application (s74(3), (4), (5), (7))

7.15   The application is to be in writing and accompanied by (a) the application fee (b) [1] a technical plan for the proposed service indicating (i) the parts of the United Kingdom which would be covered by the service (ii) the timetable in which that coverage would be achieved [2] (iii) the technical means by which it would be achieved (iv) the extent (if any) to which he proposes that the provision of the service should be undertaken by some other person under s73(5) [3] (c) the applicant's cash bid, (d) [1] such information as the ITC may reasonably require as to the applicant's present financial position and his projected financial position for the licence period and (e) [1] such other information as the ITC may reasonably require to consider the application (sub-s(3)). The applicant's cash bid for the licence is the offer to pay the ITC a specified sum for the first complete year falling within the licence period (being a sum which as increased by the 'appropriate percentage' allowing for inflation is also payable for subsequent years falling wholly or partly within the licence period) (sub-s(7)(a)). The 'appropriate percentage' for any year is established in accordance with the principle set out in s19(10) [4] (sub-s(7)(b)).

1   Before determining the application the ITC may require additional information, in the form or verified in the manner that it specifies about this part of the application (sub-ss(4), (5)).
2   See para 7.38. There must be a condition as to this timetable in the successful applicant's licence.
3   See para 7.13.
4   See para 4.31.

7.16   Particular care should be taken with the preparation of the technical and business plans as the ITC must be satisfied that these are acceptable. The local delivery system's sophistication, for example, whether cable extends to the provision of telecommunications as well as television services, is a matter for the operator to decide because the ITC is unable to give preferential treatment to a particular system. However, the applicant with a more sophisticated delivery system could make a higher cash bid than other competitors because of his expectation of more revenue. Partly because unfulfilled franchise commitments were said to have bedevilled the cable industry [1], s73 makes it possible for operators to assume realistic commitments. The 1990 Act marks a deliberate move away from technological favouritism and impliedly recognises the potential of MVDS which in some areas may be more commercially viable than cable. The ITC is guided by its general duty in s2(a) to discharge its functions as respects service licensing in the manner it considers is best calculated to ensure (i) that a wide range of services is available throughout the United Kingdom and (ii) fair and effective competition in the provision of services and services connected with them. Applicants, and the industry in general, should be aware of this overarching duty, which will influence the ITC when it examines licence applications. If the ITC should err in carrying out its s2 duty, the government expects it to err on the side of encouraging the spread of local delivery systems [2].

1   House of Commons Committee, col 917.
2   House of Commons Committee, col 926, 927.

Publication of Applications (s74(6))

7.17   The ITC must, as soon as is reasonably practicable after the closing date for applications, publish in the manner it considers appropriate (a) the name of every applicant (b) particulars of the technical plans submitted with the applications and (c) such other information connected with the application as the ITC consider appropriate (s74(6)).

Consideration of Applications (s75(1), (2))

7.18   The ITC must not proceed to consider whether to award an applicant the licence on the basis of his cash bid unless it appears to it that (a) any telecommunication system proposed to be used by the applicant in the provision of his proposed service would be acceptable to the 'relevant licensing authorities' and would be capable of being established in accordance with the timetable indicated by him in the technical plan submitted with his application and (b) he would be able to maintain that service throughout the licence period. Any reference to an applicant in s76 [1] (except in sub-s12(b)) [2] is one in whose case it appears to the ITC that the above two requirements are met (sub-s(1)). Before deciding whether the first requirement is met the ITC must consult the 'relevant licensing authorities'. Where any telecommunication system proposed to be used would be required to be licensed under the Wireless Telegraphy Act 1949, this would be the Secretary of State. If it would be required to be licensed under Part II of the Telecommunications Act 1984, this would be the Secretary of State and the Director General of Telecommunications (sub-s(2)). Coverage is an important factor in the application procedure, which does not relate to programme quality. Applicants are allowed to choose their own coverage targets. These targets and their timescale will be incorporated into the successful applicant's licence, enabling the ITC to take measures under s81 [3] should the promised service not materialise. The policy in the Cable and Broadcasting Act 1984 that cable operators should achieve 100 percent coverage in their areas was recognised [4] as making the entry costs into the market prohibitively high and is impliedly charged by the 1990 Act.

1   See paras 7.19 to 7.26.
2   See para 7.24.
3   See paras 7.36, 7.37.
4   House of Commons Committee, col 916.

Award of Licence to Person Submitting Highest Cash Bid (s76(1), (3), (4))

7.19   The general principle is that the ITC must, after considering all the applicant's cash bids, award the licence to the applicant who submitted the highest bid (sub-s(1)). However, the ITC may award the licence to an applicant who has not submitted the highest bid if it appears to it that there are exceptional circumstances which make it appropriate for it to award the licence to him (sub-s(3)). Some clarification of exceptional circumstances is given in the 1990 Act in that the ITC may regard the two following circumstances as exceptional circumstances. First, where it appears to the ITC that the coverage proposed to be achieved, as indicated in the technical plans submitted with the application, is substantially greater then that proposed to be achieved by the applicant who submitted the highest bid or by each of the applicants who submitted equal highest bids. Second, where it appears to the ITC, in the context of the licence, that any circumstances are to be regarded as exceptional circumstances, they may be so regarded by it despite the fact that similar circumstances have been so regarded by it in the context of any other licence(s) (sub-s(4)). Clearly, the exceptional circumstances provision can apply when an applicant for a local delivery licence offers to provide a service coverage for a substantially greater area than that proposed by the highest bidder. So, the successful applicant will first have satisfied the ITC about his technical competence and business plans. Then, other than in exceptional circumstances, he will have submitted the highest cash bid.

Equal Highest Cash Bids (s76(2))

7.20   When two or more applicants have submitted identical cash bids then (unless it proposes to exercise its 'exceptional circumstances' powers) the ITC must invite those applicants to submit further cash bids.

Public Interest (s76(5), (6), (7))

7.21   If it appears to the ITC, in the case of an applicant to whom it would otherwise award the licence, that there are grounds for suspecting that any 'relevant source of funds' is such that it would not be in the public interest for the licence to be awarded to him, it must (a) refer his application to the Secretary of State, together with (i) a copy of all documents submitted to it by the applicant and (ii) a summary of its deliberations on the application and (b) not award the licence to him unless the Secretary of State has given his approval (sub-s(5)). On such a reference the Secretary of State may only refuse to approve the award of the licence to the applicant if he is satisfied that the 'relevant source of funds' is such that it would not be in the public interest for the licence to be awarded (sub-s(6)). A 'relevant source of funds' is any source of funds to which the applicant might (directly or indirectly) have recourse for the purpose of (a) paying any additional payments payable by him under s77(1) or (b) otherwise financing the provision of his propose service (sub-s(7)).

7.22   When the ITC are precluded from awarding the licence to an applicant because his possible recourse to a 'relevant source of funds' is not in the public interest, the effect is as if he had not made an application for the licence (sub-s(10)). This will not happen if the ITC decide that it would be desirable to publish a fresh proposal notice to grant the licence under s74 [1] (sub-s(16)).
1   See para 7.14.

Qualifying Requirements (s76(8), (9))

7.23   When any requirements imposed by or under Parts III - V of Sch 2 [1] operate to preclude the ITC from awarding a licence to an applicant to whom it would otherwise have awarded the licence, it must award the licence in accordance with rules made by it for regulating the awarding of licences in such cases. The rules may provide for the awarding of licences by reference to orders of preference notified to the ITC by applicants when making their applications (sub-s(8)). The rules must be published by the ITC in the manner that it considers appropriate, but they do not come into force unless they have been approved by the Secretary of State (sub-s(9)).
1   See paras 10.24 to 10.53.

Publication of Applications and Grant of Licence (s76(11), (12), (15))

7.24   When the ITC have awarded a local delivery licence to any person, it must, as soon as reasonably practicable after awarding the licence (a) publish in the manner it considers appropriate certain matters and (b) grant the licence to that person (sub-s(11)). The matters to be published are (a) the name of the applicant to whom the licence has been awarded and the amount of his cash bid (b) the name of every other applicant in whose case it appeared to the ITC that the requirements of s75(1)(a) [1] concerning any telecommunication system proposed to be used were satisfied (c) when the licence has been awarded in 'exceptional circumstances' to an applicant who has not submitted the highest cash bid, by virtue of s76(3) [2], the ITC's reasons for awarding it and (d) such other information as the ITC consider appropriate (sub-s(12)). When a local delivery licence has been awarded to any person under s76, in accordance with the 1990 Act, on the revocation of an earlier grant of the licence, there is no requirement to publish the means of those in whose case the ITC were satisfied that the requirements of s75(1)(a) [1] were met but an indication of the circumstances in which the licence has been awarded to that person must be published (sub-s(15)).

1   See para 7.18.
2   See para 7.19.

Refusal to Begin Local Delivery Service (s76(13), (14))

7.25   If at any time after a local delivery licence has been granted to any person but before the licence comes into force (a) that person indicates to the ITC that he does not intend to provide the service or (b) the ITC for any other reason have reasonable grounds for believing that the person will not provide the service once the licence comes into force, then (i) the ITC must serve on him a notice revoking the licence as from the time the notice is served on him and (ii) the effect is as if he had not made an application for the licence (sub-s(13)). When the ITC have a reasonable belief that the service will not be provided, it must serve on the person granted the licence a notice stating grounds for believing that he will not provide the service. It must not serve such a notice unless it has given him a reasonable opportunity of making representations to it about the matters complained of (sub-s(14)).

7.26   The ITC may decide in a case of refusal to begin a local delivery service that after revoking the licence it would be desirable to publish a fresh proposal notice to grant the licence under s74 and then the effect of the revocation is not as if the former licence holder had failed to apply for the licence (sub-s(16)).

Additional Payments (s77(1), (2), (5))

7.27   A licence holder must pay the amount of his cash bid over the licence period as well as payments based on his qualifying revenue for that period. A local delivery licence must include conditions requiring the licence holder to pay to the ITC (in addition to any fees required to be paid under s4(1)(b) to the ITC towards its expenses) three categories of payment in respect of (a) the first complete calendar year falling within the licence period, the amount specified in his cash bid (b) each subsequent year falling wholly or partly within that period, a specified amount as increased by the appropriate percentage and (c) each accounting period of his falling within the licence period, an amount representing such percentage of the 'qualifying revenue' for that accounting period as was specified in the ITC's proposal notice to grant the licence under s74(1)(d)(ii) [1] (sub-s(1)). For the purposes of the third category of additional payments the 'qualifying revenue' for any accounting period of the licence holder consists of all payments which are received or to be received by him, or by any person connected with him [2], and are derived from the delivery in that period, in accordance with his licence, of services falling within the s72(2) [3] (whether their delivery is undertaken by him or by any person authorised by him as mentioned in s73(5) [4]. The services are any television broadcasting service, non-domestic satellite service, licensable programme service, sound broadcasting service and licensable sound programme service as described above [3] (sub-s(2)). Finally, when (a) the first complete accounting period of the licence holder falling within the licence period does not begin at the same time as that period or (b) the last complete accounting period of his falling within the licence period does not end at the same time as that period, the reference to an accounting period in the third category of additional payments includes a reference to that part of the accounting period preceding that first complete accounting period, or (as the case may be) following that last complete accounting period, as falls within the licence period

(sub-s(5)). The licensing arrangements which involve two elements, the bid and the percentage of qualifying revenue, is a responsive way of raising revenue. The same percentage does not have to apply throughout the currency of the agreement. The ITC can set a nil percentage for five years, say, and a fixed percentage thereafter. Once fixed, the percentage cannot be changed retrospectively.
1   See para 7.14.
2   See para 10.11.
3   See para 7.2.
4   See para 7.13.

Additional Payments Licence Conditions (s77(3), (4))

7.28   A local delivery licence may include conditions (a) enabling the ITC to estimate, in relation to the third category of additional payments, before the beginning of an accounting period the amount due for that period and (b) requiring the licence holder to pay the estimated amount by monthly instalments throughout that period (sub-s(3)). A licence may, in particular, include conditions (a) authorising the ITC to revise any estimate on one or more occasions and to adjust the instalments payable by the licence holder to take account of the revised estimate; (b) providing for the adjustment of any overpayment or underpayment (sub-s(4)).

Computation of Qualifying Revenue (Part I of Sch 7)

7.29   The provisions on the ITC duty to publish a statement of principles for the computation of qualifying revenue and any consequential disputes in Part I of Sch 7 apply to additional payments to be made in respect of local delivery services.

Duration and Renewal of Local Delivery Service Licences (s78)

Duration of Licence (s78(1))

7.30   A local delivery licence continues in force for a period of 15 years. It may be renewed on one or more occasions for a period of 15 years beginning with the date of renewal (s78(1)).

Renewal of Licence (s78(2)(10))

7.31   An application for the renewal of a licence may be made by the licence holder not earlier than five years before the date on which it would otherwise cease to be in force and not later than the 'relevant date', (sub-s(2)). The 'relevant date' is the date which the ITC determine to be that by which it would need to publish a proposal notice under s74 if it were to grant, as from the date on which the licence would expire if not renewed, a fresh licence to provide the local delivery service formerly provided under that licence (sub-s(10)).

Refusal to Renew Licence (s78(4), (5))

7.32   When an application for renewal of a licence has been duly made to the ITC, it may only refuse the application if (a) it proposes to grant a fresh local delivery licence for the provision of a service which would be provided for a different area from that for which the applicant's service is provided under his licence or (b) in the case of an applicant who has not achieved the coverage set out in the technical plan submitted under s74(3)(b) [1] either (i) it is not satisfied that he would, if his licence were renewed, be able to achieve that coverage in accordance with the timetable indicated in the plan or (ii) the period within which it was to be achieved has expired (sub-s(4)). The

provision safeguarding the public interest if there is suspicion that any 'relevant source of funds' may be used by the applicant and found in s76(5) - (7) apply in relation to an applicant for the renewal of a licence and were examined earlier [2] (sub-s(5)).
1   See para 7.15.
2   See para 7.21.

Determination of Post Grant Payments (s78(6), (7)).

7.33   On the grant of an application for licence renewal the ITC (a) must determine the amount to be payable to it by the applicant for the first complete calendar year falling within the period for which the licence is to be renewed and (b) may specify a different percentage than that specified in the notice proposing to grant the licence under s74(1)(d)(ii) [1] as the percentage of qualifying revenue for each accounting period of his that will be payable by him as the third category of additional payment in pursuance of s77(1)(c) during the period for which the licence is to be renewed. The ITC may, if it thinks fit, specify (a) different percentages in relation to different accounting periods falling within the licence period or (b) a nil percentage in relation to that accounting period (sub-s(6)). The amount determined by the ITC above must be such an amount as would, in its opinion, be payable to it under s77(1)(a) [2] if it were granting a fresh licence to provide the local delivery service (sub-s(7)).
1   See para 7.14.
2   See para 7.27.

Formal Renewal (s78(3), (8))

7.34   When the ITC have granted a person's application it must formally renew his licence not later than the relevant date [1] or, if that is not reasonably practicable, as soon after that date as is reasonably practicable. It must not renew its licence unless it has notified him of (a) the amount determined and (b) any percentage specified in sub-s(6) described above [2], and he has, within the period specified in the notification, notified it that he consents to the licence being renewed on those terms (sub-s(8)). Provided the application is made before the 'relevant date' [3] the ITC may postpone consideration of it for as long as it thinks appropriate having regard to sub-s(8) (sub-s(3)).
1   See para 7.31.
2   See para 7.33.

Renewed Licence Conditions (s78(9))

7.35   When a local delivery licence is renewed any conditions included in it in pursuance of s77 [1] must have effect during the renewed licence period (1) as if the amount determined by the ITC under sub-s6(a) [2] were an amount specified in a cash bid submitted by the licence holder and (ii) subject to any determination made under sub-s6(b) [2] (sub-s9(1)). Subject to this, s77 has effect for the renewed licence period as it had for the original licence period (sub-s(9)).
1   See para 7.28.
2   See para 7.33.

Power to Impose Financial Penalty or Shorten Licence Period (s81(1)(2))

7.36   The powers of the ITC to impose a financial penalty or shorten the licence period under s41 [1] apply in relation to a local delivery licence as they apply in relation to a licence to provide a Channel 3 service save with the substitution in sub-s(2) of 's77(2)' for 's19(2) to (6)' [2] and with the omission of sub-s(5).
1   See para 4.112.
2   See para 7.27.

Power to Revoke Licence (s81(1), (2))

7.37   The powers of the ITC to revoke a licence under s42 [1] apply in relation to a local delivery licence as they apply in relation to a licence to provide a Channel 3 service save with the omission of sub-s(7) [2].
1   See paras 4.113 to 4.116.
2   See para 4.115.

Technical Plan Timetable Condition (s81(3), (4))

7.38   A local delivery licence must include a condition requiring the licensed service to be established by the licence holder in accordance with the timetable indicated in the technical plan submitted under s74(3)(b) with his application (sub-s(3)). The ITC must not revoke a licence under s42 (as applied by sub-s(1)) by reason of the failure of the licence holder to comply with this condition unless it is satisfied, after consulting the Secretary of State and the Director General of Telecommunications that it would have been reasonably practicable for the licence holder to comply with it (sub-s(4)).

Prohibition on Providing Unlicensed Local Delivery Systems (s82)

7.39   Any person who provides a local delivery system without being authorised to do so by or under a 1990 Act licence is guilty of an offence (sub-s(1)). No proceedings in respect of this offence can be instituted (a) in England and Wales, except by or with the consent of the Director of Public Prosecutions or (b) in Northern Ireland, except by or with the consent of the Director of Public Prosecutions for Northern Ireland (sub-s(3)). A person guilty of this offence is liable to a fine, which is unlimited on conviction on indictment (sub-s(2)). Compliance with this prohibition is enforceable not only by a prosecution but also by civil proceedings by the Crown for an injunction or interdict or for any other appropriate relief (sub-s(4)).

Regulation of Delivery of Certain Foreign Programmes (s79)

7.40   Section 79 makes a local delivery operator responsible for the content of any foreign satellite services provided from a non-prescribed country and for advertisements inserted by him in the local delivery service. A licence to provide a licensable programme service or a licensable sound programme service may, when it is granted to the holder of a local delivery licence, authorise the provision by him of programmes for delivery on all or any of the channels on which his local delivery service is provided (s79(1)). Should any licensed local delivery service consist of or include relaying (complete and unchanged) any 'foreign satellite programmes', s6(1) so far as relating to the requirements specified in paras (a), (d) and (e) [1] and s7 [2] apply as if the delivery of those programmes constituted a licensed service (s79(2)). Accordingly, a reference in those provisions to programmes included in a licensed service is taken as a reference to foreign satellite programmes (s79(3)). A 'foreign satellite programme' means a programme transmitted by satellite from a place outside the United Kingdom, other than a programme transmitted from within any country specified in an order made by the Secretary of State (s79(5)). The holder of a local delivery licence is taken to be authorised by his licence to include in his licensed service advertisements which are inserted by him and are not included in any category of service falling within s72(2) [3] as being capable of being a local delivery service. However if advertisements are included by him, the provisions of sections 8 [4] and 9 [5] on advertisements have effect (s79(4)).
1   See para 3.27.
2   See para 3.32.

3   See para 7.2.
4   See para 3.33.
5   See paras 3.36 to 3.38.

Direction to Cease Relaying Foreign Television Programmes (s80)

7.41   If the ITC is satisfied that it is appropriate to do so because of any international agreement to which the United Kingdom is a party, it may give to the holder of a local delivery licence a direction requiring him not to relay television programmes which (a) are transmitted from a place outside the United Kingdom and (b) are included in any service specified or described in the direction (sub-s(1)). A direction may describe a service by reference to such matters as the ITC may think fit, and it may have effect during a specified period or for an indefinite period (sub-s(2)(3)).

Listed Events and Local Delivery Services

7.42   Section 14 of the Cable and Broadcasting Act 1984 provided that listed events could not be shown on cable television and on a pay-per-view basis (this is when viewers must pay an additional sum for looking at a special event). Section 14 also provided that when a channel, carried on a cable system, proposed to show a listed event, the BBC and ITV had to be offered the right to acquire the rights on comparable terms. The other applicants had the rights if the BBC and ITV did not accept the offer. Only then could a satellite or cable channel show listed events on an exclusive basis. Section 182 [1] extends the prohibition on showing listed events on pay-per-view terms to all channels and not just those carried on cable. However s182 removes the matching bid safeguard. The policy behind s182 is that only if there are compelling reasons to to so should Parliament limit the rights of people to do as they wish with their property. For example, sporting rights are a form of property and their sale is a principal means of generating income for sporting bodies [2]. It should be borne in mind that s182 does extend the scope of the pay-per-view prohibition which means that listed events could be shown only on satellite or cable television at a loss. Also levels of coverage and audience reach are relevant factors to those owning, for example, sporting rights.

1   See para 5.21.
2   House of Lords Report, cols 732-734.

Chapter 8

INDEPENDENT RADIO SERVICES

Introduction

Historical Background

8.1   Fifty two years after Samuel Morse's question 'What hath God wrought?' was sent along the telegraph wire from Baltimore to Washington, Marconi's invention of wireless telegraphy was patented in 1896. In 1920 the British Broadcasting Company was formed and it had the monopoly of public broadcasting until it was replaced by the British Broadcasting Corporation (BBC) in 1927. [1] The Sound Broadcasting Act 1972 [2] brought commercial radio to the United Kingdom but limited it to local services, called independent local radio (ILR). The private local radio stations operated under contract from the Independent Broadcasting Authority (IBA). ILR stations paid a rental for the transmitting and regulatory services provided by the IBA and derived their income from the sale of advertising time. In addition to the service provided by the BBC and the IBA, the Home Secretary licensed university radio stations and occasional special event broadcasts under the Wireless Telegraphy Act 1949 and the Cable Authority licensed and regulated community cable radio stations under the Cable and Broadcasting Act 1984. In its 1987 Green Paper 'Radio: Choices and Opportunities' (Cmnd 92) the government recognised that radio was 'poised at the beginning of a new chapter in its history' (para 2.28). All references to the Green Paper in this chapter are references to this 1987 Green Paper.

1   Agreement dated 9 November 1926 (Cmnd 2755).
2   The 1972 Acts provisions were incorporated into the Broadcasting Act 1981.

Physical Reasons for Change

8.2   Radio communication involves the radiation of energy in the form of radio waves. Radio waves belong to the same family as x-rays, ultra-violet rays, infra-red waves and light waves. All these forms of energy travel through air (or space) but a radio wave differs from other waves in two ways. First, by the length of each wave (the 'wavelength') and second, by the number of waves that pass a point in one second (the 'frequency'). Off-air radio broadcasting is divided into three bands in the United Kingdom: LF (low frequency or long wave) MF (medium frequency or medium wave) and VHF/FM (very high frequency or frequency modulation). In the United Kingdom HF (high frequency) or shortwave is used only for external services. Frequency usage in the United Kingdom is governed by the International Radio Regulations which set out the broad division of the radio spectrum amongst different types of user (broadcasting, telecommunications, navigation etc). The use of radio and television transmitters within a country must be internationally agreed if interference is to be avoided. Radio waves do not recognise frontiers and, although they travel in straight lines, they can be sent over long distances around the curved surface of the Earth. This is because the atmosphere is made up of many separate layers where the air particles are slightly different. The upper atmosphere or ionosphere acts like a mirror and reflects radio waves. Different parts of the ionosphere reflect waves of different lengths. The E-Layer, 69-75 miles above the Earth, reflects the programmes on a radio's medium waveband. The F2 Layer, 156-250 miles above the Earth, reflects short wave communication used by shipping. As a result of international agreements, additional frequencies for broadcasting in the United Kingdom will be available between 1990 and 1996. Consequently there is scope for new national and local radio services. Access to the radio spectrum in the United Kingdom is controlled not only to ensure that radio signals do not interfere with each other but also to secure the most effective use of the spectrum. Also, the United Kingdom has provisions for the regulation of programme content. These controls over access to a finite resource and programme content have resulted in the concept of a public service broadcasting so that broadcasting is used to the benefit of society as a whole, rather than for the benefit of particular groups within society, and must be of high quality. This concept has affected the nature and regulation of radio services and its influence on the deregulatory measures of the 1990 Act cannot be doubted. In having a requirement that the new Radio Authority must carry out the licensing of independent radio services in the manner that it considers best calculated to 'facilitate the provision of licensed services which (taken as a whole) are of high quality and offer a wide range of programmes calculated to appeal to a variety of tastes and interests' (s.85(3)(a)) the Government acknowledged that 'it would be strange if, in carrying out its general duties, the Radio Authority had no obligation to have a care for the quality of independent radio services taken as a whole'. [1]

1   Earl Ferrers, House of Lords Report, col 763.

Public Service Broadcasting[1]

8.3   Public service broadcasting requires that public authorities are appointed as trustees for the national interest in broadcasting. They are to be independent of government in programming matters. They must provide services which inform, educate and entertain, keep a proper balance in a wide range of subject matter and maintain high general technical standards. A sufficient amount of time must be allocated to the accurate and impartial presentation of news. Likewise, there must be due impartiality in the presentation of matters of public or industrial controversy or relating to current public policy. Unsuitable material must not be broadcast. The Peacock Committee [2] advised that the best operational definition of public service is merely any modification of purely commercial provision resulting from public policy (para 580). Consequently, in a free broadcasting market when taxpayers would wish to have available programmes which the market could not produce unaided, there would still be a need for subsidised 'public service programming (paras 682-687). The conditions identified by the Peacock Committee as necessary for the development of a free broadcasting market were spectrum abundance and a system for consumers to register their preferences by direct subscription payment. Subscription is not a practical option in the financing of radio services (with the possible exception of services provided in association with Direct Broadcasting Satellite television signals). This is because of the cheapness of radio sets and the lack of programme material which would command a commercial premium [3]. The Green Paper concluded that, as regards national radio services, the 'Peacock conditions' did not apply (paras 4.2-4.7). It argued, however, that it did not follow from this that new national services had to be in the form of public service broadcasting and suggested that a lighter regulatory system might be appropriate for them as they would have to compete with the BBC and ILR (para 4.18). As regards local radio services, the Green Paper recognised that future availability of spectrum would be sufficient for a substantial number of competing stations and that this weakened the case for the guaranteed retention of public service broadcasting. It concluded that, as at the national level, there was no need that local services should take the form of public service broadcasting. The BBC would continue to make such broadcasts, nationally and locally. The solution was to allow local commercial services to operate under the lighter regulatory system proposed for national commercial radio, subject to the general principle that the selection of stations permitted to broadcast should be such as to enhance the range of choice for listeners. This solution acknowledged that it would be unrealistic to expect many local stations, with which there would be competition for revenue, to compete within the full strength of the public service regulatory system provided by the Broadcasting Act 1981.

1   See 1987 Green Paper, para 1.14.
2   Report of the Committee on Financing the BBC (Cmnd 9824).
3   Home Office memorandum (para 3) to Home Affairs Committee Second Report 'The Government's Plans for Radio Broadcasting' 18 April 1988.

The Proposed Regulatory Authority

8.4   The Green Paper on the future of broadcasting envisaged that the IBA, the Cable Authority or a new body might regulate independent radio services (para 7.3). Early in 1988 the Home Secretary chose the option of an entirely new authority [1]. In his evidence to the Home Affairs Committee [2] Mr Renton, the minister of state, emphasised that due to the likely expansion of independent radio it was sensible to establish a body solely concerned with its regulation. For various reasons, he rejected the proposition that the IBA's Radio Division might continue to regulate it. He felt that the IBA would be fully occupied with the expansion of new television services like those provided by satellite and that there would be heavier demands on its regulatory role in those areas. Further, it might be difficult for the IBA to have responsibility for the differing levels of regulation required for radio and television. Also, the IBA should not be in the position of offering its transmitting service on a commercial basis to franchise holders and regulating them as well. The minister felt it wrong that the IBA could be a supplier of services and a judge of how those services were used. Later in 1988 the Government's White Paper 'Broadcasting in the '90s, Choice and Quality' (Cmnd 517) proposed setting up 'a new slim Radio Authority' (para 8.5). The Government proposed also to help the expansion of independent radio services 'by deregulation and the provision of a new enabling framework' (para 8.7). The White Paper asserted that 'public service radio broadcasting will continue under the aegis of the BBC' (ibid). This assertion is of crucial importance in understanding the policy behind the 1990 Act. It affects the provision of radio services at local and national levels.

1   HC Deb, 19 January 1988, cols 647-9W.
2   Home Affairs Committee Second Report 'The Government's Plans for Radio Broadcasting', 18 April 1988.

The Radio Authority

Establishment of the Radio Authority (s83)

8.5   The Radio Authority is established by the 1990 Act (sub-s(1)). It consists of a chairman and deputy chairman, who are appointed as such, and between four and ten other members (sub-s(2)). All appointments are made by the Secretary of State. Further provisions for the authority's constitution and procedure are found in Sch 8 (sub-s(3)). It is within the authority's capacity as a statutory corporation to do such things and enter into such transactions as are 'incidental or conducive' to the discharge of its functions under the 1990 Act (para 1(3)). A person is disqualified from being a member of it if he is a governor or employee of the BBC or is a member or employee of the Channel

Four Television Corporation, the Welsh Authority, the Broadcasting Complaints Commission or Broadcasting Standards Council (para 2(1)). Appointments are made for a maximum period of five years (para 3(2)). The authority may appoint advisory committees to give it advice on matters relating to its functions (para 16). The public accountability of the authority is demonstrated by the requirement that it must, at the end of each financial year send a 'general report' of its proceedings during that year to the Secretary of State who lays copies of it before Parliament (para 15(1)). The report must have attached to it the statements of accounts for the year, a copy of any auditor's report on that statement and such information as the Secretary of State may direct (para 15(2)).

8.6   The new Radio Authority is regarded as a light regulatory body with important regulatory functions, but consciously different from those that apply to television. The body will be self-financing [1]. Its members should have a diversity of experience and opinion. The ability to understand business plans submitted by applicants for independent radio service licences is important. The 1990 Act's incorporation of the Green Paper's proposal that commercial television and radio services could be separately licensed and regulated allows for the fact that the environments of each are different. In many ways its provisions for radio are even more far reaching than for television because there could be three new national stations and hundreds of new local ones. There is no equivalent to Channel 4 on commercial radio, which may incorporate public service broadcasting standards if it so wishes. Such standards are within the BBC's remit and public service broadcasting was extended on 27 August 1990 with the opening of BBC radio's Channel 5. This was made possible with a more 'efficient' use of the spectrum because of the diminution of simulcasting. Simulcasting is the broadcasting of the same service on different wavelengths. There are partly historical reasons for this duplication. It was only after LF and MF services were established that VHF/FM broadcasting was introduced. Some areas of the country are still unable to receive adequate signals on both LF/MF and VHF/FM. Consequently, simulcasting reflects the principle that geographical universality of coverage should be provided in 'public service broadcasting' which is regarded in the Green Paper [2] as imposing requirements on broadcasters not simply to refrain from transmitting material which is inaccurate, misleading or unsuitable, but positively to provide wide-ranging programmes of quality. However, simulcasting may be regarded as a waste of a finite resource and some jurisdictions, for example the United States, have forbidden its practice. The remit of public service broadcasting is not fully imposed on commercial radio by the 1990 Act and radio is more lightly regulated. The philosophy is that it serves its audience best by attracting and retaining listeners and that a market led service is suitable for a pluralistic rather than a paternalistic society [3]. In the House of Lords the Government rejected the setting up of a statutory radio fund to support independent and community radio, believing that local stations will be eligible to receive financial contributions from local and other public authorities provided that they comply with the Radio Authority's guidelines and they do not exert undue political influence [4]. The Radio Authority is intended to be a self-financing body funded by the radio industry and at the House of Common's committee stage the Government rejected a proposed Radio Development and Investment Board to be set up by the Radio Authority because it would be a drain on its resources [5]. To a greater extent than with the ITC, the 1990 Act has legislated for the Radio Authority in a broad way and left it to the Authority to provide the necessary details. Many of its provisions are permissive and reflect the principle that the responsibility for broadcasting has been given to public authorities, appointed as trustees for the national interest in broadcasting and independent of Government in programming matters. The Radio Authority should have a relationship at arm's length from the

Government and be free from its intervention in its daily affairs and programme content [6]. One example of this independence is that the authority may provide for the discharge, under the general direction of the authority, of any of its functions by a committee or by one or more of its members or employees (Sch 8, para 6(2)). Such delegation of its functions does not require the Secretary of State's approval. This power is not unique and legislative precedent exists, for example in the cases of the Civil Aviation Authority under the Civil Aviation Act 1982 and the National Rivers Authority under the Water Act 1989.

1   David Mellor MP, (minister of state, Home Office), House of Commons Committee, col 945.
2   Para 1.16.
3   House of Commons Committee, col 946.
4   House of Lords Committee, col 1392.
5   House of Commons Committee, col.962.
6   Green Paper, para 1.14.

Regulatory Function of Radio Authority

8.7   The function of the Authority is to regulate the provision of 'independent radio services'. These consist of 'sound broadcasting services' 'licensable sound programme services' and 'additional services' (s84(1)). The Secretary of State may by notice assign to the authority such frequencies as he may determine. Any frequency so assigned must be taken to be assigned for the purpose only of being used for the provision of one or more 'independent radio services' (s84(4)). Any frequency assigned by him may be assigned for use only in the areas(s) specified when the assignment is made (s84(5)). Furthermore, he may by notice revoke the assignment of a frequency, whether or not that frequency is one on which an 'independent radio service' is presently being provided s84(6). In discharging its functions, the authority may make such arrangements for frequency planning as it considers appropriate. It is to be directed towards securing that the frequencies assigned to the Authority under the 1990 Act are used as efficiently as possible. Also, the Authority may arrange for such research and development work to be done as it considers appropriate for the discharge of its functions. It must secure that, so far as is reasonably practicable, (a) both the frequency and the research and development work is carried out, under its supervision, by persons who are not members or employees of it, and (b) the research and development work is to a substantial extent financed by persons other than the Authority (s123). It must also give to the Secretary of State such information or other assistance as he may reasonably require in connection with his functions under s1 of the Wireless Telegraphy Act 1949 as respects the granting, variation or revocation of licences under that section (s124). The Authority has an international role in that one of its functions is representing the Government and persons providing independent radio services on bodies concerned with the regulation (nationally or internationally) of matters relating to broadcasting (s125). At home, as mentioned above, the Radio Authority regulates the provision of 'independent radio services', consisting of sound broadcasting services, licensable sound programme services and additional services.

Meaning of 'Independent Radio Services'

Sound Broadcasting Services

8.8   Sound Broadcasting Services consist of national, local, restricted and satellite services. A national, local and restricted service is any sound broadcasting service provided from places in the United Kingdom on a frequency or frequencies assigned to the Radio Authority by the Secretary of State under s84(2) [1] for (i) any such minimum area in the United Kingdom [2] as the Authority may determine in accordance with s98(2) (a 'national service') or (ii) a particular area or locality in the United Kingdom (a 'local service') or (iii) a particular establishment or other defined location, or a particular event, in the United Kingdom (a 'restricted service') (s84(1)(a), (2)(a)). A 'satellite service' is a sound broadcasting service (other than one provided by the BBC) provided from places in the United Kingdom which consists in the transmission of sound programmes by satellite from a place (i) in the United Kingdom for general reception there or (ii) outside the United Kingdom for general reception there to the extent that the programmes included in the service consist of material provided by a person in the United Kingdom who is in a position to determine what is to be included in the service (so far as it consists of programme material provided by him) (s84(2)(b)). In the second case, the satellite service is regarded as provided by the person by whom the programme material in question is provided (s84(3)(b)). In the first case, to the extent that the programmes included in the satellite service consists of material provided by a person in the United Kingdom who is in a position to determine what is to be included in the service (as far as it consists of programme material provided by him) then he is regarded as providing that service (whether the programmes are transmitted by him or not). Otherwise it is regarded as provided by the person by whom the programmes are transmitted (s84(3)(a)).

1   See para 8.7.
2   An area in the United Kingdom does not include or comprise the whole of England (s126(2)).

National Services

8.9   Independent local radio began in 1973. By 1990 it could be heard by 90% of the population of the United Kingdom [1]. Recognising that there will always be 'white patches' on the map not served by radio stations, the Government's view was that the prospect of more comprehensive radio coverage was maximised by expanding commercial radio, first in the direction of national radio and secondly down to the community level [2]. The language of the above provision which sets up the national independent radio channels does not envisage that transmission may actually be national. The coverage is to be determined by the Radio Authority and it is envisaged that it will want about 70% national coverage immediately [3]. Given the highly speculative nature of a national service it is likely that the three new stations, if they come into existence, will start transmitting at staggered intervals.

1   House of Commons Committee, col 991.
2   House of Commons Committee, col 946.
3   House of Commons Report, col 330.

Local Services

8.10   Local Services, as defined in the 1990 Act [1], are comprised of both community and commercially based local radio stations. No distinction is made between those run by profit-making organisations and other bodies. The IBA's incremental stations before the 1990 Act were run by both types of association and this licensing flexibility continues. The Green Paper envisaged community radio as playing an important part in the expected expansion of radio services. The Government view was that no distinction should be made between local and community services because of the problem of defining the difference and the legitimacy of proposals to provide radio services that combine commercial and community elements [2]. The aim of reinvesting the profits in the service or the community which it serves can be realised under the 1990 Act. The Radio Authority may well regard community and commercial stations as one entity in which there are distinct differences. The 1990 Act can be said to have a strong impetus for community radio written into it. The effect of s105(c) [3] is that the Radio Authority is to take into account the extent a proposed local service extends listener choice by broadening the range of programmes available and, in particular, the extent to which it caters for 'tastes and interests different from those already catered for by local services' in the area. So, it is likely that an applicant who wishes to compete with an existing pop music based station would be less likely to acquire a licence than an applicant to run a community station which adds to listener choice through social action programmes and initiatives. The 1990 Act can be said to encourage community radio in a number of ways. Very small service areas, down to neighbourhood level, may be advertised. Financial contributions to stations from local and other public authorities is permitted, despite reservations in the Green Paper, so long as the Radio Authority considers no political influence is being exercised. Provided frequencies are available, community stations may be licensed, regardless of whether the area is already served by a local station. They may have lower start-up costs than under previous legislation, be able to make their own transmission arrangements and not be subject to heavy regulation. Local consultation is, to an extent, provided for by the 1990 Act. The Radio Authority is to have regard to 'the extent to which any application for the licence is supported by persons living in that area' (s105(d)) [3]. By s104(4) [4] the Authority is also required to make available an applicant's programme proposals to anyone who wishes to see them. Otherwise, it is for the Authority to devise its own local consultation methods. When deciding where to advertise a local service it will take into account invited letters of intent from interested groups. Over 860 had been received five months before the 1990 Act received the royal assent. Aspiring community radio groups can seek advice from the Radio Authority and the Community Radio Association.

1   See para 8.8.
2   House of Lords Report, col 749.
3   See para 8.70.
4   See para 8.66.

Restricted Services

8.11   The definition of restricted services in the 1990 Act [1] seeks to make a clear distinction between them and local services because restricted services may be licensed more easily without advertisements and are not subject to the full extent of regulation which the 1990 Act provides for local services. The category of 'restricted services' is intended to ensure that these radio services are confined to within an institution or to an event. Roe Wood was the first school to have a special event radio licence and the use of Radio Woody as an education tool is clear. The distinction between restricted and local services appears to be the purpose of the radio service. The fact that a signal can be received outside a restricted place should not change the purpose of the service. However if the purpose is to serve the interests of a wider section of the community, its purpose would be that of a local service and licensed and regulated accordingly [2].

1   See para 8.8.
2   House of Commons Committee, col 958.

Satellite Services [1]

8.12   The new opportunities made available by sound channels on a system of direct broadcasting by satellite (DBS) established on a commercial basis were recognised by the Green Paper [2]. One advantage over terrestrial radio services and their requirement for a transmitter network is the comparatively small cost of delivering sound DBS alongside DBS television channels. Whereas local services, because of their low power levels, are limited to certain areas, satellite stations may focus their programmes on particular country-wide audiences, like country and western enthusiasts, who have the equipment to receive its signals. The advent of satellite commercial radio services, such as Sky Television with its additional sound service, Sky Radio, which can be received on an Astra dish, is an indication of possible changes in listening patterns and the need for its regulation in the interests of the fledgling industry.

1   For definition, see para 8.8.
2   See paras 4.23, 4.24.

Licensable Sound Programme Service (LSPS) (s 112)

8.13   This is a service consisting in the provision by any person of sound programmes with a view to their being conveyed, by means of a telecommunication system, for reception (a) in two or more dwelling-houses in the United Kingdom and (b) otherwise than for the purpose of being received there by persons who have a business interest in receiving them (sub-s(1)). This may be regarded as narrow (as opposed to broad) casting. A person has a business interest in receiving sound programmes if he has an interest in receiving them for the purposes of his business, trade, profession or employment (sub-s(5)). It is a LSPS whether the telecommunication system is run by the person providing the programmes or by someone else, and whether the programmes are to be conveyed for simultaneous reception or for reception at different times in response to requests made by different service users (sub-s(1)). A telecommunication system has the same meaning as in the Telecommunications Act 1984 (s202). It is a system for the conveyance, through the agency of electric, magnetic, electromagnetic, electrochemical or electromechanical energy [1] of (1) speech, music and other sounds, (2) visual images, (3) signals for the impartation (whether as between persons and persons, things and things or persons and things) of any matter otherwise than in the form of sounds or visual images, or (4) signals for the actuation or control of machinery or apparatus (s4(1), Telecommunications Act 1984). This definition seeks to cover all known or anticipated kinds of energy used in the means of communication between a sender and receiver. It includes electric signals conveyed by wires, radio-waves, micro-waves and light-waves used in optical-fibre cables. Two examples of a telecommunication system are cable and micro-waves (or Multipoint Video Distribution Service - MVDS). MVDS uses micro-waves to carry multiple video signals to receiving installations and is used as an alternative to cable distribution which may use optical fibres. 'Optical fibres' are thin fibres of glass down which pulses of light are sent. Sound is converted into electrical pulses or 'digital' signals. A laser or a light-emitting diode can change these electrical pulses into light pulses which are projected into the glass fibre to be converted back to electrical pulses at the receiving end. Optical fibre systems have certain advantages over ordinary metal wire cables. Much greater distances can be covered before the signal needs 'boosting' and they have a large information carrying capacity. Unlike traditional cables, optical fibres are made from a cheap raw material, sand, and are not liable to interference. In the future, optical fibre systems are likely to be an integral part of telecommunications. MVDS uses the scarce resource of the spectrum. Regarded by some cable operators as a useful adjunct in less populated areas, micro-waves are a special type of radio wave, having shorted wavelengths and higher frequencies. They are different from ordinary radio waves in that the atmosphere does not reflect them. Being able to be directed at a target, micro-waves make better use of a transmitter's power, reduce the possibility of interference from other transmitters on the same frequency and, because of the high frequencies, increase the amount of information that can be carried. The transmitting aerial must be pointed at the receiver because micro-waves travel in a straight line like other electromagnetic waves and interference will be caused by things in its path.

1   No definition is given for these various forms of energy.

Non-LSPS (s 112(2))

8.14   The 1990 Act provides that a LSPS does not consist of three types of service. First, a service where the programmes are provided for transmission in the course of the provision of a sound broadcasting service. Second, a service where the running of the telecommunication system does not have to be licensed under Part II of the Telecommunications Act 1984. Third, a two-way service. An essential feature of a two-way service is that while visual images and/or sounds are being conveyed by the service provider there is or may be sent from each place of reception by means of the same telecommunication system, or the part of it by means of which they are conveyed, visual images and/or sounds for reception by the service provider or others receiving it (other than signals sent for the operation or control of the service do not amount to a two-way service) (s46(2)(c)).

Additional Services

8.15   Additional Services are services provided from places in the United Kingdom and consist in the sending of telecommunication signals for transmission by wireless telegraphy by means of the use of 'spare capacity within the signals' carrying any sound broadcasting service provided (a) on a frequency assigned under s84(4) [1] by the Secretary of State to the Radio Authority or (b) on any other allocated frequency notified to the Authority by the Secretary of State (s114(1)). The Green Paper acknowledged the possibility of radio engineers using the spare capacity within radio frequencies to carry information 'piggy-back' and so realise more fully the potential of existing signals [2]. In this way, sound radio channels can be used to generate a visual display, to transmit computer software and carry other information or to provide automatic retuning of car radio receivers as the vehicle moves from one transmitter's service area to another. The 1990 Act gives the holder of a licence to provide a local, restricted or satellite service the right to all spare signal capacity within the frequency on which the service is provided. If they wish, the licence holder can sub-contract that capacity (s115(8)) [3]. The spare capacity of the three national services is licensed separately from the spare signal capacity within the frequency on which the national service is provided. However, the Radio Authority must, when determining the extent and nature of this spare signal capacity, have regard to the need of the national service provider to be able to use part of the signals carrying the service for providing ancillary services (s114(3)) [4]. This provision can be used to exempt the Radio Data System (RDS) sub carrier and safeguard the national service licence holder's right to it. RDS is coded information and uses some of the spare capacity of the FM signal. It may provide automatic tuning of car radio and a read-out of the station can be heard, with the time and date displayed. The BBC, in 1989, transmitted a RDS service that automatically switched a car radio to travel information that was relevant to the area in which the driver was driving. More sophisticated road traffic information services may be expected in the future. Today, RDS compatible radio sets are made for receiving financial information transmitted on spare FM signal capacity [5].

1   See para 8.8,
2   See paras 2.26 and 2 27.
3   See para 8.97.
4   See para 8.93.
5   House of Commons Committee, col 1075.

Licensing Function of Radio Authority

8.16   The Radio Authority may grant such licences to provide independent radio services as it may determine (s85(1)). The overarching duty of the Authority is to carry out its functions as respects the licensing of such services in the manner that it considers best calculated (a) to facilitate the provision of licensed services which (taken as a whole) are of high quality and offer a wide range of programmes calculated to appeal to a variety of tastes and interests, and (b) to ensure fair and effective competition in the provision of such services and services connected with them (s85(3)). The discharge by the Director General of Fair Trading, the Secretary of State or the Monopolies and Mergers Commission of any of their functions is not affected by the Radio Authority's duty to ensure fair and effective competition (s85(4)). The Government had been reluctant to import subjective quality criteria (incorporated in s85(3)(a) above) into the licensing tests for both national and local radio. This was because radio was considered different from television, there would be difficulty in having subjective regulatory judgements about quality in a licensing process originally based on the concept of diversity and expanding listener choice, the Radio Authority would not wish to make such judgments and excessive quality requirements could seriously impede the growth of independent radio [1]. The overarching duty in s85(3) is to be read with the specific licensing criteria for national and local radio contained in ss99 [2] and 105 [3] respectively and neither of these sections includes a quality requirement. The significance of s85(3) is that where the Radio Authority consider applications for a national service licence, exceptional quality differences in the programme proposals may be regarded by it as a relevant factor in its consideration of whether 'exceptional circumstances' applied and made it appropriate for the authority to award the license to an applicant who had not submitted the highest bid for the licence (s100(3)) [4]. Again, if the Radio Authority considered that applicants for a particular local service licence equally met the licensing criteria in s105, it can now licence the proposed services it considers best in terms of the across-the-board quality of radio services.

1   House of Lords Report, cols 762, 763.
2   See para 8.52.
3   See para 8.70.
4   See para 8.53.

Particular National Service Duty

8.17   The Radio Authority must do all it can to secure the provision within the United Kingdom of a diversity of national services each catering for tastes and interests different from those catered for by the others and of which one is a service the greater part of which consists in the broadcasting of spoken material and another is a service which consists, wholly or mainly, in the broadcasting of music which, in the opinion of the authority is not pop music (s85(2)(a)). 'Pop music' is defined as including rock music and other kinds of modern popular music which are characterised by a strong rhythmic element and a reliance on electronic amplifications for their performance (whether or not, in the case of a particular piece of rock or other such music, the music in question enjoys a current popularity as measured by the number of recordings sold) (s85)(6)). The Broadcasting Bill originally had an internal diversity text which may have resulted in there being three national radio channels broadly the same. The 1990 Act has substituted for that an external diversity test, with requirements to be set by the Radio Authority, so that one national station must be largely speech-based, one most be based on the broadcasting of music other than pop music and the last station's base is unspecified but it may be assumed that it will broadcast pop music. The need for the definition arose because of the possibility that a service based on rock, and not pop, music might otherwise be eligible to apply for the national licence specifically restricted to non-pop music [1]. To permit this would result in two of the three stations broadcasting what to many people would be virtually pop music. The external diversity requirement can be justified by the fact that the three national channels will be using prime scarce spectrum. One of the channels will be on FM and two on AM, the latter being better suited to speech-based programming than high quality music sound [2]. The three stations are subject to the consumer protection provisions of the law [3]. An argument could be made for not imposing onerous regulations on the quality of their programming content because they have no guaranteed audience or income. Of total advertising spending, 2% goes to radio [4], and it is important not to stifle the productivity base of new ventures. In other words, the best guarantee of quality is the ability of the radio station to attract and retain an audience [5]. In the event, the 1990 Act does require the Radio Authority to facilitate the provision of licensed services which (taken as a whole) are of high quality [6]. Powers are contained in the 1990 Act which allow certain variations on the type of national services. The Secretary of State may, by order, make such amendments of s85(2)(a) as he considers appropriate for (a) including a requirement that one of the national services should be a service of a particular description or (b) removing such a requirement (s85(5)). Such an order requires the approval of each House of Parliament (s85(7)).

1   House of Lords' Report, col 752.
2   House of Commons Committee, col 967.
3   See Chapter 9.
4   House of Commons Committee, col 981.
5   House of Commons Committee, col 988.
6   See para 8.16.

Particular Local Service Duty

8.18   The 1990 Act simply provides that the Radio Authority must do all that it can to secure the provision within the United Kingdom of a range and diversity of local services (s85(2)(b)). In 1990 independent local radio (ILR) could be heard by 90% of the population. The Government anticipates that the expansion of radio will allow some of the 'white' areas like parts of Cornwall, not covered by ILR transmissions, to be covered. An example was given by Mr Mellor, minister of state [1]. The Radio Authority will be able to discover whether applicants wish to provide a country-wide service or whether there is greater interest in offering a more local service covering individual towns and districts. Then, the Authority could analyse those options in terms of frequency usage, publish results and allow further time for subsequent applications so that some of the 'white' areas could be covered. Remoter areas will have the advantage of being more likely than cities to have frequency assignments more readily available. When determining whether, and to whom, to grant a local licence, the Radio Authority must have regard to certain requirements, including the extent to which the proposed service could cater for tastes and interests different from those already catered for by ILR and the extent to which the application has local support (s105(b)(d)) [2]. Clearly the intention is that the Authority will be expected to prefer applicants who propose to do more than merely replicate existing ILR services.

1   House of Commons Committee, col 991.
2   See para 8.70.

Prohibition on Providing Unlicensed Independent Radio Services (s97)

8.19   Any person who provides any independent radio service without being authorised to do so by or under a licence under the 1990 Act is guilty of an offence (sub-s(1)). The Secretary of State may, after consultation with the Radio Authority, by order, provide that an offence is not committed with respect to such services or descriptions of services as are specified in that order (sub-s(2)). The order is subject to annulment by a resolution of either House of Parliament (sub-s(6)). In England and Wales, the consent of the Director of Public Prosecutions is required to bring a prosecution. In Northern Ireland, the Director of Public Prosecutions is required to give his consent (sub-s(4)). On conviction a fine may be imposed and there is no limit to that fine if the conviction is on indictment (sub-s(3)). Compliance with the prohibition on providing unlicensed services can also be enforceable by civil proceedings by the Crown for an injunction, interdict or any other appropriate relief (sub-s(5)). The combination of criminal and civil proceedings against people who carry out illegal pirate broadcasts, perhaps because they have been unsuccessful in persuading the Radio Authority to award them a licence, should prove a formidable deterrent both to actual and would-be offenders.

General Provisions about Licences

8.20   A fundamental duty placed on the Radio Authority is that (a) it must not grant an independent radio service licence to any person unless it is satisfied that he is a 'fit and proper' person to hold it, and (b) it must do all that it can to ensure that he does not remain the licence holder if it ceases to be so satisfied (s86(4)). The phrase 'fit and proper' is not defined in the 1990 Act. However, a person is not 'fit and proper' and is disqualified for holding a licence if within the last five years he has been convicted of (a) an offence under s1 of the Wireless Telegraphy Act 1949 which involved the making of an unlicensed transmission by wireless telegraphy (b) an offence under the Marine, & c., Broadcasting (Offences) Act 1967 or (c) an offence under s97 [1] (s89(1)). This provision is retrospective to the extent that it does not apply to an offence committed under either s1 of the 1949 Act or the 1967 Act before 1 January 1989 (s89(2)). To critics of retrospective legislation the point can be made that the then Home Secretary outlined the proposal of this provision in a speech to the Radio Academy Festival on 6 July 1988 and formally confirmed it in a parliamentary Written Answer on 2 November. The 1990 Act therefore distinguishes those who disregarded the proposal, knowingly or not, and spent the time since 1 January 1989 unlawfully acquiring experience and establishing an audience from those former 'pirates' who stopped transmitting in the expectation of an opportunity to obtain a licence from the Radio Authority. The mischief caused by 'pirate' broadcasts is that the interference they may cause can disrupt frequencies used by life safety services as well as other broadcasters [2]. The scope of s89 is wide and every independent radio service licence must include conditions requiring the licence holder to do all that he can to ensure that no person who is disqualified from holding a licence because of the s89(1) provision is concerned in the operation of any station for wireless telegraphy used in the provision of the licensed service (s89(3)).

1   See para 8.19.
2   House of Lords Committee, cols 1428, 1429.

Restrictions on the Holding of Licences (s88)

8.21   The Radio Authority must do all that it can to secure that (a) a person does not become or remain a licence holder if he is a 'disqualified person' in relation to that licence by virtue of Part II of Sch 2 [1] and (b) any requirements imposed by or under Parts III - V of Sch 2 [2] are compiled with by or in relation to licence holders to whom those requirements apply (sub-s(1)). To facilitate the discharge of this duty the Radio Authority may require an applicant for a licence to provide it with such information as it may reasonably require to determine (i) whether he is a 'disqualified person' (ii) whether any requirements imposed by Parts III to V of Sch 2 would preclude it from granting a licence to him and (iii) if so, the steps required to be taken by or in relation to him so that the requirements are met (sub-s(2)(a)). To secure compliance with those requirements the Authority may make the grant of a licence conditional on the taking of any specified steps that appear to it to be required to be taken so that those requirements are met (sub-s(2)(c)). Where the Authority determine that any such condition imposed by it has not been satisfied, the effect is as if the person to whom the licence was awarded or granted had not made an application for it (sub-s(3)(b)). However, the Authority may decide that it is more desirable to publish a fresh notice proposing to grant a licence (or, if appropriate, a further licence) to provide the service (sub-s(4)). The 1990 Act also provides that the Radio Authority may, so as to secure compliance with the requirements imposed by Parts III - V of Sch 2, impose conditions in any licence enabling it to give the licence holder directions requiring him to take, or arrange for the taking of, any specified steps appearing to it to be required in the circumstances (sub-s(2)(e)).

1   See paras 10.13 to 10.23.
2   See paras 10.24 to 10.53.

Relevant Change (s88)

8.22   A body to which a licence has been awarded or granted may undergo a 'relevant change'. A 'body' means a body of persons whether incorporated or not and includes a partnership (s202(1)). A 'relevant change' means (a) any change affecting the nature or characteristics of the body or (b) any change in the persons having control over or interests in the body, being (in either case) a change which is such that, if the Radio Authority had to determine whether to award the licence to the body in the new circumstances of the case, it would be induced by the change to refrain from awarding the licence (sub-s(7)). Certainly a 'relevant change' would be when a body holding a licence becomes disqualified in relation to that licence by virtue of Part II of Sch 2 [1] or any requirements imposed by or under Parts III - V of that Sch [2] are not complied with by or in relation to bodies holding licences to which those requirements apply. The Authority may revoke the award of a licence to a body where a relevant change takes place after the award but before the grant of the licence (sub-s(2)(b)). Should it do this, the effect is as if the person to whom the licence was awarded had not made an application for it (sub-s(3)(a)). However, the Authority may decide that it is more desirable to publish a fresh proposal notice to grant a licence (or, if appropriate, a further licence) to provide the service (sub-s(4)).

1   See paras 10.13 to 10.23.
2   See paras 10.24 to 10.53.

8.23   To facilitate the operation of the provisions on relevant change, the Radio Authority must include in every licence conditions that it considers necessary or expedient to ensure that where (a) the licence holder is a body and (b) a relevant change takes place after the grant of the licence, the Authority may revoke the licence by notice served on the licence holder. The revocation takes effect forthwith or on a date specified in the notice (s88(5)). The Authority must give the licence holder a reasonable opportunity of making representations to it, about the matters complained of, before serving the notice (s88(6)). A more particular power is given to the Radio Authority where the licence holder is a body corporate. The Authority may impose conditions in the licence requiring the body corporate to give to it advance notice of proposals affecting (i) shareholdings in the body or (ii) the directors of the body, where such proposals are known to the body (s88(2)(d)).

The Form, Scope, Duration, Variation and Transfer of a Licence (s86)

8.24   A licence must be in writing and may be granted by the Radio Authority for the provision of either the service specified in the licence or the service of such a description as is specified. It may be granted for the provision of a service which to any extent consists in the simultaneous broadcasting of different programmes on different frequencies (sub-s(1)(2)). Not surprisingly, no provision is made for simulcasting [1]. The maximum period that a licence to provide an independent radio service licence (other than a restricted service [2]), a licensable sound programme service and additional services can be in force is eight years (sub-s(3)). No maximum period is laid down for a restricted service licence. The Radio Authority needs to be satisfied that a licence holder's service can be provided for the duration of the licence period. Given the substantial investment necessary to establish, for example, a national service, a licence period of eight years would be more attractive to a licence holder than a lesser period of time which may be appropriate for a local service. The Radio Authority may vary a licence by notice served on the licence holder if in the case of (a) a variation of the period for which the licence is to continue in force, the licence holder consents [2] or (b) any other variation, the licence holder has been given a reasonable opportunity to make representations to the Authority about the variation (sub-s(5), (6)). The prior written consent of the Radio Authority is required for the transfer of a licence to another person. This consent is to be given only if the Authority is satisfied that the proposed new licence holder would be in a position to comply with all of the licence conditions for the remainder of the licence period (sub-s(7), (8)). Section 86 concludes with a warning that holding of an independent radio services licence does not relieve the holder of any requirement to hold a licence under s1 of the Wireless Telegraphy Act 1949 or s7 of the Telecommunications Act 1984 in connection with the provision of that service (sub-s(9)).

1 See para 8.6.
2 See para 8.11.
3 This does not affect the Authority's power to serve a notice reducing the licence period under s110(1)(b)(sub-s(6)), see para 8.81.

General Licence Conditions (s87)

8.25 The 1990 Act specifies a number of general conditions which the Radio Authority may include in licences. The overriding discretion given to the Authority is that a licence may include those conditions which appear to it to be appropriate, having regard to any duties which are or may be imposed on it, or the licence holder, by or under the 1990 Act (sub-s(1)(a), (6)). Other licence conditions may enable the Authority to supervise and enforce technical standards in connection with the provision of the licensed service (sub-s(1)(b)). Should unnecessarily high technical standards be imposed on, for example, restricted and local services their development may be restricted. The Green Paper [1] suggested that the important principle is that the equipment of a licensed service should not interfere with the provision of other licensed services. To prevent interference with other users of the spectrum, the Radio Authority needs to specify matters like bandwidths and permitted power levels. Only for this purpose can the Radio Authority be sure to be acting within its 1990 Act's powers of having a 'technical standards' condition [2].

1 See paras 7.24 to 7.25.
2 House of Commons Committee, col 1001.

8.26 The Radio Authority is intended to be self-financing and a licence may include conditions requiring the payment by the licence holder to the Authority (whether on the grant of the licence and/or at other times determined by or under the licence) of a fee(s) (sub-s(1)(c)). These fees must be in accordance with the tariff currently fixed by the Authority. The fee to be paid by the holder of a licence of a particular class or description must represent what appears to the Authority to be his appropriate contribution towards meeting the sums which the Authority regard as necessary in order to discharge its duty under para 12(1) of Sch 8 (sub-s(3)). This duty is to so conduct its affairs that its revenues become, at the earliest possible date and continue to be, at least sufficient to enable it to meet its obligations and discharge its functions under the 1990 Act. The tariff fixed by the Radio Authority may specify different fees in relation to different cases or circumstances, and is to be published in the manner that the Authority considers appropriate (sub-s(4)).

8.27   The Radio Authority will wish to avoid unnecessary expense for itself. Consequently, it is possible to have licence conditions requiring the licence holder to furnish the Authority, in the manner and at the times it may reasonable require, with information so as to exercise its 1990 Act functions (sub-s(1)(d)). Likewise, a licence can include conditions requiring the licence holder, if found by the Radio Authority to be in breach of a licence condition, to reimburse to the Authority in specified circumstances any costs reasonably incurred by it in connection with the breach of that condition (sub-s(1)(e)). As a 'stop gap' provision a licence may have conditions providing for such incidental and supplemental matters as appear to the Radio Authority to be appropriate (sub-s(1)(f)).

8.28   The 1990 Act, as an enabling statute, provides that a licence may in particular include two sets of conditions. First, conditions requiring the licence holder (i) to comply with any direction given by the Authority as to such matters as are specified in the licence or are of a description so specified or (ii) (except to the extent that the Radio Authority consents to his doing or not doing them) not to do or to do such things as are specified in the licence or are of a description so specified. Also, conditions requiring the licence holder to permit (i) any employee of, or person authorised by, the Radio Authority or (ii) any officer of, or person authorised by, the Secretary of State, to enter premises used in connection with the broadcasting of the licensed service and to inspect, examine, operate or test any equipment on the premises which is used in that connection (sub-s(2)). Clearly the latter condition can be included in a licence which contains a 'technical standards' condition [1].

1   See para 8.25.

8.29   To facilitate the Radio Authority's powers, under s110 [1], to impose a financial penalty, suspend or shorten the licence period for breach of a licence condition or to revoke the licence for a breach of condition under s111 [2], the 1990 Act provides that where a licence holder (a) is required by virtue of any condition imposed under the 1990 Act to provide the Radio Authority with any information and (b) in purported compliance with that condition provides them with information which is 'false in a material particular,' he is to be taken to have broken that condition (sub-s(5)).

1   See paras 8.81 to 8.83.
2   See paras 8.84 to 8.87.

8.30   Not surprisingly, there is no provision in s87 for a condition requiring that the costs incurred in respect of the broadcasting services are to be shared by the licence holders. Such a provision failed to be inserted at the House of Lords Report stage and was a 'last ditch' attempt to ensure that rural areas do not suffer as a result of the privatisation of the transmission system. The Government saw little justification for re-introducing a radio cross-subsidy system under the 1990 Act's regime [1]. In a more competitive environment, new licence holders incur lower start-up costs because of the lighter touch regulation and the Government considered it unfair to expect some stations to subsidise others. In areas with little or no local service provision frequency availability may attract service providers. The Government considered that radio and television should not be treated similarly for the purpose of transmission cross-subsidy. There is the possibility of many more terrestrial radio than terrestrial television services. The need for relay transmitters is less for radio than for television and radio transmission costs are cheaper. Independent sound broadcasting services have not achieved the geographical coverage of the United Kingdom in the way ITV did. Channel 3 companies have less freedom to determine their transmission costs than radio stations. The government's approach in the 1990 Act is to give radio stations freedom to establish their costs while providing transitional arrangements to enable existing stations to adjust to the new regime. The opportunity of entering into transitional transmission contracts with the IBA's privatised transmission successor is offered to radio stations existing when the 1990 Act's provision come into effect. The 1990 Act seeks to ensure that during the transitional period stations whose transmission costs exceed what would have been their rental payments will not have to pay more than the latter amount. The opportunity of buying transmitting equipment from the IBA is offered to licence holders during the transitional period.

1   House of Lords Report, cols 768, 769.

General Provisions for Licensed Services (s90) [1]

8.31   The Radio Authority must do all it can to secure that every licensed service complies with the requirements that (a) nothing is included in its programmes which offends against good taste or decency, is likely to encourage or incite to crime, to lead to disorder or to be offensive to public feeling; (b) any news given (in whatever form) in its programmes is presented with due accuracy and impartiality; and (c) its programmes do not include any technique which exploits the possibility of conveying a message to, or otherwise influencing the minds of, persons listening to the programmes without their being aware, or fully aware of what has occurred (sub-s(1)). For the main part these requirements are long-standing requirements and are similar to ones found in the Broadcasting Act 1981 and the Cable and Broadcasting Act 1984. Taken with the additional requirements in sub-s2 [2] they reflect the requirements in s6(1) that the ITC must do all that it can to secure compliance by services licensed by it. Radio can be tasteless or offensive, although it is a different medium from television, and it is especially important that it should not be when listeners may be vulnerable or lonely [3]. Listener protection safeguards should be known by all licence applicants as they will be included among their licence conditions. Under the deregulated regime there will be many more stations, including those whose programming may relate to potentially sensitive matters. An increase in stations catering specifically for local ethnic minority groups is anticipated and the Radio Authority needs sufficient power to ensure that its licensees conform to a minimum programme standard, albeit a subjective one, especially perhaps regarding good taste and decency. Although there appears to be no evidence that any subliminal messages have been broadcast on the radio [4], this consumer protection requirement addresses the possibility that techniques may be developed for broadcasting such messages in sound transmissions and it provides a safeguard against any future abuse in the same way as the 1990 Act does in the case of television in s6(1)(e) [5].

1   Nothing in ss90 - 96 has effect in relation to any licensed service which is an additional service (s90(7)).
2   See para 8.32.
3   House of Lords Committee, col 1432.
4   House of Lords Report, col 771.
5   See para 3.27.

8.32   The Radio Authority must, in the case of every licensed service which is a national, local, satellite or licensable sound programme service (but not, it may be noted, a restricted or additional service) do all that it can to secure that the service complies with additional requirements. First, there are excluded from its programme all expressions of the views and opinions of the person providing the service on matters (other than sound broadcasting) which are of political or industrial controversy or relate to current public policy (sub-s(2)(b)). Second, that due responsibility is exercised with respect to the content of any of its programmes which are religious programmes and, in particular, that the programmes do not involve (i) any improper exploitation of any susceptibilities of the programme's listeners or (ii) any abusive treatment of the religious views and beliefs of those belonging to a particular religion or religious denomination (sub-s(2)(c)).

8.33   In the case of a national service, the Radio Authority must do all that it can to secure that due impartiality is preserved by the service provider as respects matters of political or industrial controversy or relating to current political policy (sub-s(2)(a), (3)(a)). In applying this requirement a series of programmes may be considered as a whole (sub-s(4)). The Radio Authority must draw up and from time to time review a code giving guidance as to the rules to be observed (i) in determining what constitutes a series of programmes and (ii) in 'other respects' in applying the above requirement to a national service (sub-s(5)(a)). The areas which the ITC's impartiality code should cover are set out in the 1990 Act (s6(5)(6)) [1]. There is no similar 'contents list' provided for the Radio Authority in the 1990 Act.

1   See para 3.30.

8.34   The lesser requirement that undue prominence is not given in the programmes of a local, satellite or licensable sound programme service to the views and opinions of particular persons or bodies on matters of political or industrial controversy or relating to current political policy is in the 1990 Act (sub-s(3)(b)). In applying this requirement, the programmes included in that service must be taken as a whole and the Radio Authority must draw up, and from time to time review a code giving guidance as to relevant rules to be observed (sub-s(4)(5)(a)(iii)). It must publish the code providing for this requirement (and the above requirement imposed on a national service) and every revision of it in the manner it considers appropriate (sub-s(6)). Also, the Radio Authority must do all it can to secure that the provisions of the code are observed in the provision of licensed services and it may make different provision in the code for different cases or circumstances (sub-s(5)(b)). Clearly, the 1990 Act reflects the policy that it is more appropriate to review local, satellite and licensable sound programme services as a whole because it is inappropriate to treat them as a national service when balance within a programme or across a series is more relevant to preserving a proper perspective [1].

1   House of Commons Committee, col 1003.

General Code for Programmes (s91) [1]

8.35   The Radio Authority must draw up and from time to time review a code giving guidance as to: (a) the rules to be observed regarding the inclusion in programmes of sounds suggestive of violence, particularly in circumstances such that large numbers of children and young persons may be expected to be programme listeners; (b) the rules to be observed regarding the inclusion in programmes of appeals for donations; and (c) 'other matters' concerning standards and practice for programmes as the Radio Authority may consider suitable for inclusion in the code (sub-s(1)). When considering what 'other matters' ought to be included in the code, the Authority must have special regard to programmes included in licensed services in circumstances such that large numbers of children and young persons may be expected to be listening to them (sub-s(2)). Before drawing up or revising the code the Authority must, to the extent that it considers it reasonably practicable to do so, consult every licence holder (sub-s(3)). It must publish the code and every revision of it, in the manner it considers appropriate and do all that it can to secure that the provisions of the code are met in the provision of licensed services (sub-ss(1), (4)). Similar provisions for the ITC to draw up a general code on programme standards are present in s7 [2]. An obvious source of reference for the ITC and Radio Authority when drawing up their respective codes is the Broadcasting Standards Council code relating to broadcasting standards (s152) [3]. The latter code should not conflict with either the ITC or Radio Authority's codes which will have a direct impact on broadcasters.

1   Section 91 has no application to additional services.
2   See para 3.32.
3   See para 9.15.

General Provisions for Advertisements (s92) [1]

8.36   The Radio Authority must do all it can to ensure that the following rules are complied with in relation to licensed services (sub-s(1)). First, a licensed service must not include any advertisement which (i) is inserted by or on behalf of any body whose objects are wholly or mainly of a political nature, (ii) is directed towards any political end, or (iii) has any relation to any industrial dispute (other than an advertisement of a public service nature inserted by or on behalf of a government department). Second, in the acceptance of advertisements for inclusion in a licensed service there must be no unreasonable discrimination either against or in favour of any particular advertiser. Third, a licensed service must not, without the Authority's prior approval, include a programme sponsored by any person whose business consists, wholly or mainly, in the manufacture of a product or the provision of a service, which the license holder is prohibited from advertising because of any provision of s93 [2] (sub-s(2)). After consultation with the Authority, the Secretary of State can make regulations, which require approval by a resolution of each House of Parliament, that amend, repeal, or add to the above rules (sub-s(4)). Should there be any doubt about the matter, there is no prohibition on the inclusion in a licensed service of any party political broadcast which complies with the rules made by the Radio Authority for the purposes of s107 [2] (sub-s(3)). However, there is a prohibition on the Authority acting as an advertising agent (sub-s(5)) [3]. Section 92 mirrors s8 which was considered in paras 3.33 and 3.34.

1   Section 92 has no application to additional services.
2   See paras 8.37, 8.38.
3   See para 10.3, footnote 1.

Control of Advertisements (s93) [1]

8.37   The Radio Authority must, after appropriate consultation, draw up and from time to time review an 'advertisements and sponsorship code' (sub-s(1)). It must consult with (a) the ITC (b) such bodies or persons as appear to the Authority to represent (i) listeners (ii) advertisers and (iii) professional organisations qualified to give advice in relation to the advertising of particular products, as the Authority think fit and (c) such other bodies or persons who are concerned with advertising standards of conduct, again as the Authority think fit. Also the Authority must, to the extent that it considers it reasonably practicable, consult with every licence holder (sub-s(2)). The code must (i) govern standards and practice in advertising and in the sponsoring of programmes and (ii) prescribe the advertisements and methods of advertising or sponsorship to be prohibited or to be prohibited in certain circumstances. The code may contain different provisions for different kinds of licensed service (sub-s(1)). The Authority must publish the code, and every revision of it, in the manner it considers appropriate but only after taking account of any international obligations of the United Kingdom as the Secretary of State may notify to it (sub-s(3)(8)). It must do all it can to secure that the provisions of the code are observed in the provision of licensed services (sub-s(1)). From time to time the Authority must consult with the Secretary of State as to the classes and descriptions of advertisements which must not be included in licensed services and the methods of advertising and sponsorship which must not be employed in, or in connection with, their provision. Any directions which he may consequently give to the Authority must be carried out by it (sub-s(4)).

1   Section 93 has no application to additional services.

8.38   In the discharge of its general responsibility for advertisements and methods of advertising and sponsorship, the Authority may impose requirements which go beyond those imposed by the 'advertisements and sponsorship code' (sub-s(5)). The methods of control exercisable by the Authority so as to ensure that the provisions of the code as well as any requirements which go beyond them are complied with include a power to give directions to a licence holder with respect to the (a) classes and descriptions of advertisements and methods of advertising or sponsorship to be excluded, or excluded in particular circumstances or (b) exclusion of a particular advertisement, or its exclusion in particular circumstances (sub-s(6)). Directions may be general, specific, qualified or unqualified (sub-s(7)). The provisions on the control of advertisements by the Radio Authority are less extensive than those provided by s9 [1] for the ITC. One reason given for this is that the possibility that there will be many more radio services to choose between means that licence holders must take account of listeners' tolerance of advertisements and sponsorship, as this will be an important determinant in listener choice of radio station [2].

1   See paras 3.36 to 3.38.
2   House of Commons Committee, col 1008.

Government Control Over Licensed Services (s94) [1]

8.39   The Secretary of State or any other Crown Minister [2] may, if it appears to him necessary or expedient to do so, because of his functions, by notice require the Radio Authority to direct the holders of any specified licences to publish in their licensed services, at specified times a specified announcement. The Authority must comply with the notice and when a licence holder publishes the announcement, he may announce that he is doing so because of such a direction (sub-ss(1), (2)). The announcements are anticipated to be generally used in civil emergencies, for example when there is danger to life or property from escaping toxic gas or water pollution, and in the past the practice has been to request, not direct, broadcasters to make the announcements. In the eventuality of a war the government has the power to have an announcement made in its own terms.

1   Section 94 has no application to additional services.
2   This includes the head of any Northern Ireland department when the licensed service is provided from a place in Northern Ireland (sub-s(6)).

8.40   At any time, the Secretary of State may, by notice, require the Radio Authority to direct the holders of any specified licences to refrain from including in their programmes any specified matter or classes of matter. Again, the Authority must comply with the notice and when it has (a) given the licence holder its direction or (b) revoked the direction because the Secretary of State has revoked the notice (or where the notice has expired) the licence holder may publish in the licensed service an announcement of the giving or revocation of the direction (or the expiration of the notice) as is appropriate (sub-ss(3), (4)). A direction may require, for example, that licence holders refrain from broadcasting interviews with members of terrorist groups. In considering whether the Secretary of State should have this power, it is important to distinguish the existence of the power from its exercise. If misused, the existence of the power will be brought into disrepute. The powers conferred on the Secretary of State by s94 are additional to any other power conferred on him elsewhere in the 1990 Act (sub-s(5)). The provisions of s94 are mirrored in s10 [1] as regards services licensed by the ITC. In neither section is there a requirement for prior consultation with the ITC or Radio Authority by the Crown Minister. Dropped from the Broadcasting Bill was a clause enabling the Radio Authority to direct licensees to exclude any programme from a licensed service [2]. Similar powers were given, under s15 of the Cable and Broadcasting Act 1984, to the Cable Authority in relation to licensed cable services and, under s6(4) of the Broadcasting Act 1981, to the IBA in relation to the television and radio schedules of its contractors. It was thought that an explicit reserve power for use in exceptional circumstances would enable the Radio Authority to prevent the broadcasting of material that would contravene the provisions on taste, decency and editorialising contained in s90 [3]. The government considered the clause unnecessary as s93 [4] empowers the Radio Authority to exclude particular classes or descriptions of advertisements and s109 [5] empowers it to require advance production of scripts and recordings because of failure to comply with licence conditions.

1 See para 3.39.
2 House of Commons Committee, cols 1010, 1011.
3 See paras 8.31 to 8.34.
4 See para 8.37.
5 See para 8.79.

Monitoring of Programmes (s95) [1]

8.41 The Radio Authority may make and use recordings of programmes included in licensed services for the purpose of maintaining supervision over them (sub-s(1)). To facilitate this power, a licence must include conditions requiring the licence holder (a) to retain for a period not exceeding 42 days, a recording of each programme included in the licensed service (b) at the Authority's request, to produce to it the recording for examination or reproduction and (c) at the Authority's request, to produce to it any script or transcript of a programme included in the licensed service (sub-s(2)). This provision may be regarded as an example of the lighter regulatory regime introduced by the 1990 Act in that the original maximum period for retention in the Bill was 90 days. Forty-two days would appear to be a reasonable time for evidence to be held and the lesser time period means a saving of storage space. In the case of monitoring by the ITC of programmes included in its licensed services the maximum period of retention is 90 days under s11 [2]. The existence of the enabling powers in s95 facilitates the consideration of complaints by the Broadcasting Complaints Commission and the Broadcasting Standards Council. It is the duty of the licence holder providing the service that included the programme which is the subject of complaint to provide those respective bodies with a sound recording of it if he has it in his possession (ss145(4)(a), 155(3)(a)). It is thought that as regards transcripts, a Welsh language radio station must merely submit it in the language in which it was broadcast [3]. The Radio Authority is not required to listen to programmes in advance of their being included in licensed services.

1 Section 95 has no application to additional services.
2 See para 3.41.
3 House of Commons Committee, col 1018.

Audience Research (s96) [1]

8.42   The Radio Authority must make arrangements for (a) ascertaining the state of public opinion concerning programmes included in licensed services and (b) assisting it to perform its functions in connection with programmes to be included in national and local services and for ascertaining the types of programme that members of the public would like to be included in licensed services (sub-s(1)). These arrangements must (a) ensure that, so far as is reasonably practicable, any research is undertaken by people who are neither members or employees of the Authority and (b) include provision for full consideration by the Authority of the research results (sub-s(2)). A similar requirement for audience research is imposed on the ITC by s12 [2] and the Welsh Authority by s64 [3]. The Broadcasting Standards Council (BSC) may commission research under s157 [4]. The 1990 Act anticipates that the research arranged by the Radio Authority will be carried out mainly by 'out-of-house' organisations. There is no requirement that the research be published. This may be because some will be of low quality. The research to assist the Radio Authority perform its functions in connection with national and local service programmes does not extend to additional services, where there may be only some form of data transmission, or satellite services, where there may not be a competition for licences which could usefully be informed by audience research. The shadow Radio Authority suggested during the progress of the Broadcasting Bill that it would be inappropriate for a light touch regulatory body to arrange research into the effects of programmes on listeners [5]. The BSC arranges such research itself under s157. There is no such requirement imposed on the Radio Authority in the 1990 Act.

1   Section 96 has no application to additional services.
2   See para 3.42.
3   See para 4.199.
4   See para 9.23.
5   House of Lords Committee, col 1436.

National Radio Services

8.43   A proposed national service is not expected to cover the whole of the United Kingdom. In determining the minimum area of the United Kingdom for which a national service is to be provided the Radio Authority must have regard to the following considerations: (a) the service should, so far as is reasonably practicable, make the most effective use of the frequency or frequencies on which it is to be provided; (b) the area for which it is to be provided should not be so extensive that the costs of providing it would be likely to affect the ability of the person providing the service to maintain it (s98(2)). These considerations are of fundamental importance to the licensing of national services.

8.44   It is practically impossible to impose a requirement for universal coverage. The BBC is subject to universality obligations but its national coverage is still not complete. It expects to spend £26 million in the near future on new transmitters and this will not result in total coverage [1]. Not surprisingly the 1990 Act allows flexibility for the development of national services over a period of time. Section 106(3) [2] enables the Radio Authority to control their degree of growth by requiring national service licence holders to extend the provision of their service beyond the originally determined coverage area. In practice, it is likely that licence holders will seek to achieve as much coverage as is possible in the shortest period of time so as to increase its audience and be more attractive to advertisers and sponsors.

1   House of Lords Report, col 774.
2   See para 8.75.

8.45   It may be anticipated that the Radio Authority will select at least 80% as the minimum national service coverage area, including a reasonable proportion within each of the national regions of the United Kingdom. One limiting factor is that the minimum area must not comprise or include the whole of England (s126(2)). Independent national services are to attain as much coverage as they can without harming their financial resources for sustaining their development. Also frequencies are to be effectively used. Any frequencies which are unused by national services will be available for local services.

Licensing of National Services

Proposal Notice (s98(1))

8.46   When the Radio Authority propose to grant a licence to provide a national service, it must publish, in the manner that it considers appropriate, a notice (a) stating that it proposes to grant a national licence (b) specifying (i) the period for which the licence is to be granted (ii) the minimum area of the United Kingdom for which the service is to be provided [1] (iii) if the service is to be one where the greater parts consists in the broadcasting of spoken material or one consisting, wholly or mainly, in the broadcasting of music which in the opinion of the Authority is not pop music, that the service is to be such a service (iv) if there is an existing licensed national service, that the service is to be one which caters for tastes and interests different from those already catered for by any such service (as described in the notice) (c) inviting applications for the licence and specifying the closing date for applications and (d) specifying (i) the application fee and (ii) the percentage of qualifying revenue for each accounting period that would be payable by an applicant in pursuance of s102(1)(c) [2] if he were granted a licence (s98(1)).

1   See s98(2), para 8.43.
2   See para 8.60.

8.47   The 1990 Act does not allow for all three national services to be allocated to the category where the profitability is likely to be greatest, which is pop music. A broader range is sought. Although the proposal notice must state whether the proposed service is speech or non pop music based, there is no statutory requirement for the Radio Authority to publish illustrative guidelines of the kinds of programmes 'calculated to appeal to a variety of tastes and interests', which the applicant must submit with his application (s98(3)(a)(ii)) [1]. There is such a statutory requirement on the ITC when it publishes a notice proposing to grant a licence to provide a Channel 3 service 'calculated to appeal to a wide variety of tastes and interests' (s(15(2)) [2]. However the Radio Authority is free to provide illustrative programming schedules. There is no requirement that a certain percentage of independent productions are to be transmitted on a national service. One reason given is that investment in a national service is highly speculative and there is no guarantee of it becoming a permanent part of broadcasting in the United Kingdom [3].

1   See para 8.48.
2   See para 4.5.
3   House of Commons Committee, col 1027.

Application (s98(3))

8.48   The written application must be accompanied by the applicant's (a) proposals for providing a service that would both (i) comply with any requirement specified in the proposal notice relating to the fact that the proposed service is to be one where the greater part consists in the broadcasting of spoken material or one consisting, wholly or mainly, in the broadcasting of music which in the opinion of the Radio Authority is non pop music and (ii) consist of a diversity of programmes calculated to appeal to a variety of tastes and interests [1] (b) application fee (c) proposals for training or retraining persons employed or to be employed by him in order to help fit them for employment in, or in connection with, the making of programmes [2] to be included in his proposed service [1] (d) cash bid, which is an offer to pay to the authority, in respect of the grant of the licence, a specified amount of money which is to be payable by equal annual instalments throughout the period for which the licence is in force (being an amount which, as increased by the appropriate percentage is also to be payable in respect of subsequent years falling wholly or partly within that period) (s98(8)) (e) such information as the authority may reasonably require as to (i) the applicant's present financial position and his projected financial position during the period for which the licence would be in force and (ii) the arrangements which the applicant proposes to make for, and in connection with, the transmission of his proposed service [1] and (f) such other information as the authority may reasonably require for the purpose of considering the application [1] (s98(3)). No deposit is required.

1   Before determining the application the Radio Authority may require the applicant to furnish additional information on this part of his application in such form or verified in such manner as it may specify (s98(4), (5)).
2   In s98 'programme' does not include an advertisement (s98(7)).

8.49   The applicant's proposals for a 'diversity of programmes calculated to appeal to a variety of tastes and interests' means that they must contain his programming schedules in the light of how he interprets this requirement. The Radio Authority must ensure there is a diversity of interests (s99(1)(a)(ii)) [1]. Consequently, an applicant for a speech-based national service could not expect proposals solely consisting of spoken material to be successful. The proposals are extremely important because they will be incorporated into the licence awarded to the successful applicant and he will be generally bound by them during the currency of the licence (s106(1)) [2].

1   See para 8.52.
2   See para 8.73.

8.50   There is no requirement that a national service must carry news and current affairs. Whereas in 1990 terrestrial television had a duopoly, with ITV and Channel 4 broadly matching BBC1 and BBC2 as regards programming obligations and coverage, there was no equivalent for radio. So, it may be argued, false parallels between radio and television could be drawn. The 1990 Act provides a framework for independent national services to develop. The policy is to have the BBC radio networks continue providing public service broadcasting and allow the national services to be more lightly regulated [1].

1   House of Lords Committee, col 1497.

Publication of Applications (s98(6))

8.51   The Radio Authority must, as soon as reasonably practicable after the closing date for applications, publish in the manner it considers appropriate (a) the name of every applicant for the proposed service (b) his proposals for providing a service that would both (i) comply with any requirement specified in the proposal notice relating to the fact that the proposed service is to be one where the greater part consists in the broadcasting of spoken material or one consisting, wholly or mainly, in the broadcasting of music which in the opinion of the Radio Authority is not pop music and (ii) consist of a diversity of programmes calculated to appeal to a variety of tastes and interests (c) such other information connected with his application as the authority consider appropriate (s98(6)). The Authority may not consider it appropriate, for reasons of confidentiality, to publish the applicants' business plans concerning his present and projected financial position submitted with his application.

Consideration of Applications (s99(1))

8.52 When a person has made an application for a national licence, the Radio Authority must not proceed to consider whether to award him the licence on the basis of his cash bid unless it appears to it that (a) his proposed service would both (i) comply with any requirement in the authority's proposal notice that if the proposed service is to be one which is speech-based or pop music based, that the service is to be such a service or that if there is an existing licensed national service, that the service will cater for different tastes and interests and (ii) consist of a diversity of programmes calculated to appeal to a variety of tastes and interests and (b) he would be able to maintain the service throughout the period for which the licence would be in force (s99(1)).

Award of National Licence (s100(1), (3))

8.53 The general principle is that the Radio Authority must, after considering all the cash bids submitted by the applicants for a national licence, award it to the applicant who submitted the highest bid (sub-s(1)). The important exception to these general principles is that the Authority may award the licence to an applicant who has not submitted the highest bid if it appears to it that there are 'exceptional circumstances' which make it appropriate for it to award the licence to that applicant (sub-s(3)). The 1990 Act does not define 'exceptional circumstances'. However, where it appears to the Authority, in the context of the licence, that any circumstances are to be regarded as exceptional, these circumstances may be so regarded by it despite the fact that similar circumstances have been so regarded by it in the context of any other licence(s) (ibid). This offers the same clarification as for television in s17(4)[1]. Exceptional circumstances will not cease to apply in relation to applications for the third national service simply because the Authority had invoked the exceptional circumstances provision in the case of the two preceding national radio competitions. In determining what constitutes exceptional circumstances, there is the overarching requirement in s85(3)(a) that the Radio Authority must 'facilitate the provision of licensed services which (taken as a whole) are of high quality and offer a wide range of programmes calculated to appeal to a variety of tastes and interests' [2].

1 See para 4.20.
2 See para 8.16.

Identical Cash Bids (s100(2))

8.54 When two or more applicants for a particular licence have submitted cash bids specifying an identical amount which is higher than the amount of any other cash bid submitted, the Radio Authority must invite them to submit further cash bids in respect of that licence. However, the Authority may propose to exercise their s100(3) power [1] and award the licence to an applicant because it appears to it that there are 'exceptional circumstances' which make this appropriate (sub-s(2)).

1 See para 8.53.

The Public Interest (s100(4) - (7), (11))

8.55 National service licences should not be awarded to a qualified applicant if this is contrary to the public interest. Accordingly, if it appears to the Radio Authority in the case of an applicant to whom it would otherwise award the licence, that there are grounds for suspecting that any 'relevant source of funds' is such that it would not be in the public interest for the licence to be awarded to him, it must (a) refer his application to the Secretary of State, together with (i) a copy of all documents submitted to it by the applicant and (ii) a summary of its deliberations on the application and (b) not award the licence to him unless the Secretary of State has given his approval (s100(4)). On such a reference the Secretary of State may only refuse to give such approval if he is satisfied that any 'relevant source of funds' is such that it would not be in the public interest to award the licence to him (s100(5)).

8.56 A 'relevant source of funds' is any source of funds to which an applicant might (directly or indirectly) have recourse for the purpose of (a) paying any additional payments in respect of the licence under s102(1)[1] or (b) otherwise financing the provision of his proposed service (s100(6)). Money from the illegal trade of controlled drugs may be a relevant source. Should the Radio Authority be precluded from awarding the licence to an applicant because his relevant source of funds is such that to do so that it would not be in the public interest, the effect is as if he had not made an application for the licence. Alternatively, the Authority may decide that it would be desirable to publish a fresh notice proposing to grant the licence under s98 [2] and again invite applications for it (s100(7), (11)).

1   See para 8.60.
2   See para 8.46.

Grant of Licence (s100(8) - (10))

8.57 When the Radio Authority have awarded a national licence to any person, it must, as soon as is reasonably practicable, (a) publish certain matters in the manner that it considers appropriate and (b) grant the licence to that person (sub-s(8)). The matters to be published are (a) the name of the person to whom the licence has been awarded and the amount of his cash bid (b) the name of every other applicant who appeared to the Authority to satisfy the requirement of s99(1)(a) [1] (c) when the licence has been awarded, because of the 'exceptional circumstances' provision in s100(3)[2], to an applicant who has not submitted the highest cash bid, the Authority's reasons for so awarding the licence and (d) such other information as the Authority consider appropriate (sub-s(9)). When a licence has been awarded to any person under s100 on the revocation of an earlier grant of it the Authority must publish all the above matters, except the names of other applicants who satisfied the s99(1)(a) requirements, and give an indication of the circumstances in which the licence has been awarded (sub-s(10)).

1   See para 8.52.
2   See para 8.53.

Failure to Begin National Service (s101(1), (2))

8.58 If, after a national licence has been granted to a person but before it has come into force, (a) he indicates to the Radio Authority that he does not intend to provide the service or (b) the Authority for any other reason have reasonable grounds for believing that he will not provide the service once the licence has come into force, then (i) the Authority must serve on him a notice revoking the licence as from the time the notice is served and (ii) the effect is as if he had not applied for the licence. Alternatively, the Authority may, if it considers this desirable, publish a fresh notice proposing to grant the licence under s98(1) [1] and invite applications for it (sub-s(1)). When the Authority reasonably believe that he will not begin to provide the national service, it must serve on the person awarded the licence a notice stating its grounds for its belief, after giving

him a reasonable opportunity of making representations to it about the matters complained of (sub-s(2)).
1   See para 8.46.

Financial Penalties on Licence Revocation (s101(3) - (5))

8.59   When the Radio Authority revoke a national licence under s101 [1] or under any other provision in the 1990 Act, it must serve on the licence holder a notice requiring him to pay to it, within a specified period, a financial penalty of the 'prescribed amount' (sub-s(3)). Should the licence be revoked either under s101 for failure to begin providing the service or within the first complete accounting period of the licence holder falling within the period for which the licence is in force, the 'prescribed amount' is 7% of the amount which the Authority estimate would have been the 'qualifying revenue' for that accounting period. In any other case, it is 7% of the 'qualifying revenue' for the last complete accounting period of the licence holder so falling. The 'qualifying revenue' is determined in accordance with s102(2) - (6) [2] (sub-s(4)). Any financial penalty payable by a body is recoverable by the Radio Authority from that body, whether or not the licence is in force, and from any person who controls that body (sub-s(5)).
1   See para 8.58.
2   See paras 8.61, 8.62.

Additional Payments for National Licences (s102(1), (9), (10))

8.60   In addition to any fees required to be paid because of a licence condition under s87(1)(c) [1], a national licence must include conditions requiring the licence holder to pay to the Radio Authority additional payments that fall into three categories. The first, in respect of the first complete calendar year falling within the period for which the licence is in force, is the amount specified in his cash bid (sub-s(1)(a)). The second, in respect of each subsequent year falling wholly or partly within that period, is the amount specified as increased by the 'appropriate percentage' (sub-s(1)(b)). In any relevant year 'the appropriate percentage' is the percentage corresponding to the percentage increase between (a) the retail prices index published by the Central Statistical Office of the Chancellor of the Exchequer for the November in the year preceding the first complete calendar year falling within the period for which the licence is in force and (b) the retail prices index for the November preceding the relevant year (sub-s(10)). The third category of payment, in respect of each accounting period of his falling within the period for in the first category, is an amount representing such percentage of the 'qualifying revenue' for that accounting period as was specified in the notice proposing to grant a national licence under s98(1)(d)(ii) [2] (sub-s(1)(c)). When (a) the first complete accounting period of the licence holder falling within the licence period in the first category of additional payments does not begin with the licenced period or (b) the last complete accounting period of his falling within that licensed period does not end with that licence period, an accounting period in the third category includes that part of the accounting period preceding the first complete accounting period or (as the case may be) following that last complete accounting period as falls within the licence period (s102(9)). These provisions relate to payment by licence holders of the amount of their cash bids over the licence period (allowing for 'inflation') as well as payments based on their qualifying revenue over that period. Part II of Sch 7 contains provisions relating to the completion of qualifying revenue (s121). The Authority must draw up a statement of principles for ascertaining qualifying revenue for any accounting period of a licence holder (para 1(1)). The Secretary of State must lay copies of it before each House of

Parliament (para 1(4)). Disputes are determined by the Authority and are subject to judicial review (para 2).

1   See para 8.26.
2   See para 8.46.

Qualifying Revenue (s102(2), (6))

8.61   For the purposes of the above third category of additional payment, 'qualifying revenue' in a licence holder's accounting period consists of all payments received or to be received by him or by any connected person (a) in consideration of inclusion in the national service in that period of advertisements or other programmes or (b) in respect of charges made in that period for the reception of programmes included in that service (sub-s(2)). The purpose is to include all relevant incomes, not only from advertisements but also sponsorship. Consequently, if in any accounting period of the licence holder, he or any connected person derives, in relation to any programme to be included in the national service, any financial benefit (whether direct or indirect) from payments made by any person, by way of sponsorship, for the purpose of defraying or contributing towards costs incurred or to be incurred in connection with that programme, the qualifying revenue for that accounting period is taken to include the amount of the financial benefit derived by the licence holder or the connected person (sub-s(6)).

8.62   If, in connection with the inclusion of any advertisements or other programmes where inclusion is paid for by payments falling within s102(2) [1], payments are made to the licence holder or any connected person to meet any payments falling within the third category, they are to be regarded as made in consideration of the inclusion of the programmes (s102(3)). When an advertisement is included under arrangements made between (a) the licence holder or any connected person and (b) a person acting as an advertising agent [2], the amount of any receipt by the licence holder or any connected person that represents a payment by the advertiser from which the advertising agent has deducted an amount by way of commission must be the amount of the payment by the advertiser after the deduction of the commission (s102(4)). However, if the amount deducted by way of commission exceeds 15% of the advertiser's payment, the amount of the receipt is taken to be the amount of the payment less 15% (s102(5)).

1   See para 8.61.
2   For example, carrying on a business involving the selection and purchase of advertising time or space for persons wishing to advertise (s202(7)).

Additional Payment Licence Conditions (s102(7), (8))

8.62A A national licence may include conditions (a) enabling the Radio Authority to estimate before the beginning of an accounting period the amount due for that period because of the existence of the third category of additional payment [1] and (b) requiring the licence holder to pay the estimated amount by monthly instalments throughout that period (sub-s(7)). In particular, there may be conditions (a) authorising the Authority to revise any estimate on one or more occasions, and to adjust the instalments payable by the licence holder to take account of the revised estimate and (b) providing for the adjustment of any over or under payment (sub-s(8)).

1   See para 8.60.

Restriction on Changes in Control over National Licence Holder

Moratorium on Takeovers (s103)

8.63   Section 103 provides for a limited moratorium on takeovers of national radio licences so that there can be a period of stability at the commencement of the licence period. When (a) any change in the persons having control over (i) a body to which a national licence has been duly awarded or transferred or (ii) an associated programme provider takes place between the date of the award of the licence and the first anniversary of the date of its coming into force and (b) that change takes place without the prior approval of the Radio Authority, it may refuse to grant the licence to the body to whom it was awarded or transferred or, if it has been granted, serve on that body a notice revoking it (sub-s(1)). The body must be given a reasonable opportunity of making representations to the Authority about the matter complained of before the refusal to grant a licence or notice revoking it is served (sub-s(5)). An 'associated programme provider' is any body connected with the body to whom a licence has been awarded or transferred and appears to the Radio Authority to be, or to be likely to be, involved to any extent in the provision of programmes for inclusion in the national service. When a body has been awarded but not yet granted a national licence it will be regarded as a national service holder for the purposes of para 3 in Part I of Sch 2 [1] (sub-s(2)). When the Radio Authority refuse to grant a licence to any body the effect is as if that body had not made an application for the licence. Alternatively, the Authority may, if it decides it desirable, publish a fresh notice proposing to grant the licence under s98 [2] and invite applications for it. When the Authority serve on any body a notice revoking its licence, the notice is to take effect as from the time when it is served on the licence holder. However, if it appears to the Authority to be appropriate to do so for the purpose of preserving continuity in the provision of the national service, it may provide in the notice for it to take effect as from a date specified in it (sub-s(6)).

1　See para 10.11.
2　See para 8.46.

8.64　The Radio Authority has a discretion as to how to act in the above circumstances. However it must refuse to approve any change if it appears to it that the change would be prejudicial to the provision under the licence, by the body to which a national licence has been duly awarded or transferred, of a service which accords with the proposals submitted under s98(3)(a) [1] by that body (or, as the case may be, by the person to whom the licence was originally awarded (sub-s(3)). It may refuse to approve any change in other circumstances if it considers it appropriate to do so (sub-s(4)).

1　See para 8.48.

Licensing of Local Services

Proposal Notice (s104(1))

8.65　When it proposes to grant a licence to provide a local service, the Radio Authority must publish, in the manner it considers appropriate, a notice. The notice must (a) state that it proposes to grant a local service licence (b) specify the area or locality in the United Kingdom for which the service is to be provided (c) invite applications for the licence and specify the closing date for applications and (d) state the fee payable on the application (s104(1)). Over 860 letters of intent from interested groups had been received by the Radio Authority at the House of Lords Committee stage of the Broadcasting Bill [1]. The Authority will take account of these and other expressions of interest when deciding where to advertise a local service.

1　House of Lords Committee, col 1383.

Application (s104(2) - (4))

8.66　The written application must be accompanied by (a) the application fee (b) the applicant's proposals for providing a service that would (i) cater for the tastes and interests of persons living in the area or locality for which it would be provided or for any particular tastes and interests of such persons and (ii) broaden the range of programmes [1] available by way of local services to persons living in that area or locality [2] (c) such information as the Authority may reasonably require as to (i) the applicant's present financial position and his projected financial position during the period for which the licence would be in force and (ii) the arrangements which the applicant proposes to make for, and in connection with, the transmission of his proposed service [2] and (d) such other information as the Authority may reasonably require for the purpose of considering the application [2] (sub-s(2)). The Radio Authority must, on request of any person and on his payment of such sum (if any), as it may reasonably require, make available for his inspection any information furnished under part (b) above by the applicants (sub-s(4)). There is no duty on the Authority to publish particulars of applications received. Nor is it required to explain the reasons for its licensing decision. Should an unsuccessful applicant inquire of the Authority why they were unsuccessful, there is no reason that those explanations should not be given. The basic reason will be that the successful applicant produced better programme suggestions. The successful applicant's proposals are of fundamental importance as they will be incorporated into his licence and he will generally be bound by them (s106(1)) [3].

1   Programme does not include an advertisement in ss104 - 106 (s104(7)).
2   Before determining an application the Radio Authority may require the applicant to furnish additional information on these matters (sub-s(3)).
3   See para 8.73.

8.67   The policy behind the lack of a requirement for the Radio Authority to publish its reasons for awarding a licence to a particular applicant is pragmatic [1]. Such a requirement would slow down the licensing process and add to the Authority's costs which would be passed onto its licensees. Any reasons given could possibly be the subject of judicial review. Section 105 [2] sets out the criteria to which the Authority must have regard when considering local licence applications. Should an unsuccessful applicant examine his competitors' applications under s104(4) [3], he will be able to examine them in the knowledge of the criteria used by the Authority. There is no requirement that independent local services must carry news and current affairs, although the BBC local services have public service obligations. This results in a lighter regulatory regime for them and the hope that they will expand in a way which genuinely adds to listener choice [4].

1   House of Lords Report, col 782.
2   See para 8.70.
3   See para 8.66.
4   House of Lords Committee, col 1497.

8.68   Whereas s103 [1] provides for a one-year moratorium on the takeover of national radio licences, no such rule applies to a local radio. A number of reasons can be given for this [2]. There will be only three national service licences. It is possible that some interested persons may stay out of the tender process until the licence has been awarded. In the case of local services the position is different. Several hundred licences will be available in the near future and more than one licence could be offered in some areas. Also, should a moratorium apply to local services existing when the 1990 Act comes into effect, they would be able to obtain licences from the Radio Authority without facing competition. Further, the licensing of local radio services will be a gradual process over a number of years. Normally licences will be readvertised every eight years. A moratorium provision could result in a set of moratoria extending over a long time. Finally, it can be doubted whether listeners are concerned about who provides a local service so long as it continues to provide the programmes promised in its application proposals.

1   See para 8.63.
2   House of Lords Report, cols 779, 800.

Renewal of Local Licences (s104(5), (6)(a))

8.69   When the Radio Authority propose, on the expiry of a local licence for any reason other than because it exercised its s110 power to shorten the licence period, to grant a further local licence it must publish a notice of the proposed grant. However, the authority need not do this if it appears to it that to do so would not serve to broaden the range of programmes available by way of local services to persons living in the area or locality for which the service has been provided (sub-s(5)). In these circumstances an application must be made in a manner to be determined by the authority and accompanied by any fee (if any) that the authority may determine (sub-s(6)(a)). The Radio Authority will normally be expected to readvertise a local licence which had expired if it is proposed to issue a further service licence. However, it has the power not to invite further competition in certain circumstances. For example, there is little point inviting applications for a service whose licence is due to expire in an area where the number of expressions of interest sent to the Authority was exceeded by the number of available spare frequencies. The Authority need not invite local licence applications if this would not be relevant to the general objective of broadening listener choice.

Special Requirements in Granting Local Licences (s105)

8.70   When the Radio Authority have published a proposal notice under s104(1) [1], it must, in determining whether and to whom to grant the local licence, have regard to four requirements. These are: (a) each applicant's ability to maintain, throughout the period for which the licence is to be in force, the service which he proposes to provide; (b) the extent to which the proposed service would cater for the tastes and interests of persons living in the area or locality for which the service would be provided, and, where it is proposed to cater for any particular tastes and interests of such persons, the extent to which the service would so cater; (c) the extent to which the proposed service would broaden the range of programmes available by way of local services to persons living in the area or locality for which it would be provided, and, in particular, the extent to which the service would cater for tastes and interests different from those already catered for by local services provided for that area or locality and (d) the extent to which any application for the licence is supported by persons living in that area or locality (s105). The test in the third requirement is whether a proposed service would contribute to listener choice. For example, if in an area a pop music based service was proposed but one already existed, a community based service would be better placed to be awarded the licence. However, the 1990 Act is not protectionist. It is designed to attempt to increase the uptake of the available radio wavelengths [2]. As there is no competitive tendering procedure the Radio Authority has a large discretion, guided as it is by these four requirements which together constitute the criteria by which the Radio Authority will judge applications.

1   See para 8.65.
2   Mr David Mellor, (minister of state), House of Commons Committee, col 978.

Applications for a Licence to Provide a Satellite or Restricted Service (s104(6)(b))

8.71   An application to provide a satellite or restricted service is to be made in the manner determined by the Radio Authority. It must be accompanied by the fee (if any) which the Authority determines (s104(6)(b)). Consequently, the licensing process is not competitive and is more in the nature of a certification process.

Character and Coverage of National and Local Services (s106)

8.72   The 1990 Act enables the Radio Authority to make certain requirements as to the character and coverage of national and local services.

Joint Requirement as to Character (sub-s(1))

8.73   A national or local licence must include such conditions as appear to the Radio Authority to be appropriate for securing that the character of the licensed service, as proposed by the licence holder when making his application, is maintained during the period in which the licence is in force, except to the extent that the Authority consents to any departure on the grounds that it would not (a) narrow the range of programmes available by way of independent radio services to persons living in the area or locality for which the service is licensed to be provided or (b) that it would not substantially alter the character of the service. Clearly this is of practical importance because it means that the licence holder is generally bound by the programming proposals that he submitted with his successful application. However, particular types of programme may go out of fashion and they may be dropped but only if the Radio Authority are satisfied that the character of the service would not be substantially altered.

Joint Requirement as to Coverage (sub-s(2))

8.74   A national or local licence must include conditions requiring the licence holder to ensure that the licensed service serves so much of the area or locality for which it is licensed to be provided as is for the time being reasonably practicable.

National Requirement as to Coverage (sub-s(3))

8.75   A national licence must include conditions enabling the Radio Authority, where it appears to it to be reasonably practicable for the licensed service to be provided for any additional area falling outside the minimum area determined by it in accordance with s98(2), [1] to require the licence holder to provide the licensed service for any such additional area. There is no commitment to universal coverage in the 1990 Act. A combination of commercial viability and practicality will be key determining factors in the expansion of national services [2].

1   See para 8.43.
2   House of Commons Committee, col 1069.

Local Requirement as to Coverage (sub-ss(4) - (6))

8.76   The Radio Authority may, if it thinks fit, authorise the holder of a local licence, by means of a variation of his licence to that effect, to provide the licensed service for any additional area or locality adjoining the area or locality for which that service has previously been licensed to be provided (sub-s(4)). The Authority may only exercise this power if it appears to it that to do so would not result in a substantial increase in the area or locality for which the service is licensed to be provided (sub-s(5)). As soon as practicable after the Authority have exercised that power in relation to any service, it must publish, in the manner it considers appropriate, a notice (a) stating that they have exercised that power in relation to that service and (b) giving details of the additional area or locality for which that service is licensed to be provided (sub-s(6)). Section 106(4) seeks to solve a problem that arose under the Broadcasting Act 1981 [1]. The effect

of the 1981 Act was that when an independent local radio station sought approval for a new transmitter so as to improve the coverage within its contract area, it could be thwarted if listeners outside the contract area might receive the service from the proposed relay transmitter. A significant extension of the contract area meant that the IBA had to readvertise the franchise. Some local radio stations preferred not to improve reception for its listeners if the alternative was readvertisement. The Radio Authority's use of its s106(4) power is limited by the fact that it must not result in a substantial increase in the licence area (sub-s(5)). The power may be used when the additional area cannot support its own service.
1   House of Lords Committee, col 1504.

Party Political Broadcasts (s107)

8.77   A national licence must include conditions requiring the licence holder to (a) include party political broadcasts in the licensed service and (b) observe the rules with respect to party political broadcasts as the Radio Authority may determine (sub-s(1)). The Authority may determine both (a) the political parties on whose behalf party political broadcasts may be made and (b) the length and frequency of such broadcasts (sub-s(2)). Any rules made by the Radio Authority may make different provision for different cases or circumstances (sub-s(3)). This provision is a statutory mechanism which enables agreements reached on party political broadcasts to be applied to independent radio services.

Promotion of Equal Opportunities (s108)

8.78   A national licence must include conditions requiring the licence holder to make, and from time to time review, arrangements for promoting, in relation to employment by him, equality of opportunity between men and women and between persons of different 'racial groups' (sub-s(1)). 'Racial group' has the same meaning as in the Race Relations Act 1976.

Enforcement of Licences

Power to Require Scripts, etc (s109(1), (2))

8.79   If the Radio Authority is satisfied that the holder of a sound broadcasting licence has failed to comply with any licence condition or with any direction given by the Authority under or by virtue of the 1990 Act, it may serve on him a notice (a) stating that it is so satisfied (b) stating that if at any time during a specified period not exceeding 12 months the Authority is satisfied that the licence holder has again failed to comply with a licence condition or direction given by the Authority under or by virtue of the 1990 Act (whether or not the same as the one specified in the notice), it may issue a direction to him. The Authority may direct him (a) to provide the Authority in advance with such scripts and particulars of programmes to be included in the licensed service as are specified in the direction and (b) in relation to those programmes as will consist of or include recorded matter, to produce to the Authority in advance for examination or reproduction such recordings of the matter specified. The direction is to have effect for a specified period not exceeding six months.

Power to Require Broadcasting of Correction or Apology (s109(3) - (5))

8.80   If the Radio Authority is satisfied that (a) the holder of a sound broadcasting service licence has failed to comply with any condition of the licence and (b) the failure can be appropriately remedied by the inclusion in the licensed service of a correction and/or apology, it may direct the licence holder to include in the licensed service a correction and/or apology in such form and at such time(s) as it may determine (sub-s(3)). Before giving such a direction the Authority must give the licence holder a reasonable opportunity of making representations to it about the matters complained of (sub-s(4)). When a licence holder includes such a correction or apology he may announce that he is doing so in pursuance of such a direction (sub-s(5)).

Power to Impose Financial Penalty or Suspend or Shorten Licence Period (s110)

8.81   If the Radio Authority is satisfied that the holder of a sound broadcasting services licence has failed to comply with a licence condition or a direction given by it under or by virtue of the 1990 Act, it may serve on him (a) a notice requiring him to pay, within a specified period, a specified financial penalty to it (b) a notice reducing the licence period by a period not exceeding two years or (c) a notice suspending the licence for a specified period not exceeding six months (sub-s(1)). Before serving a notice the Authority must give the licence holder a reasonable opportunity of making representations to it about the matters complained of (sub-s(4)). Any exercise by the Radio Authority of its powers to serve such a notice does not preclude the exercise by it of its powers under s109 [1] to require scripts etc or the broadcasting of a correction or apology (sub-s(6)).
1   See paras 8.79, 8.80.

8.82   The amount of any financial penalty imposed by the Radio Authority in pursuance of the above s110 powers on the holder of any licence other than a national licence must not exceed £50,000 (sub-s(3)). The Secretary of State may by order substitute a different sum. His order is subject to annulment by resolution of either House of Parliament (sub-s(7)). In the case of a national licence holder the amount, if such a penalty has not been imposed on him during any period for which his licence has been in force ('the relevant period'), must not exceed 3% of the qualifying revenue for his last complete accounting period. This is determined in accordance with s102(2) - (6) [1]. Otherwise, the amount must not exceed 5% of the qualifying revenue for that accounting period. Should the first complete accounting period fall within the relevant period not yet ended, it is 3 or (as the case may be) 5% of the amount which the Authority estimate to be the qualifying revenue for that accounting period (sub-s(2)).
1   See paras 8.61 to 8.62.

8.83   When a licence is due to expire on a particular date by virtue of a notice served on any person reducing the period for which it to be in force under s110(1)(b) [1], the Radio Authority may, on his application, revoke that notice by a further notice served on him at any time before that date. This is subject to the requirement that the Authority is satisfied that, since the date of the earlier notice, his conduct in relation to the operation of the licensed service has been such as to justify the revocation of that notice (sub-s(5)).
1   See para 8.81.

Power to Revoke Licences (s111(1) - (3))

8.84   If the Radio Authority is satisfied that (a) the holder of a sound broadcasting services licence is failing to comply with any condition of the licence or with any direction given by it under or by virtue of the 1990 Act and (b) the failure is such that, if not remedied, it would justify the revocation of the licence, it must serve on the licence holder a notice (sub-s(1)). The notice must (a) state that the authority is satisfied that there is the above failure (b) specify the respects in which, in its opinion, the licence holder is failing to comply with any mentioned condition or direction and (c) state that the authority will revoke his licence if the licence holder does not take, within the period specified in the notice, specified steps to remedy the failure (sub-s(2)). If, at the end of the period specified in the notice the authority is satisfied that (a) the person on whom the notice was served has failed to take the steps specified in it and (b) it is necessary in the public interest to revoke his licence, it must serve on him a notice revoking his licence (sub-s(3)).

8.85 A further ground for revocation of a sound broadcasting services licence exists. If the authority is satisfied that (a) the licence holder provided them, in connection with his application for the licence, with information which was false in a material particular or (b) in connection with his application for the licence, he withheld any material information with the intention of causing the Authority to be misled, it may serve on him a notice revoking his licence (s110(5)).

8.86 A more particular power is that if, in the case of any national licence, the Radio Authority is satisfied that (a) the licence holder has ceased to provide the licensed national service before the end of the period for which the licence is to continue in force and (b) it is appropriate for it to do so, it must serve on him a notice revoking his licence (s110(4)).

8.87 There are three important provisions in the 1990 Act concerning a notice of revocation which is served for any s111 ground given above. The Authority must not serve a notice on someone unless it has given him a reasonable opportunity of making representations to it about the matters complained of (sub-s(8)). Any notice of revocation takes effect as from the time when it is served on the licence holder (sub-s(6)). However, the Authority may provide in the notice for it to take effect as from a date specified in it, if it appears to the Authority to be appropriate to do so for the purpose of preserving continuity in the provision of the service in question (sub-s(7)).

Licensable Sound Programme Services

Meaning of Licensable Sound Programme Services (s112)

8.88 The meaning of licensable sound programme services (LSPS) was examined earlier in this chapter [1]. Further clarification is given in s112 which declares that a person who (a) uses a telecommunication system for conveying sound programmes as mentioned in s112(1) [2] and/or (b) runs a telecommunication system which is so used, is not to be regarded as providing a LSPS in respect of any such programmes except to the extent that they are provided by that person with a view to their being so conveyed by means of that system (sub-s(3)). It is further declared that where (a) any service constitutes a service as is mentioned in s112(1) and (b) the sound programmes in respect of which the service is provided are provided for transmission in the course of the provision of any additional service, that service is licensable as a LSPS (sub-s(4)).

1   See paras 8.13 to 8.14.
2   See para 8.13.

Application for LSPS Licence (s113)

8.89 An application for a licence to provide a LSPS must (a) be made in the manner which is determined by the Radio Authority and (b) be accompanied by the fee (if any) determined by the Authority (sub-s(1)).

Granting of LSPS Licence (s113)

8.90   When an application is duly made to the Radio Authority, it may only refuse to grant it if it appears to the Authority that the service which would be provided would not comply with the requirements of s90(1) [1] and (2) [2]. Consequently, the licensing process is more in the nature of a certification process. The presumption that a LSPS licence will be granted is only displaced if the proposed programme standards are unacceptable to the Radio Authority.

1   See para 8.31.
2   See paras 8.32 to 8.33.

Enforcement of LSPS Licence (s113)

8.91   The provisions in s109 [1] (power to require scripts etc or broadcasting of correction or apology) and s110 [2] (power to impose financial penalty or suspend or shorten the licence period) enable the Radio Authority to enforce LSPS in the same way as it enforces sound broadcasting service licences. Similarly the Authority may utilise the powers contained in s111 [3] (power to revoke licences), save the power in s111(7) [4] which allows the Authority, if it appears appropriate to it to do so for preserving continuity in the provision of a service, to provide in a notice of revocation for it to take effect as from a date specified in it (sub-ss(3), (4)).

1   See para 8.79 to 8.80.
2   See para 8.81 to 8.83.
3   See para 8.84 to 8.87.
4   See para 8.87.

Additional Services Provided on Sound Broadcasting Frequencies

Meaning of Additional Services (s114(1), (5), (6))

8.92   'Additional service' means any service which consists in the sending of telecommunication signals for transmission by wireless telegraphy by means of the use of the spare capacity within the signals carrying any sound broadcasting service provided on (a) a frequency assigned under s84(4) [1] or (b) any other allocated frequency notified to the Radio Authority by the Secretary of State (sub-s(1)). An 'allocated frequency' is a frequency allocated to the United Kingdom for the provision of sound broadcasting services (sub-s(6)). The Secretary of State may, when making a notification, specify a date beyond which the frequency is not to be used for the provision of additional services (sub-s(5)). 'Telecommunication signals' means anything falling within paragraphs (a) - (d) of s4(1) of the Telecommunication Act 1984 [2] (sub-s(6)). Examples of additional services are given in para 8.15.

1   See para 8.7.
2   See para 8.13.

Spare Capacity (s114(2) - (4))

8.93   The spare capacity within the signals carrying a sound broadcasting service is, when the service is provided on a frequency assigned under s84(4), any part of those signals which is not required for the purposes of the provision of that service and is determined by the Radio Authority to be available for the provision of additional services (sub-s(2)(a)). When determining the extent and nature of the spare capacity available on a frequency on which a national service is provided, the Authority must have regard to any need of the person providing that service to be able to use part of the signals carrying it for providing services which are ancillary to programmes included in the service (sub-s(3)). A person holding a national licence is taken to be authorised

by his licence to provide these ancillary services (sub-s(4)). When the service is provided on a frequency notified to the Radio Authority by the Secretary of State under s114(1)(b) [1] the spare capacity within the signals is that part of the signals which the Secretary of State may specify when making the notification (sub-s(2)(b)).
1   See para 8.92.

Licensing of Additional Services

Duty of Radio Authority (s115(1))

8.94   The Radio Authority must do all that it can to ensure that in the case of any (a) frequencies assigned under s84(4) and used for the provision of a national service and (b) frequencies notified to the Authority under s114(1)(b) [1] by the Secretary of State, all of the spare capacity available for the provision of additional services on that frequency is so used under additional services licences granted by the Authority (sub-s(1)). There is the duty as regards frequencies assigned under s84(4) [2] and used for providing a national licence partly because the holder of a licence to provide a local, restricted or satellite service is taken to be authorised by his licence to provide, or to authorise another person to provide, additional services on the frequency on which the licensed service is provided (sub-s(8)). As regards national service frequencies assigned under s84(4), the Authority must have regard to the need of the service provider to be able to use part of the signals for providing services ancillary to programmes included in the service, which is taken to be authorised by his licence (s114(3), (4)).
1   See para 8.92.
2   See para 8.7.

Scope of Additional Services Licences (s115(2))

8.95   An additional services licence may relate to the use of spare capacity within more than one frequency. Two or more additional services licences may relate to the use of spare capacity within the same frequency where it is to be used at different times, or in different areas, in the case of each of the licences.

Additional Services Not to Interfere with Other Transmissions (s119(1), (2))

8.96   Additional services use the spare capacity within the signals carrying any sound broadcasting service. An additional services licence may include such conditions as the Radio Authority consider appropriate for securing that the provision of any additional service under the licence does not cause any interference with (a) the sound broadcasting services(s) on whose frequency or frequencies it is provided or (b) any other wireless telegraphy transmissions. Before imposing any conditions the Authority must consult the relevant licensing authorities (the Secretary of State and the Director General of Telecommunications) (sub-s(2)).

Authorisation by Licence Holder of Another to Provide Additional Services (s115)

8.97   It has been seen that the holder of a licence to provide a local, restricted or satellite service is taken to be authorised to permit another person to provide additional services on the frequency on which the licensed service is provided (sub-s(8)). An additional services licence may include provisions enabling the licence holder, subject to such conditions as the Radio Authority may impose, to authorise any person to provide an additional service on the spare capacity allocated by the licence (sub-s(3)). The person authorised must not be a disqualified person in relation to an additional services licence by virtue of Part II of Sch 2 [1] (sub-s(4)). To ensure the licence holder cannot avoid his obligations when he authorises another person to provide additional services, any conditions included in an additional services licence apply in relation to the provision of additional services by an authorised person as they apply in relation to the provision of such services by the licence holder. Any failure by an authorised person is treated as a failure by the licence holder to comply with those conditions (sub-s(5)).

1   See paras 10.13 to 10.23.

8.98   Every licence to provide a national service must include such conditions as appear to the Radio Authority to be appropriate for securing that the licence holder grants to (a) any person who holds a licence to provide additional services on the frequency on which that national service is provided and (b) any person who is duly authorised by that additional services licence holder to provide additional services on the frequency, access to facilities reasonably required by that person for the purposes of, or in connection with, the provision of those additional services (s115(6)). Any person who grants to another person access to facilities in accordance with these national service licence conditions may require that other person to pay a reasonable charge for the access. Any dispute as to the amount of the charge is to be determin d by the Radio Authority (s115(7)).

Proposal Notice (s116(1), (2))

8.99   When the Radio Authority propose to grant a licence to provide additional services, it must publish in the manner it considers appropriate, a notice. The notice must (a) state its proposal to grant such a licence (b) specify (i) the licence period (ii) the sound broadcasting service or services on whose frequency or frequencies the services are to be provided (iii) the extent and nature of the spare capacity to be allocated by the licence (subject to the Secretary of State's approval) (c) invite applications for the licence and specify the closing date for applications and (d) specify (i) the application fee and (ii) the percentage of qualifying revenue for each accounting period that will be payable by an applicant under s118(1)(c) [1] if he were granted a licence (sub-s(1)). The Authority may, if it thinks fit, specify (a) different percentages in relation to different accounting periods falling within the licence period (b) a nil percentage in relation to any accounting period so falling (sub-s(2)). It may be anticipated that the Radio Authority may issue a press notice for general applications and advertise in national newspapers and periodicals appropriate to reach the proposed licence area. 'Advertisements that were placed only in a magazine for canary fanciers would hardly be reasonable' [2].

1   See para 8.104.
2   Mr David Mellor MP, (minister of state), House of Commons Committee, col 1077.

Application (s116(3) - (5))

8.100   The written application must be accompanied by (a) the application fee (b) a technical plan indicating (i) the nature of any additional services which are proposed [1] and (ii) so far as known to the applicant, the nature of any additional services which any other person proposes to provide in accordance with s115(3) [2] (c) the applicant's cash bid and (d) such information as the Authority may reasonably require as to the applicant's present financial position during the licence period [1] (sub-s(3)). Any information furnished to the Authority must be in the form or verified manner that it specifies (sub-s(5)).

1   Before determining an application the Radio Authority may require the applicant to furnish it with additional information about this item (sub-s(4)).
2   See para 8.97.

Publication of Applications (s116(6))

8.100A The Radio Authority must, as soon as reasonably practicable after the date specified in the proposal notice as the closing date for applications, publish in the manner that it thinks appropriate (a) the name of each applicant, (b) particulars of the technical plan submitted with the application and (c) such other information as it considers appropriate (sub-s(6)).

Consideration of Applications (s117(1), (2), (7))

8.101 When a person has made an application for an additional services licence under s116 [1], the Radio Authority must not proceed to consider whether to award him the licence on the basis of his cash bid unless it appears to it that two requirements are met. First, that the technical plan submitted with the application is, so far as it involves the use of any telecommunication system, acceptable to the relevant licensing authorities (sub-s(1)(a)). These authorities are the Secretary of State and the Director General of Telecommunications (sub-s(7)). Before deciding whether the first requirement is satisfied, the Radio Authority must consult them (sub-s(2)). The second requirement is that the services proposed to be provided under the licence would be capable of being maintained throughout the licence period (sub-s(1)(b)). For present purposes, an applicant who can satisfy the Authority on these two requirements will be described as a 'qualified applicant'.
1   See para 8.100.

Award of Additional Services Licence (s117(3), (4))

8.102 The provisions of s100 [1] as to the award of a national licence apply, with appropriate modification, to the award of an additional services licence (s117(3)). The two modifications are that in s100(6)(a) [2], the relevant source of funds is any source of funds to which the applicant might have recourse for the purpose of paying any amounts payable by him by virtue of s118(1) which provides for additional payments in respect of additional services licences (sub-s(4)(a)). In s100(9)(b) [3], the Radio Authority having awarded an additional services licence must publish the name of every applicant whose technical plan submitted with their application under s116(3)(b) appeared to it, so far as it involved the use of any telecommunication system, acceptable to the Secretary of State and Director General of Telecommunications (sub-s(4)(b)).
1   See paras 8.53 to 8.57.
2   See para 8.56.
3   See para 8.57.

Failure to Begin Providing Licensed Additional Services (s117(5), (6))

8.103 If, after an additional services licence has been granted to any person but before the licence has come into force (a) that person indicates to the Radio Authority that none of the services will be provided once the licence has come into force or (b) the Authority for any other reason have reasonable grounds for believing that none of those services will be provided, then (i) the Authority must serve on him a notice revoking the licence as from the time the notice is served on him and (ii) the effect is as if he had not applied for the licence. Alternatively, the Authority may, if it considers this desirable, publish a fresh notice proposing to grant the licence under s116 and invite applications (sub-s(5)). When the Authority reasonably believe that he will not begin to provide the additional services, it must serve on the person awarded the licence, a notice stating its grounds for its belief, after giving him a reasonable opportunity of making representations to it about the matters complained of (sub-s(6)).

Additional Payments for Additional Services Licences (s118(1), (2), (5))

8.104   In addition to any fees required to be paid because of a licence condition under s87(1)(c) [1], an additional services licence must include conditions requiring the licence holder to pay to the Radio Authority additional payments that fall into three categories. The first, in respect of the first complete calendar year falling within the period for which the licence is in force, is the amount specified in his cash bid (sub-s(1)(a)). The second, in respect of each subsequent year falling wholly or partly within that period, is the amount specified as increased by the appropriate percentage (sub-s(1)(b)). The third, in respect of each accounting period of his falling within the period referred to in the first category, is the amount representing such percentage of the qualifying revenue for that accounting period as was specified in the notice proposing to grant an additional services licence under s98(1)(d)(ii) [2] (sub-s(1)(c)). For the purposes of the third category the qualifying revenue for any accounting period of the licence holder must consist of all amounts which are received or to be received by him or any connected person and are referable to the right under his licence to use, or to authorise any other person to use, in that period the spare capacity allocated by the licence (sub-s(2)). When (a) the first complete accounting period of the licence holder falling within the licence period in the first category of additional payments does not begin with that licence period or (b) the last complete accounting period of his falling within that licence period does not end with that licence period, an accounting period in the third category includes that part of the accounting period preceding the first complete accounting period or (as the case may be) following that last complete accounting period as falls within the licence period (sub-s(5)).

1   See para 8.26.
2   See para 8.46.

Additional Payment Licence Conditions (s118(3), (4))

8.105   An additional services licence may include conditions (a) enabling the Radio Authority to estimate before the beginning of an accounting period the amount due because of the existence of the third category of additional payment and (b) requiring the licence holder to pay the estimated amount by monthly instalments throughout that period (sub-s(3)). The licence may in particular include conditions (a) authorising the Authority to revise any estimate on one or more occasions and to adjust the instalments payable by the licence holder to take account of the revised estimate (b) providing for the adjustment of any overpayment or underpayment (sub-s(4)).

Enforcement of Additional Services Licences

Power to Impose a Financial Penalty (s120(1) - (3))

8.106   If the Radio Authority is satisfied that the holder of an additional services licence has failed to comply with any licence conditions or with any direction given by it under or by virtue of the 1990 Act, it may serve on him a notice requiring him to pay, within a specified period, a specified financial penalty to the Authority (sub-s(1)). Before serving a notice the Authority must give the licence holder a reasonable opportunity of making representations to it about the matters complained of (sub-s(3)). The amount of the financial penalty, if such a penalty has not been imposed on him during any period for which his licence has been in force ('the relevant period') must not exceed 3% of the qualifying revenue for his last complete accounting period. This is determined in accordance with s118(2) [1]. Otherwise, the amount must not exceed 5% of the qualifying revenue for that accounting period. When the first complete accounting period falling within the relevant period has not yet ended it is three (or as the case may be) 5% of the amount which the Authority estimate to be the qualifying revenue for that accounting period (sub-s(2)).

1   See para 8.104..

Power to Revoke Additional Services Licences (s120(4))

8.107 The powers and duties of the Radio Authority to revoke sound broadcasting licences under s111 [1] apply in relation to an additional services licence, with one modification. The provision in s111(7) [2] giving the Authority a discretion, if it appears to it appropriate for preserving continuity in the provision of the service, to provide in the notice of revocation for it to take effect as from a specified date, does not apply in relation to additional services licences.

1   See paras 8.84 to 8.87.
2   See para 8.87.

Chapter 9

CONSUMER PROTECTION

Introduction

9.1   The 1990 Act is parliamentary recognition that technological developments make change in broadcasting inevitable. In the near future there will be the possibility of many television channels, most of which may be delivered by satellite, cable or microwave. Also there could be three new national independent radio stations and two to three hundred local independent radio stations. Confidently the White Paper 'Broadcasting in the 90's: Competition, Choice and Quality' (Cmnd 517) affirmed that 'The Government is . . . clear that there need be no contradiction between the desire to increase competition and widen choice and concern that programme standards on good taste and decency should be maintained' (para 1.2). The case for a consumer-orientated market is particularly strong in broadcasting because it involves the basic right of freedom of expression. Article 10 of the European convention on Human Rights provides:

> 'Everyone has the right to freedom of expression. This right shall include the freedom to hold opinions and to receive and impart information and ideas without interference by public authority and regardless of frontiers. This Article shall not prevent States from requiring the licensing of broadcasting, television or cinema enterprises.
> 'The exercise of these freedoms, since it carries with it duties and responsibilities, may be subject to such formalities, conditions, restrictions or penalties as are prescribed by law and are necessary in a democratic society in the interests of national security, territorial integrity or public safety for the prevention of disorder or crime, for the protection of health and morals, for the protection of the reputation or rights of others, for preventing the disclosure of information received in confidence, or for maintaining the authority and impartiality of the judiciary'.

9.2   The principle that freedom of expression is to be balanced against the needs of society is clearly easier to state than to put into practice, as the continuing controversy surrounding *The Satanic Verses* illustrates. The provisions of the 1990 Act do not allow consumer preference to operate unchecked. The ITC and Radio Authority must draw up, and from time to time review, codes on programme standards (ss7, 91) [1] and advertising and sponsorship (ss9, 93) [2] . They have the power to monitor programmes included in licensed services (ss11, 95) [3]. The Government is given control over services licensed by those two bodies and the broadcasts of the Welsh Authority (ss10, 63, 94) [4]. This chapter is concerned with the Broadcasting Complaints Commission (the BCC), the Broadcasting Standards Council (the BSC) and the prohibition on inclusion of obscene and other material in programme services.

1   See paras 3.32 and 8.35.
2   See paras 3.3 to 3.38 and 8.37, 8.38.
3   See paras 3.41 and 8.41.
4   See paras 3.39, 4.198, 8.39 and 8.40.

The Broadcasting Complaints Commission (BCC)

Re-Establishment of BCC (s142)

9.3   The BCC, which was set up as a body corporate by the Broadcasting Act 1980, continues in existence but is constituted in accordance with, and has the functions conferred by, the 1990 Act (sub-s(1)). It consists of at least three members appointed by the Secretary of State (sub-s(2)). He appoints one member to be chairman and may appoint another to be deputy chairman (sub-s(3)). Further provisions for the BCC's constitution and procedure are to be found in Sch 13. These include the provision that it is within the BCC's capacity as a statutory corporation to do things, and enter into transactions, which are 'incidental or conducive' to the discharge of its functions under the 1990 Act (para 1(2)). A person is disqualified from being a member if he is a governor or employee of the BBC or is a member or employee of the Independent Television Commission, the Radio Authority, the Channel Four Television Corporation, the Welsh Authority or the Broadcasting Standards Council. Likewise excluded is anyone who appears to the Secretary of State to be concerned with, or have an interest in (1) the preparation or provision of programmes for broadcasting by the BBC or the Welsh Authority or (2) the provision of a licensed service (or the preparation or provision of programmes for inclusion in such a service) (para 2(1)). Appointments are made for a maximum period of five years (para 3(2)). The BCC must keep proper accounts (para 12(1)).

Function of the BCC (s143).

9.4   The BCC's function is to consider and adjudicate on complaints of (a) unjust or unfair treatment in programmes or (b) unwarranted infringement of privacy in, or in connection with the obtaining of material included in, programmes (sub-s(1)) 'Programmes' in the 1990 Act include advertisements (s202(1)). Programmes about which complaints may be made are television or sound programmes broadcast by the BBC, television programmes broadcast by the Welsh Authority and television or sound programmes included in a licensed service [1]. The date when they are to be subject to BCC consideration and adjudication is to be specified in an order made by the Secretary of State (sub-s(2)). There is no requirement for the BCC (unlike the BSC) to draw up a code of practice in programmes to be reflected in any codes relating to standards and practice published by the BBC, Welsh Authority, ITC and Radio Authority.

1   A television programme includes a teletext transmission (s150).

The Person Affected (s144(7)(a), 150).

9.5   'Unjust or unfair treatment' includes treatment which amounts to that because of the way in which material in a programme has been selected or arranged. A person is affected by unjust or unfair treatment if, as a participant in a programme, he was the subject of that treatment or, whether as a participant or not, he had a direct interest in the subject matter of the treatment. He is a 'participant' if he appeared, or his voice was heard, in a programme (s150). The BCC may refuse to entertain a complaint of unfair or unjust treatment if the allegedly affected person was not himself the subject of the complained of treatment and it appears to the BCC that he did not have a sufficiently direct interest in the subject matter of that treatment to justify the making of a complaint with him as the person affected (s147(a)). The High Court considered in the pre-1990 Act case of *R v Broadcasting Complaints Commission, ex p Owen* [1] the type of treatment which may fall within the jurisdiction of the BCC. A person is affected by an unwarranted infringement of privacy if his privacy is infringed (s150). The key word 'unwarranted' means such an infringement is possible in the wake of a well-publicised tragedy, for example, a ferry disaster. Relatives of the deceased could experience an unwarranted infringement of privacy by the electronic media. 'Privacy' is undefined in the 1990 Act.

1   [1985] 1QB 1153. Dr Owen, the SDP leader, complained to the BCC that, having regard to the comparable number of votes received by the parties in the 1983 General Election, the SDP had received a disproportionately small amount of coverage in programmes broadcast during the same period compared with that received by the Labour Party. The BCC was held to have jurisdiction to entertain the complaint of unjust or unfair treatment although it was a political complaint made by a political leader. In the circumstances, the BCC had good and sufficient reasons to exercise its discretion not to entertain the complaint.

Making of Complaints (s144(1), (2), (3), (7)(b))

9.6   Complaints must be made in writing (sub-s(1)). They may be made by an individual or body of persons, whether incorporated or not. Complaints are not entertained by the BCC unless made by the person affected or by someone authorised by him to complain (sub-s(2)). Should the person affected be dead, or otherwise unable both to complain himself or authorise another to do so, a complaint may be made by his personal representative, family member or someone else closely connected with him. They may, for example, be connected with him as his employer or as a body of which he is or was, at his death, a member (sub-s(3)). However, the BCC may, for example, refuse to entertain a complaint by a person other than the person affected or someone authorised by him, if it appears to the BCC that the complainant's connection with the person affected is not sufficiently close to justify a complaint by him (sub-s 7(b)). An example of someone having 'locus standi' would arise should a radio programme describe an eight-year-old boy as the 'worst behaved boy in Europe'. If the unfortunate youngster is brain damaged and clearly unable to make a complaint to the BCC himself, his mother can complain.

Entertaining of Complaints (s144(4) - (6))

9.7   The BCC is not to entertain or proceed with the consideration of a complaint if it appears to it that (a) the complaint relates to the broadcasting of a programme, or its inclusion in a licensed service, more than five years after the death of the person affected or (b) the alleged unjust or unfair treatment or unwarranted infringement of privacy is either the subject of proceedings in a United Kingdom court or (c) a matter in which the person affected has a remedy by way of proceedings in a United Kingdom court and that in the particular circumstances it is not appropriate for the BCC to consider a complaint about it or (d) the complaint is frivolous or it appears for any other reason inappropriate to entertain or proceed with its consideration [1] (sub-s(4)). The BCC is intended to provide an inexpensive remedy for complaints that cannot be remedied by court action. The BCC may refuse to entertain a complaint if it appears to it not to have been made within a reasonable time after the programme was broadcast or included in a licensed service (sub-s(5)). If it was broadcast or included in a licensed service within five years of the death of the person affected, the complaint must be made within a reasonable time of the programme being broadcast or included (sub-s(6)). The circumstances of a particular case would determine what amounts to a reasonable time.

1   The BCC was held to have acted reasonably in refusing to accept a complaint although it had jurisdiction to hear it in *R v Broadcasting Complaints Commission, ex p Owen* [1985] 1QB 1153 - see para 9.5.

Consideration of Complaints (s145(1) - (3))

9.8   Every duly made complaint to the BCC must be considered by it, either at a hearing or if it thinks fit, without a hearing (sub-s(1)). If there is a hearing it must be in private and the following must be given an opportunity to be heard: (a) the complainant (b) the 'relevant person', which is the BBC and the Welsh Authority if they broadcast the programme and the licence holder providing the licensed service if the programme was included in it (c) the ITC and Radio Authority if they licensed a service including the programme (d) anyone else who appears to the BCC to have been responsible for the making or provision of the programme and (e) anyone whom the BCC consider might be able to assist at its hearing (sub-s(2)). Before considering a complaint the BCC must send a copy of it to the 'relevant person' and the ITC and Radio Authority if they licensed a service including the programme (sub-s(3)).

Assistance of 'Relevant Person' [1] *to the Consideration (s145(4) - (9))*

9.9   On receiving a copy of the complaint, the relevant person must, if required by the BCC (a) provide the BCC with a visual or sound recording of the programme or a specified part of it (b) make suitable arrangements for enabling the complainant to view or hear the programme, or a specified part of it (c) provide the BCC and the complainant with a transcript of the programme or a specified part of it (d) provide the BCC and the complainant with copies of any correspondence about the complaint between themselves and the person affected or the complainant in connection with the complaint and (e) furnish the BCC and the complainant with a written answer to the complaint (sub-s(4)). To facilitate this provision, the BBC and Welsh Authority must retain a recording of every television programme for 90 days from its broadcast and a recording of every sound programme for 42 days from its broadcast (sub-s(5)). Likewise ss11 [2] and 95 [3] empower the ITC and Radio Authority to have television and sound programmes kept for a similar period. Should the BBC or Welsh Authority receive a complaint from the BCC, it must arrange for one or more of its governors, members or employees to assist it. When it is a licence holder which is a body, it must arrange for one or more of those who either take part in its management or control or are employed by it (or, if it is an individual, either him or his employee(s)) to assist it (sub-s(6)). When the relevant person receives a copy of a complaint and the BCC request certain things of someone else, the relevant person must take reasonable steps to ensure that the request is met (sub-s(7)). The request may be to (a) make suitable arrangements for the complainant and any member or employee of the BCC to view or hear the programme or a specified part of it (b) provide the BCC and the complainant with a transcript of the programme or a specified part (c) provide the BCC and the complainant with copies of correspondence between the person requested and the person affected or the complainant (d) furnish the BCC and the complainant with a written answer to the complaint and (e) attend or, in the case of a body, arrange for a representative to attend, and assist the BCC (sub-s(8)). The BCC may provide travelling or subsistence allowance to anyone who attends it (sub-s(9)).

1   The 'relevant person' is the BBC and the Welsh Authority if they broadcast the programme complained of and the licence holder providing a licensed service if it was included in it (s145(10)).
2   See para 3.41.
3   See para 8.41.

Publication of BCC's Findings (s146)

9.10   Having considered and adjudicated on a complaint, the BCC may direct, when the programme was broadcast by the BBC or Welsh Authority, that it publish in the manner, and within the period specified, a summary of the complaint and the BCC's findings on the complaint or a summary of them (sub-s(1)(a), (2)). The form and content of the summary must be approved by the BCC (sub-s(3)). Similar directions may be given to the ITC or Radio Authority when the programme was included in a service

licensed by them (sub-s(1)(b), (2), (3)). The BBC, Welsh Authority, ITC and Radio Authority must comply with these directions (sub-s(4)). To facilitate this, every licence to provide a licensed service which is granted by the ITC or Radio Authority must include conditions requiring the licence holder to comply with directions given to him by it enabling it to comply with a BCC direction (sub-s(5)). The BCC can only impose the requirement to publish its adverse findings. Some may say that as a watchdog it more resembles a poodle than a rottweiler. Although possibly lacking in bite, publication can cause severe embarrassment to broadcasting and regulatory authorities. The upholding of a serious or repeated complaint may indicate an infringement of licence conditions, in which case various sanctions are available to the ITC [1] and Radio Authority [2]. The BCC must publish at intervals and in the manner that it thinks fit, reports containing a summary of every complaint received, the action taken and where it makes an adjudication, a summary of its findings (sub-s(6)). There is no requirement for the BCC to publish complaints which it is precluded from entertaining because they were made by someone other than the person affected or a person authorised by him or the 1990 Act, as required by s144(2) [3] (sub-s(7)). The BCC may omit from a summary in the report information which could lead to the disclosure of the identity of a person connected with the complaint unless it is the BCC, Welsh Authority, the ITC, Radio Authority or licensed service provider (sub-s(8)).

1   Under ss40 - 42: see paras 4.111 to 4.117.
2   Under ss109 - 111: see paras 8.79 to 8.87.
3   See para 9.6.

Duty to Publicise BCC (s147)

9.11   The BBC, Welsh Authority, ITC and Radio Authority must arrange for the publication (by means of broadcasts or otherwise) of regular announcements publicising the BCC (sub-s(1)). The announcements may contain a statement of the difference between the kinds of complaints that may be considered by the BCC and the Broadcasting Standards Council (sub-s(2)). A licence to provide a licensed service which is granted by the ITC or Radio Authority must include conditions requiring the licence holder to comply with any directions given to him by them to publicise the BCC (sub-s(3)).

Annual Reports (s148)

9.12   At the end of every financial year the BCC must prepare a report of its proceedings during that year and transmit it to the Secretary of State who must lay copies of it before each House of Parliament (sub-s(1)). The report must have attached to it the statement of accounts for the year and a copy of any report made by the auditors on that statement (sub-s(2)). There is no guarantee that this report will be debated by Parliament. The BCC must send a copy of the report to the BBC, the Welsh Authority, the ITC, the Radio Authority and every person providing a licensed service (sub-s(3)).

Contributions Towards Cost of BCC (s149)

9.13   For each financial year the Secretary of State must notify to (a) the ITC and the Radio Authority the sum which he considers to be the appropriate contribution of each body in respect of persons providing licensed services under licences granted by it, towards the expenses of the BCC and (b) the Welsh Authority, the sum which he considers to be its appropriate contribution towards those expenses (sub-s(1)). The ITC, Radio Authority and Welsh Authority must pay to the Secretary of State that sum (sub-s(2)).

The Broadcasting Standards Council (BSC)

Establishment of BSC (s151)

9.14   The BSC is set up as a body corporate by the 1990 Act which provides for its constitution and confers its functions (sub-s(1)). It consists of a chairman and a deputy chairman, appointed as such, and not less than four other members. All appointments are made by the Secretary of State (sub-s(2)). Further provisions for the BSC's constitution and procedure are to be found in Sch 14. These include the provision that it is within the BSC's capacity as a statutory corporation to do such things and enter into such transactions as are 'incidental or conducive' to the discharge of its functions under the 1990 Act (para 1(2)). A person is disqualified from being a member if he is a governor or employee of the BBC or is a member or employee of the ITC, Radio Authority, the Channel Four Television Corporation, Welsh Authority or the Broadcasting Complaints Commission (para 2(1)). BSC members are disqualified from sitting in the House of Commons or Northern Ireland Assembly (para 5). Appointments are made for a maximum period of five years (para 3(2)). The BSC must prepare in respect of each financial year a statement of accounts in the prescribed form and send copies to the Secretary of State and the Comptroller and Auditor General. The latter must certify and report on them and lay a copy of each statement and his report before each House of Parliament (para 13).

The BSC Code (s152)

9.15   The BSC must draw up, and from time to time review, a code giving guidance on three matters: the practices to be followed in connection with the portrayal of violence in television or sound programmes broadcast by the BBC, television programmes broadcast by the Welsh Authority and television or sound programmes included in a licensed service; the practices to be followed in connection with the portrayal of sexual conduct [1] in those programmes; the standards of taste and decency for those programmes generally (sub-ss(1), (2)). Before drawing up or revising its code, the BSC must consult with (a) the BBC, Welsh Authority, ITC and Radio Authority and (b) any one else that appears to it appropriate (sub-s(5)). The BSC must publish its code, the general effect of which is to be reflected in the codes on standards and practices in programmes drawn up by the BBC, Welsh Authority, ITC and Radio Authority (sub-ss(3), (4)). These bodies are not required to consult with the BSC when drawing up, or revising their codes. The BSC code has no direct influence on programmes because it operates on the regulators and it is the codes of the regulators that have a direct influence on programmes.

1   'Sexual conduct' means any form of sexual activity or other sexual behaviour (s161(1)). When explaining why this definition is given, Mr Mellor, (minister of state, Home Office) felt it to be unnecessary and suggested that 'it was in case anyone thought it meant eating liquorice allsorts' (House of Commons Committee, col 1178).

9.16   The provision in the pre-1990 Act BSC Code that deals with violence in news and current affairs programmes warns of the need to avoid leaving the audience 'with an unjustified aggravation of any real threat to its own physical or mental security'. Difficult value judgements may be involved in evaluating what constitutes an unjustified aggravation. Recently, both BBC and ITV News showed in the early evening, when many young children could have been watching, Israeli soldiers in the occupied territories breaking their prisoners' limbs. There is no suggestion by the BSC that similar future incidents involving any nationals should not be shown. Certainly, the BSC Code should deter the televising of clearly recognisable people dying in a disaster of the type that occurred in Hillsborough football stadium in April 1989. Excessive violence and obscenity involve relative judgements which take into account their context and purpose. Different practices are to be expected in a late night documentary about the Mafia than in a children's programme. The BSC can be expected to strike a balance between an electronic media exercising free speech and the protection of vulnerable people for the sake of themselves, and sometimes others. A programme on deeply-held religious beliefs may cause deep offence to many people, but perhaps as many or more would defend the right for it to be shown and heard. When reviewing its code, the BSC can be expected to respond to the changing values of society if they can be ascertained. There is the statutory duty to consult with persons that appear to it appropriate. This could be myriad organisations including, for example, audience rating, television and polling companies.

Monitoring of United Kingdom Broadcasting Standards (s153(1) - (3))

9.17 The BSC must monitor programmes so as to enable it to (a) make reports, which it may publish, on the portrayal of violence and sexual conduct in, and the standards of taste and decency attained by, programmes generally and (b) determine whether to issue complaints about them under s154(7) [1] (sub-ss(1), (3)). The report may include an assessment of the attitudes of the public towards the portrayal of violence or sexual conduct in, or towards the standards of taste and decency attained by, programmes. Also an assessment may be included of any effects or potential effects on the attitudes or behaviour of particular categories of people of the portrayal of violence or sexual conduct in programmes or of the failure by programmes to attain those standards (sub-s(2)). The BSC was established to act as a forum for public concern about the portrayal of sex and violence. It is not intended to monitor the quality of broadcasting generally. This can be taken as an example on the basic philosophy behind the 1990 Act of having a light regulatory regime for television and radio.
1   See para 9.19.

Monitoring of Foreign Broadcasting Standards (s153(4), (5)).

9.18 Additionally, the BSC must monitor, so far as is reasonably practicable, all television and sound programmes which are transmitted or sent from outside the United Kingdom but are capable of being received there with a view to ascertaining (a) how violence and sexual conduct are portrayed in these programmes and (b) the extent to which those programmes meet standards of taste and decency (sub-s(4)). The BSC may make a report to the Secretary of State on any issues identified by it in the course of carrying out this duty and appearing to it to raise questions of general broadcasting policy (sub-s(5)). It can be assumed that the provisions of the EEC Directive 'Television Without Frontiers' [1] and the Council of Europe convention on Transfrontier Television [2] will influence the BSC's monitoring of foreign broadcasts containing excessive violence or pornography. 'Programmes' in the 1990 Act includes advertisements [3] and as much of transfrontier transmissions includes advertisements it may be anticipated that they will be closely monitored by the BSC.
1   See paras 1.20, 1.21.
2   See para 1.23.
3   Section 202.

Consideration of Broadcasting Standards Complaints (s154)

9.19 The BSC must consider written complaints relating to (a) the portrayal of violence or sexual conduct in programmes or (b) alleged failures by programmes to attain standards of taste and decency. Its findings must take account of its code [1] (sub-ss(1), (2)). The BSC may itself issue a complaint giving particulars of the matters complained of (sub-ss(7), (8)). Unless it appears to the BSC that it is appropriate to do so, it must not entertain a complaint about (a) a television programme which is made more than two months after the relevant date, or (b) a sound programme which is made more than three weeks after the relevant date (sub-s(3)). The 'relevant date' is the date when the programme was broadcast by the BBC or Welsh Authority or included in a licensed service or, as the case may be, last broadcast or included (sub-s(4)). The provision dovetails into the s11 [2] powers of the ITC relating to the production of programme recordings by licensees who are to keep them for 90 days and the s95 [3] powers of the Radio Authority to require licensees to retain recordings for 42 days and produce them on request. The fact that the BSC can issue a complaint even if no one else complains may seem strange, perhaps especially as it was set up as a forum of public concern. However, bodies that regulate standards in other areas may also be said to have an initiating role, for example the Commission for Racial Equality and the Equal Opportunities Commission. There is an argument that the BCC and the BSC should be amalgamated. The BCC argued strongly against amalgamation on the basis that it would be wrong to associate what it considered to be its objective, quasi-judicial function with the essentially different areas of taste and decency that is within the remit of the BSC. An illustration of the different roles of the BSC and BCC was given by Mr Mellor (minister of state, Home Office). Should an investigative programme apparently involve an unwarranted invasion of Mr X's privacy, this is a factual consideration and a matter for the BCC. If a programme includes sexually explicit scenes in a play and complaint is made of lack of broadcasting controls, this relates to standards in general rather than issues of fact regarding an allegation against a particular individual. This is more likely to be the concern of the BSC [4].

1   See para 9.15.
2   See para 3.41.
3   See para 8.41.
4   House of Commons Committee, col 1165.

9.20   The BSC must not entertain or proceed with the consideration of a complaint if it appears to it that (a) the matter complained of is the subject of proceedings in a United Kingdom court or (b) it is a matter for which the complainant has a remedy by way of proceedings in a United Kingdom court, and that in the particular circumstances it is not appropriate for the BSC to consider a complaint about it or (c) the complaint is frivolous or (d) for any other reason it is inappropriate for it to entertain or proceed with the consideration of the complaint (sub-s(5)). The BSC is meant to provide an inexpensive remedy for complaints that cannot be remedied by taking court action. When the BSC consider two or more complaints which appear to it to raise the same, or substantially the same, issue(s) in relation to a particular programme, it may determine that these complaints are to be treated as constituting a single complaint (sub-s(6)). In these circumstances the BSC determines which of the complainants is to be given the opportunity to be heard at a BSC hearing of the complaint (s155)(5)).

Consideration of Complaints (s155)

9.21   Provided the complaint is duly made to, or issued under s154 [1] by the BSC, it must be considered by the BSC either without a hearing or, if it thinks fit, at a hearing. A hearing is held in private unless the BSC decide otherwise (sub-s(1)). Before the BSC consider a complaint it must send a copy of it to (a) the 'relevant person' who is the BBC and Welsh Authority, if it broadcast the programme, and the licence holder providing the service, if it was included in it and (b) the ITC and Radio Authority if they licensed a service that included the programme (sub-ss(2), (7)). When the relevant person receives a copy of the complaint they must, if required by the BSC, provide it with (a) a visual or sound recording of the programme or any specified part of it (b) a transcript of as much of the programme, or any specified part of it, as consisted of speech (c) any copies of correspondence between themselves and the complainant about the complaint and (d) a written answer to the complaint (sub-s(3)). Should a hearing be held in respect of a complaint, the following persons must be given an opportunity to be heard: (a) the complainant (b) the relevant person (c) the ITC or Radio Authority if either licensed a service that included the programme (d) any other person who appears to the BSC to have been responsible for the making or provision of that programme and (e) anyone else whom the BSC consider might be able to assist at the hearing (sub-s(4)). When the BSC have made a determination in respects of complaints being treated as a single complaint under s154(6) [1] it has a discretion as to which of the complainants is to be given an opportunity to be heard at the hearing. Should the BSC itself issue the complaint under s154(7), the requirement that the complainant be given an opportunity to be heard is ignored (sub-s(5)). The BSC may provide travelling or subsistence allowance to anyone who attends the hearing (sub-s(6)).

1   See para 9.20.

Publication of BSC's Findings (s156)

9.22   When the BSC has considered and made its findings on a complaint it may direct the BBC and Welsh Authority, when the programme was broadcast by them, to publish in a specified manner and within a specified period (a) a summary of the complaint and (b) the BSC's findings and any observations by it on the complaint, or a summary of those findings and any observations (sub-ss(1)(a), (2)). The form and content of any summary must be approved by the BSC (sub-s(3)). When the programme was included in a service licensed by the ITC and Radio Authority, the BSC may direct them to direct the licence holder to similarly publish a statement (sub-ss(1)(b), (2). The BBC, Welsh Authority, ITC and Radio Authority must comply with these directions from the BSC (sub-s(4)). To assist the ITC and Radio Authority to do this, any licence to provide a licensed service granted by them must include conditions requiring the licence holder to comply with directions given to him by the ITC or Radio Authority to enable them to comply with the BSC directions (sub-s(5)). The BSC, like the BCC, can only require the publication of a statement. Similarly, this can embarrass the publisher and may be indicative of an infringement of licence conditions, in which case the ITC and Radio Authority can impose various sanctions under ss40 - 42 [1] and 109 - 111 [2] respectively.

1   See paras 4.111 to 4.117.
2   See paras 8.79 to 8.87.

Power to Commission Research (s157)

9.23   The BSC may make arrangements for the undertaking of research into matters related to or connected with (a) the portrayal of violence or sexual conduct in programmes or (b) standards of taste and decency for programmes generally (sub-s(1)). Matters into which research may be undertaken include, in particular, (a) the attitudes of the public towards the portrayal of violence or sexual conduct in, or towards the standards of taste and decency attained by, programmes and (b) any effects or potential effects on the attitudes or behaviour of particular categories of persons of the portrayal of violence or sexual conduct in programmes or of any failure on the part of programmes to attain those standards (sub-s(2)). Research arrangements must ensure, so far as is reasonably practicable, any research subsequently undertaken is carried out by persons who are neither members or employees of the BSC (sub-s(3)). The BSC may publish the results of that research (sub-s(4)).

Duty to Publicise the BSC (s159)

9.24 The BBC, Welsh Authority, ITC and Radio Authority must arrange for the publication (by means of broadcasts or otherwise) of regular announcements publicising the BSC (sub-s(1)). The announcements may contain a statement of the difference between the kinds of complaints that may be considered by the BSC and the Broadcasting Complaints Commission (sub-s(2)). A licence to provide a licensed service which is granted by the ITC or Radio Authority must include conditions requiring the licence holder to comply with any directions given to him by them to publicise the BSC (sub-s(3)).

International Representation (s158)

9.25 The functions of the BSC include representing the Government, at the request of the Secretary of State, on international bodies concerned with setting standards for television programmes.

Annual Reports (s160)

9.26 At the end of each financial year the BSC must prepare a report of its proceedings during that year and transmit it to the Secretary of State who must lay copies of it before each House of Parliament (sub-s(1)). There is no guarantee the report will be debated in Parliament. The report must include a report by the ITC on the portrayal of violence and sexual conduct in, and the standards of taste and decency attained by, programmes generally (sub-s(2)). The BSC must send a copy of the report to (a) the BBC, Welsh Authority, ITC and Radio Authority and (b) every person providing a licensed service (sub-s(3)).

Prohibition on Inclusion of Obscene and other Material in Programmes [1] **Included in Programme Services** [2]

Meaning of Obscenity

9.27 Part VII of the 1990 Act applies the law on obscenity, racial hatred and defamation to programme services. The Obscene Publications Act 1959 can be regarded as a 'backstop measure' should the ITC and Radio Authority codes on programme standards (ss7 and 91) and advertising and sponsorship (ss9 and 93) together with the powers to monitor programmes (ss11 and 95) fail in their objectives. Section 1(1) of the Obscene Publications Act 1959 provides that an article shall be deemed to be obscene if its effect or (where the article comprises two or more distinct items) the effect of any one of its items is, if taken as a whole, such as to tend to deprave and corrupt persons who are likely, having regard to all relevant circumstances, to read, see or hear the matter contained or embodied in it. An article may be obscene within the 1959 Act if it has a tendency to deprave and corrupt, though it is not filthy, lewd or disgusting. This has enabled the courts to extend the notion of obscenity beyond sexual morality to promoting the pleasures of drug taking [3] and to conditioning young children to engage in violence [4] Lawyers may agree with the aphorism that obscenity, like an elephant, cannot be defined but is recognised when seen. The looseness of the definition of obscenity and the inconsistency of jury decisions leads to uncertainty about the law. In 1966, when the publishers first submitted *Last Exit to Brooklyn* to the DPP, they received, in the words of the Court of Appeal, 'an inconclusive reply' ending with the sentence, 'if you find - as I am afraid you will - that this is a most unhelpful letter, it is not because I wish to be unhelpful, but because I can get no help from the Acts' [5]. Uncertainty persists. The jury decide whether an article is obscene without regard to what the defendant thought and however reasonably he may have believed that the article would not deprave and corrupt. Unless the defendant seeks to prove that he had not examined the article and had no reason to suspect its nature or a defence of 'public good' is submitted, 'the nebulous nature of the question gives the jury an extraordinary roving commission' [6]. The 1959 Act test for obscenity retains, in substantially the same form, the common law test. Using that test Radclyffe Hall's novel *The Well of Loneliness* was condemned as obscene by a magistrate in 1936. In 1974 the BBC broadcast it as a 'Book at Bedtime'. Not surprisingly, then, is the view that if the legislator wishes to use criminal sanctions to control obscene behaviours he must accept the responsibility of defining the prohibited conduct, even if the resulting legislation makes distasteful reading [7].

1　'Programme' includes an advertisement and, in relation to any service, includes any item included in that service (s202(1)).

2　'Programme service' means any of the following services (whether or not it is, or requires to be, licensed under the 1990 Act), namely — (a) any television broadcasting service or other television programme service (see para 3.8) (b) any sound broadcasting service (see para 8.8) or licensable sound programme service (see paras 8.13, 8.14 and 8.88) (c) any 'other service' which consists in the sending, by means of a telecommunication system, of sounds or visual images or both either for reception at (i) two or more places in the United Kingdom (whether they are sent for simultaneous reception or at different times in response to requests made by different users of the service) or (ii) a place in the United Kingdom for the purpose of being presented there to members of the public or to any group of persons. The meaning of 'other service' does not apply to a local delivery service (see para 4.140), a service where the running of the telecommunication system does not require to be licensed under Part II of the Telecommunications Act 1984 or a two-way service as defined by s46(2)(c) (s201).

3　*Calder (John) Publications Ltd v Powell* [1965] 1 All ER 159.

4　*Director of Public Prosecutions v A and BC Chewing Gum Ltd* [1967] 2 All ER 504.

5　[1968] 1QB 151 at 165.

6　Glanville Williams *Textbook of Criminal Law* (2nd edn) 143.

7　D A Thomas *Reshaping the Criminal Law* (Glazebrook, editor), (London, 1978) 32.

Obscenity in Programme Services: England and Wales

Publication of Obscenity (s1(3), Obscene Publications Act 1959 as Amended by s162(1))
9.28　It is an offence if anyone 'publishes' an obscene article whether for gain or not or 'has' an obscene article for publication for gain (s2(1) of the Obscene Publications Act 1959 as amended by the Obscene Publications Act 1964). Before the 1990 Act, a person 'published' an article containing or embodying matter to be looked at or a record when he showed, played or projected it provided this was not done in the course of television or sound broadcasting (s1(3) of the Obscene Publications Act 1959). The 1990 Act repeals this exemption for television and sound broadcasting (s162(1)(a)). It provides that three sub-sections be added after s1(3) of the Obscene Publications Act 1959) (s162(1)(b)). The effect of these are that for the purposes of the Obscene Publications Act 1959 a person publishes an article if any matter recorded on it is included by him in a programme included in a programme service. When the inclusion of matter in a programme would, if it were recorded matter, constitute the publication of an obscene article it is to be treated as recorded matter. 'Programme' [1] and 'programme service' [2] have the same meaning as in the 1990 Act.

1　See para 9.27, footnote 1.

2　See para 9.27, footnote 2. For police powers to copy recordings see para 9.45.

9.29   Schedule 15 supplements the repeal of the exemption of television and sound broadcasting formerly found in s1(3) of the Obscene Publications Act 1959) (s162(2)). In Sch 15 'programme' means a programme included in a programme service'.

Liability for Providing Live Programme Material (Sch 15, para 2)
9.30   When any matter is included by a person in a programme in circumstances where its inclusion, if it were recorded matter, would constitute the publication of an obscene article and (b) that matter has been provided, for inclusion in that programme, by some other person, the Obscene Publications Act 1959 has effect as if that matter had been included by both persons.

Obscene Articles Kept for Inclusion in Programmes (Sch 15, para 3)
9.31   When a person has an obscene article in his ownership, possession or control with a view to the matter recorded on it being included in a programme, the article must be taken for the purposes of the Obscene Publications Act 1959 to be an obscene article had or kept by him for publication or gain. Apparently an article is not obscene under this provision if it has not been transmitted and there is no intention to transmit it.

Requirement for Consent of Director of Public Prosecutions (Sch 15, para 4)
9.32   Proceedings for an offence under s2 of the Obscene Publications Act 1959 (the 1959 Act) for publishing an obscene article cannot be instituted except by or with the consent of the Director of Public Prosecutions (DPP) when (a) the relevant publication, or (b) the only other publication which followed from the relevant publication, took place in the course of the inclusion of a programme in a programme service. 'Relevant publication' means the publication in respect of which the defendant would be charged if the proceedings were brought (para 4(1)). Also, proceedings for an offence under s2 of the 1959 Act for having an obscene article for publication cannot be instituted except by or with the consent of the DPP when (a) the relevant publication, or (b) the only other publication which could reasonably have been expected to follow from the relevant publication, was to take place in the course of the inclusion of a programme into a programme service. 'Relevant publication' means the publication which, if proceedings were brought, the defendant would be alleged to have had in contemplation (para 4(2)). Without prejudice to the duty of the court to make a forfeiture order for an article under s1(4) of the Obscene Publications Act 1964, when, by virtue of para 4(2), proceedings under s2 of the 1959 Act for having an article for publication for gain cannot be instituted except by or with the consent of the DPP, no order for the articles' forfeiture can be made under s3 of the 1959 Act unless the warrant under which the article was seised was issued on an information laid by or on behalf of the DPP (para 4(3)). At the committee stage of the Broadcasting Bill, Mr Mellor, (minister of state, Home Office) said that the prosecuting authorities would normally proceed by way of prosecution rather than forfeiture, when licensees of the ITC and Radio Authority intended to include forbidden material into a programme service [1].
1   House of Commons Committee, col 1190.

Defences (para 5)
9.33   No one can be convicted of an offence under s2 of the 1959 Act for the inclusion of any matter in a programme if he proves that he did not know and had no reason to suspect that the programme would include matter rendering him liable to be convicted of the offence (para 5(1)). This provision provides the innocent broadcaster with a defence in circumstances genuinely beyond his control. When the publication in issue in any proceedings under the 1959 Act consists of the inclusion of any matter in a programme, s4(1) of the 1959 Act which provides a general defence of public good does

not apply. However, (a) a person is not to be convicted of an offence under s2 of the 1959 Act and (b) an order for forfeiture cannot be made under s3 of the 1959 Act, if it is proved that the inclusion of the matter in the programme is justified as being for the public good because it is in the interests of (i) drama, opera, ballet or any other art, (ii) science, literature or learning or any other objects of general concern (para 5(2)). The admissibility of opinions of experts, provided for by s4(2) of the 1959 Act applies to this defence as it does for the purposes of s4(1) and (1A) of that Act (para 5(3)).

Exclusion of Common Law Proceedings (para 6)
9.34   A person cannot be proceeded against for an offence at common law for (a) a programme, or anything said or done in a programme, when it is of the essence of the common law offence that the programme, or (as the case may be) what was said or done was obscene, indecent, offensive, disgusting or injurious to morality or (b) an agreement to cause a programme to be included in a programme service or to cause anything to be said or done in the course of a programme which is to be included, when the common law offence consists of conspiring to corrupt public morals or to do any act contrary to public morals or decency.

Obscenity in Programme Services in Scotland

9.35   The 1990 Act amends s51 of the Civic Government Scotland Act 1982 (the '1982 Act') to create a new crime (s163). Any person who (a) is responsible for the inclusion of any obscene material in a programme included in a programme service or (b) with a view to its eventual inclusion in a programme so included, makes, prints, has or keeps any obscene material is guilty of an offence (s51 (2A), the 1982 Act)[1]. A person has a defence if he proves that he had used all due diligence to avoid committing the offence (s51(4), the 1982 Act). 'Programme' and 'programme service' have the same meaning as in the 1990 Act (s51(8), the 1982 Act). The decision whether to bring a prosecution is vested in the procurator fiscal. Material expunged as part of the editorial process would not normally be caught by the new crime as there would be no 'view to its eventual inclusion in a programme'. Section 51(6)(a) of the 1982 Act is deleted.
1   For police powers to copy recordings, see para 9.45.

Racially Inflammatory Material

9.36   The 1990 Act makes provision for programmes included in programme services to be brought within the scope of the legislation covering incitement to racial hatred. An offence under s22[1] of the 1986 Act is only committed if there is an intent to stir up racial hatred or if, given all the circumstances, racial hatred is likely to be stirred up. Under s23[2] of the 1986 Act an offence is only committed if racially inflammatory material is held with a view to broadcasting it with the intention thereby of stirring up racial hatred, or in the likelihood that racial hatred will be stirred up having regard to all the circumstances. It seems that much more than mere gathering of material for possible inclusion in a programme is needed. The possibility of an offence may only arise when the first edited version of the programme has emerged[3]. Also the statutory defences in ss22 and 23 are retained and prosecutions for incitement to racial hatred can be instituted only by, or with the consent of, the Attorney-General (s27(1) of the 1986 Act). He will need to be satisfied that the evidence affords a realistic prospect of securing a conviction and that the institution of criminal proceedings is in the public interest.
1   See para 9.38.
2   See para 9.39.
3   House of Lords Committee, col 1598 (Earl Ferrers).

Inclusion in Programme Services in Great Britain of Racially Inflammatory Material

Exemption from Prohibitions (ss18(6), 20(3)(c) and 21(4) of the Public Order Act 1986 as Amended by s164(2))

9.37   Three amendments in the 1990 Act relate to exemptions from prohibitions in the Public Order Act 1986 (the '1986 Act'). Section 18(1) of the 1986 Act provides that a person who uses threatening, abusive or insulting words or behaviour, or displays any written material which is threatening, abusive or insulting is guilty of an offence if (a) he intends thereby to stir up racial hatred or (b) having regard to all the circumstances racial hatred is likely to be stirred up thereby. Section 18 does not apply to words or behaviour used, or written material displayed, 'solely' for the purpose of being included in a programme included in a programme service (s18(6)). Section 20(1) of the 1986 Act provides that if a public performance of a play is given which involves the use of threatening, abusive or insulting words or behaviour, any person who presents or directs the performance is guilty of an offence if (a) he intends thereby to stir up racial hatred or (b) having regard to all the circumstances (and in particular, taking the performance as a whole) racial hatred is likely to be stirred up thereby. Section 20 does not apply to a performance given 'solely or primarily' for the purpose of enabling the performance to be included in a programme service (s20(3)(c)). Section 21(1) of the 1986 Act provides that a person who distributes, or shows or plays, a recording of visual images or sounds which are threatening, abusive or insulting is guilty of an offence if (a) he intends thereby to stir up racial hatred or (b) having regard to all the circumstances racial hatred is likely to be stirred up thereby. Section 21 does not apply to the showing or playing of a recording 'solely' for the purpose of enabling the recording to be included in a programme service (s21(4)). These exemptions, on a literal interpretation, are given a limited effect by the use of the words 'solely' and 'solely or primarily'.

Including Programmes in a Programme Service (s22 of the 1986 Act as Amended by s164(3))

9.38   Section 22 of the 1986 Act is amended so that if a programme involving threatening, abusive or insulting visual images or sounds is included in a programme service then the (a) service provider (b) any person by whom the programme is produced or directed and (c) any person by whom offending words or behaviour are used, is guilty of an offence if (a) he intends thereby to stir up racial hatred or (b) having regard to all the circumstances racial hatred is likely to be stirred up thereby (s22(1)(2)) [1]. A person who is not shown to have intended to stir up racial hatred is not guilty of a s22 offence if he did not know, and had no reason to suspect, that the offending material was threatening, abusive or insulting (s22(6)). Apart from this general defence, three particular defences are found in s22. If the service provider, or someone by whom the programme was produced or directed, is not shown to have intended to stir up racial hatred, it is a defence for him to prove that (a) he did not know and had no reason to suspect that the programme would involve the offending material and (b) having regard to the circumstances in which the programme was included in a programme service, it was not reasonably practicable for him to secure the removal of the material (s22(3)). It is a defence for a person by whom the programme was produced or directed who is not shown to have intended to stir up racial hatred to prove that he did not know and had no reason to suspect that the (a) programme would be included in a programme service or (b) circumstances in which the programme would be so included would be such that racial hatred would be likely to be stirred up (s22(4)). Also, it is a defence for a person by whom offending words or behaviour were used and who is not shown to have intended to stir up racial hatred to prove that he did not know and had no reason to suspect that (a) a programme involving the use of the offending material would be included in a programme service or (b) the circumstances in which a programme involving the use of the offending material would be included, or in which a programme included would involve the use of the offending material, would be such that racial hatred would be likely to be stirred up (s22(5)). Section 22(7) and (8) of the 1986 Act are repealed by the 1990 Act.

1   For police powers to copy recordings, see para 9.45.

Possession of Racially Inflammatory Material (s23 of the 1986 Act as Amended by s164(4))

9.39   Section 23 of the 1986 Act is amended so that a person who has in his possession written material which is threatening, abusive or insulting, with a view to its being displayed, published, distributed or included in a programme service (whether by himself or another) is guilty of an offence if (a) he intends racial hatred to be stirred up thereby or (b) having regard to all the circumstances, racial hatred is likely to be stirred up thereby (s23)(1)) [1]. Section 23(1) further provides that a person who has in his possession a recording of visual or sounds which are threatening, abusive or insulting, with a view to its being distributed, shown, played or included in a programme service (whether by himself or another) is guilty of an offence if (a) he intends racial hatred to be stirred up thereby or (b) having regard to all the circumstances, racial hatred is likely to be stirred up thereby. For these purposes regard must be had to such display, publication, distribution, showing, playing or inclusion in a cable programme service as the accused has, or it may reasonably be inferred that he has, in view (s23(2)). In proceedings for an offence under s23 it is a defence for an accused who is not shown to have intended to stir up racial hatred to prove that he was not aware of the content of the written material or recording and did not suspect, and had no reason to suspect, that it was threatening, abusive or insulting (s23(3)). Section 23(4) of the 1986 Act is repealed by the 1990 Act.

1   For police powers to copy recordings, see para 9.45.

Interpretation of the 1986 Act (s29 of the 1986 Act as Amended by s164(4))

9.40   Section 29 of the 1986 Act is amended so that the definitions of 'broadcast' and 'cable programme service' are omitted. The definition of 'programme' is any item which is included in a programme service. 'Programme service' has the same meaning as in the 1990 Act.

Inclusion in Programme Services in Northern Ireland of Material Likely to Stir up Hatred

Exemption From Prohibitions (Arts 9(5) and 11(4) of the Public Order (Northern Ireland) Order 1987 as Amended by s165(2))

9.41   Two amendments in the 1990 Act relate to exemptions from prohibitions in the Public Order (Northern Ireland) Order 1987 (the '1987 Order'). Article 9(1) of the 1987 Order provides that a person who uses threatening, abusive or insulting words or behaviour, is guilty of an offence if (a) he intends thereby to stir up hatred or arouse fear or (b) having regard to all the circumstances hatred is likely to be stirred up or fear is likely to be aroused thereby. Article 9 does not apply to words or behaviour used, or written material displayed, 'solely' for the purpose of being included in a programme included in a programme service (Art 9(5)). Article 11(1) of the 1987 Order provides that a person who distributes, or shows or plays, a recording or visual image or sounds which are threatening, abusive or insulting is guilty of an offence if (a) he intends thereby to stir up hatred or arouse fear or (b) having regard to all the circumstances hatred is likely to be stirred up or fear is likely to be aroused thereby. Article 11 does not apply to the showing or playing of a recording 'solely' for the purpose of enabling the recording to be included in a programme service (Art 11(4)). These exemptions, on a liberal interpretation, are given a limited effect by the use of the word 'solely'.

Including Programmes in a Programme Service (Art 12 of the 1987 Order as Amended by s165(3))

9.42   Article 12 of the 1987 Order is amended so that if a programme involving threatening, abusive or insulting visual images or sounds is included in a programme service then (a) the service provider (b) any person by whom the programme is produced or directed and (c) any person by whom offending words or behaviour are used, is guilty of an offence if (a) he intends thereby to stir up hatred or arouse fear or (b) having regard to all the circumstances hatred is likely to be stirred up or fear is likely to be aroused thereby (Art 12(1), (2)) [1]. A person who is not shown to have intended to stir up hatred or arouse fear is not guilty of an offence under this article if he did not know, and had no reason to suspect, that the offending material was threatening, abusive or insulting (Art 12(6)). Apart from this general defence, three particular defences are found in Art 12. If the service provider, or a person by whom the programme was produced or directed, is not shown to have intended to stir up hatred or arouse fear, it is a defence for him to prove that (a) he did not know and had no reason to suspect that the programme would involve the offending material and (b) having regard to the circumstances in which the programme was included in a programme service, it was not reasonably practicable for him to secure the removal of the material (Art 12(3)). It is a defence for a person by whom the programme was produced or directed who is not shown to have intended to stir up hatred or arouse fear to prove that he did not know and had no reason to suspect that (a) the programme would be included in a programme service or (b) the circumstances in which the programme would be so included would be such that hatred would be likely to be stirred up or fear would be likely to be aroused (Art 12(4)). Also, it is a defence for a person by whom offending words or behaviour were used and who is not shown to have intended to stir up hatred or arouse fear to prove that he did not know and had no reason to suspect (a) that a programme involving the use of the offending material would be included in a programme service or (b) that the circumstances in which a programme involving the use of the offending material would be so included, or in which a programme so included would involve the use of the offending material, would be such that hatred would be likely to be stirred up or fear would be likely to be aroused (Art 12(5)). Article 12(7) and (8) of the 1987 Order are repealed by the 1990 Act.

1   For police powers to copy recordings, see para 9.45.

Possession of Matter Intended or Likely to Stir up Hatred or Arouse Fear (Art 13 of the 1987 Order as Amended by s165(4))

9.43   Article 13 of the 1987 Order is amended so that a person who has in his possession written material which is threatening, abusive or insulting, with a view to its being displayed, published, distributed or included in a programme service, whether by himself or another is guilty of an offence if he intends hatred to be stirred up or fear to be aroused thereby or, having regard to all the circumstances, hatred is likely to be stirred up or fear is likely to be aroused thereby (Art 13(1)) [1]. Article 13(1) also provides that a person who has in his possession a recording of visual images or sounds which are threatening, abusive or insulting, with a view to its being distributed, shown played or included in a programme service, whether by himself or another, is guilty of an offence if he intends hatred to be stirred up or fear to be aroused thereby, or having regard to all the circumstances, hatred is likely to be stirred up or fear is likely to be aroused thereby. For these purposes regard must be had to such display, publication, distribution, showing, playing or inclusion in a programme service as he has, or it may reasonably be inferred that he has, in view (Art 13(2). In proceedings for an offence under Art 13 it is a defence for an accused who is not shown to have intended to stir up hatred or arouse fear to prove that he was not aware of the content of the written material or recording and did not suspect, and had no reason to suspect, that it was threatening, abusive or insulting (Art 13(3)). Article 13(4) of the 1987 Order is repealed by the 1990 Act.

1   For police powers to make copies of recordings, see para 9.45.

Interpretation of the 1987 Order (Art 17 of the 1987 Order as Amended by s165(5))

9.44   Article 17 of the 1987 Order is amended so that the definitions of 'broadcast' and 'cable programme service' are omitted. 'The definition of programme means any item which is included in a programme service. 'Programme service' has the same meaning as in the 1990 Act.

Copying Recordings

Power to Make Copies of Recordings (s167)

9.45   If a justice of the peace is satisfied by information on oath laid by a constable that there is reasonable ground for suspecting that a 'relevant offence' has been committed by any one in respect of a programme included in a programme service, he may make an order authorising any constable to require that person (a) to produce to the constable a visual or sound recording of any matter included in that programme, if and so far as he is able to do so and (b) on the production of the recording, to afford the constable an opportunity of causing a copy of it to be made (sub-s(1)). The order must describe the programme in a manner sufficient to enable it to be identified (sub-s(2)). Any one who, without reasonable excuse, fails to comply with the requirements of the constable is guilty of an offence and liable on summary conviction to a fine not exceeding the third level on the standard scale (sub-s(3)). What constitutes a 'relevant offence' varies in the United Kingdom. In England and Wales it is an offence under s2 of the Obscene Publications Act 1959 [1] or s22 of the Public Order Act 1986 [2] (sub-s(5)). In Scotland it is an offence under s51 of the Civil Government (Scotland) Act 1982 [3] or s22 of the Public Order Act 1986 [2] (sub-s(6)(a)). In Scotland a sheriff may make the order and evidence on oath is given (sub-s6(b), (c)). In Northern Ireland it is an offence under Art 12 of the Public Order (Northern Ireland) Order 1987 [4] (sub-s(7)(a)). A resident magistrate makes the order and a complaint on oath is made (sub-s7(b), (c)). No order can be made under s167 for a recording in respect of which a warrant could be granted under any of the three following provisions (sub-s(4)): s3 of the Obscene Publications Act 1959, which authorises a justice of the peace to issue a warrant authorising a constable to search for, seize and remove any articles which he has reason to believe to be obscene and to be kept for publication for gain; s24 of the Public Order Act 1986, which authorises a justice of the peace to issue a warrant authorising a constable to enter and search premises where it is suspected that written material or a recording in contravention of s23 of the Public Order Act 1986 [5] is situated; Art 14 of the Public Order (Northern Ireland) Order 1987, which authorises a resident magistrate to issue a warrant authorising a constable to enter and search premises where it is reasonably suspected that written material or a recording in contravention of Art 13 [6] is situated and to seize and remove anything he reasonably suspects to be that material or recordings.

1   See para 9.28.
2   See para 9.38.

3   See para 9.35.
4   See para 9.42.
5   See para 9.39.
6   See para 9.43.

9.46   Section 167 recasts the original provision in the Broadcasting Bill on police powers to obtain copies of recordings. It was introduced at the House of Commons Reports stage because of criticism that the original provision would have enabled the police to go on 'fishing trawls' looking for incriminatory evidence that might have been thought to have contravened the relevant legislation. The police, under s167, still have the powers to enforce certain provisions of the 1990 Act but those powers are subject to safeguards.

Defamation

Introduction

9.47   Section 166 provides that defamatory statements in a programme included in a programme service are to be treated as libel for the purposes of the law of defamation. Libel is both a crime and a tort. Section 166 also applies ss7 of the Defamation Act 1952 and the Defamation Act (Northern Ireland) 1955 with their provisions on qualified privilege to reports in a programme service. Finally, s166 applies the provisions in s3 of each of the Defamation Acts on slander of title, slander of goods or other malicious falsehoods to programmes included in a programme service.

Publication of Defamatory Material in England, Wales and Northern Ireland (s166(1), (5))

9.48   For the purposes of the law of libel and slander (including the law of criminal libel so far as it relates to the publication of defamatory matter) the publication of words in any programme included in a programme service is treated as publication in a permanent form (sub-s(1)). This provision does not extend to Scotland (sub-s(5)). The fact that false defamatory words spoken in a programme constitute a libel as they are treated as being in permanent form means that they are actionable per se. No proof of special damage must be proved by the plaintiff. The tortious aspect of libel is much more important than the criminal aspect. Criminal libel is rarely prosecuted. Before the 1990 Act it was uncertain whether broadcasting (except from a script) could constitute criminal libel. Libel has a different meaning in tort and criminal law. Traditionally, criminal courts described libel as a false defamatory statement made in permanent form which tends to vilify a man and bring him into hatred, ridicule and contempt [1]. The maximum penalty that can be imposed is one year's imprisonment (s5 of the Libel Act 1843). The commonly accepted test applied in the law of tort is whether the words would tend to lower the plaintiff in the estimation of right thinking members of society generally [2].

1   *Goldsmith v Pressdram Ltd* [1977] QB 83 at 87 (Wien J).
2   *Sim v Stretch* [1936] 2 All ER 1237 at 1240 (Lord Atkin).

Differences between the Crime and the Tort of Libel

9.49   The crime of libel is wider that the tort. While publication to the person defamed suffices in crime, publication to a third party is required in tort. Also, the truth of the defamatory statement provides the defence of justification in tort but in crime the accused must prove not only that the statement is true but that it is for the public benefit that it be published (s6 of the Libel Act 1843). The common law defence of privilege applies in crime as it does in tort but there is uncertainty whether the defence of fair comment on a matter of public interest is available in crime. Authoritative works suggest that it is available [1]. A libel on a class of persons is not actionable in the civil courts unless the class is so small, for example a board of directors, that it may be taken to refer to an individual. However, it is possible that a libel meant to excite public hatred against a class, for example the clergy of Swindon or primary school teachers in Slough is a crime, although no individual cleric or teacher's reputation is harmed [2]. Similarly, a libel on a dead person is not actionable in the civil courts. However, it seems that it can be a crime if the libel is meant to bring the deceased's surviving relations into hatred or contempt or was intended to provoke them [3].

1   28 Halsbury's Laws of England (4th edn), para 285.
2   *Williams* (1822) 5 B & Ald 595.
3   *Ensor* (1987) 3 TLR 366.

Qualified Privilege

Application of s7 of the Defamation Acts (s166(3))
9.50   Section 7 and the Schedule of both the Defamation Act 1952 and the Defamation Act (Northern Ireland) 1955 (the 'Defamation Acts') have identical wording. They apply in relation to (a) reports or matters included in a programme service and (b) any inclusion in the service of those reports or matters, as they apply in relation to reports and matters published in a newspaper and to publication in a newspaper (s166 (3)). Section 7 and the Schedule of each of the Defamation Acts extends qualified privilege to libel to two categories of reports and statements. In cases falling within the first category (Part I of the Schedule) the report or statement is privileged 'without explanation or contradiction'. In cases falling within the second category (Part II of the Schedule) the report or statement is 'subject to explanation or contradiction'. Consequently, in the latter case the defence of privilege is not available under the statute if it is proved that the defendant has been requested by the plaintiff to publish in the programme service in which the original publication was made, a reasonable letter or statement by way of explanation or contradiction of the words complained of, and has refused or neglected to do so, or has done so in a manner not adequate or not reasonable having regard to all the circumstances (s7(2) of the Defamation Acts as amended by s166(3)). In all cases proof that the publication was made with malice will defeat the privilege (s7(1) of the Defamation Acts). Section 7 does not protect the publication of any matter the publication of which is prohibited by law, or is not of public concern for the public benefit (s7(3) of the Defamation Acts). Also, any privilege existing at common law or by statute (apart from the privilege formerly conferred by s4 of the Law of Libel Amendment Act 1888) is unaffected by s7 (s7(4) of the Defamation Acts). The Defamation Acts substituted a longer list of protected reports than that contained in s4 of the 1888 Act.

Statements Privileged Without Explanation or Contradiction (Part I of the Schedule in the Defamation Acts)
9.51   In Part I of the Schedule to s7 of the Defamation Acts is a list of the reports and statements in a programme included in a programme service in which qualified privilege is conferred 'without explanation or contradiction' and a complainant has no statutory right of reply, as is given in cases falling within Part II of the Schedule. The reports and statements in Part I are a fair and accurate report of any proceedings (1) in public of the legislature of any part of Her Majesty's Dominions outside Great Britain [1] (2) in public of an international organisation of which the United Kingdom or Her Majesty's Government in the United Kingdom is a member, or of any international

conference to which that Government sends a representative (3) in public of an international court² (4) before a court exercising jurisdiction throughout any part of Her Majesty's Dominion outside the United Kingdom, or of any proceedings before a court-martial held outside the United Kingdom under the Naval Discipline Act, the Army Act or the Air Force Act³ (5) in public of a body or person appointed to hold a public inquiry by the government or legislature of any part of Her Majesty's Dominions outside the United Kingdom (6) a fair and accurate copy or extract from any register kept in pursuance of an Act of Parliament⁵ which is open to inspection by the public or of any other document which is required by the law of any part of the United Kingdom to be open to inspection by the public and (7) a notice or advertisement published by or on the authority of any court within the United Kingdom or any judge or officer of that court.

1   'Legislature' and 'part of Her Majesty's Dominions' are defined in Part III of the Schedule, paras 13 and 14. A fair and accurate report of parliamentary proceedings in Great Britain is privileged of common law.
2   'International court' means the International Court of Justice and any other judicial or arbitral tribunal deciding matters in dispute between states (Part III of the Schedule).
3   For countries and territories (including India and the Republic of Ireland) in relation to which the Schedule's provisions have effect as they do in relation to Her Majesty's Dominions, see Part III of the Schedule, para 14.
4   'Act of Parliament' includes an Act of Parliament of Northern Ireland (Part III of the Schedule, para 13).

Statements Privileged Subject to Explanation or Contradiction (Para 8 of Part II of the Schedule to the Defamation Acts)

9.52   In Part II of the Schedule to s7 of the Defamation Acts is a list of the reports and statements in a programme included in a programme service on which qualified privilege is conferred 'subject to explanation or contradiction'. In the following cases, listed in paras 8 - 12 of the Schedule, the defence of qualified privilege given by s7 is not available if it is proved that the defendant has been requested by the plaintiff to publish in the programme service in which the original publication was made, a reasonable letter or statement by way of explanation or contradiction, and has refused or neglected to do so or has done so in a manner not adequate or not reasonable having regard to all the circumstances (s7(2) of the Defamation Acts as amended by s 166(3)).

Domestic Tribunals (Para 8 of Part II of the Schedule to the Defamation Acts)
9.53   A fair and accurate report of the findings or decisions of the following associations (or their committee or governing body) relating to a member, or someone who is subject, because of a contract, to its control is privileged subject to explanation or contradiction. Associations formed in the United Kingdom for the purpose of (a) promoting or encouraging the exercise of, or interest in, any art, science, religion or learning and empowered by it constitution to exercise control over or to adjudicate on matters of interest or concern to the association or the actions or conduct of anyone subject to that control or adjudication or (b) promoting or safeguarding the interests of any trade, business, industry or profession or of anyone carrying on or engaged in those activities, and empowered by its constitution to exercise control over or adjudicate on matters connected with activities or the actions and conduct of those people or (c) promoting or safeguarding the interests of any game, sport or pastime to the playing or exercise of which members of the public are invited or admitted, and empowered by its constitution to exercise control over or adjudicate on people connected with or taking part in those activities (para 8 of Part II of the Schedule to the Defamation Acts). An example of the findings and decision of the domestic tribunals of the types of

association specified in para 8 may be provided by the Stewards of the Jockey Club. After inquiring into the performance of a horse at a race, their decision may be that: 'Having satisfied themselves that a drug had been administered to the horse for the purpose of the particular race, the stewards disqualified the horse for that race and warned the trainer of the horse off Leicester race course'. A fair and accurate report of that decision in a programme included in a programme service is privileged. Other cases falling within Part II of the Schedule to the Defamation Acts are public meetings (para 9), meetings of local authorities etc (para 10), company meetings (para 11) and public notices (para 12).

Public Meetings (Para 9 of Part II of the Schedule to the Defamation Acts)
9.54   A fair and accurate report of any public meeting held in the United Kingdom is privileged subject to explanation or contradiction (para 9). A public meeting is defined as 'a meeting bona fide and lawfully held for a lawful purpose and for the furtherance or discussion of any matter of public concern, whether the admission to the meeting is general or restricted' (ibid). Whether a meeting is a public meeting is a question of law and consequently a question for the judge to decide. Clearly a meeting to which all community charge payers of a district are admitted to discuss the charge would constitute a public meeting. Eighty-five years ago a meeting of 'passive resisters' in the streets, called to protest about the rating system, was held to constitute a public meeting [1]. However, a meeting of a congregation at chapel for worship is not a 'public meeting' and so a report of the sermon preached at the service is not privileged [2]. Likewise no privilege attaches to a report of an unlawful meeting, for example a meeting in Hyde Park that contravened the Park's regulations. The meeting must be 'lawfully held for a lawful purpose' (para 9).

1   *Spearing v Wandsworth News* (1906) Times, 3 July.
2   *Chaloner v Lansdown* (1894) 10 TLR 290.

Meetings of Local Authorities etc (para 10 of Part II of the Schedule to the Defamation Acts)
9.55   A fair and accurate report of certain proceedings is privileged subject to explanation or contradiction (para 9). These are proceedings at a meeting or sitting in any part of the United Kingdom of (a) any local authority or its committee or local authorities (b) any justice(s) of the peace acting otherwise than as a court exercising judicial authority (c) any commission, tribunal, committee or person appointed for the purposes of an inquiry by Act of Parliament, by Her Majesty, or by a Minister of the Crown (d) any person appointed by a local authority to hold a local inquiry in pursuance of an Act of Parliament (e) any other tribunal, board, committee or body constituted by or under, and exercising functions under, an Act of Parliament, not being a meeting or sitting admission to which is denied to representatives of newspapers and other members of the public (para 10). This paragraph extends the range of public bodies of whose proceedings a fair and accurate report in a programme included in a programme service is privileged in the absence of proof of malice.

Company Meetings (para 11 of Part II of the Schedule to the Defamation Acts)
9.56   A fair and accurate report of the proceedings at a general meeting of a company or association, constituted, registered or certified by or under any Act of Parliament or incorporated by Royal Charter, not being a private company within the meaning of the Companies Act 1985 is privileged subject to explanation or contradiction (para 11).

Public Notice (para 12 of Part II of the Schedule to the Defamation Acts)
9.57   A copy or fair and accurate report or summary of a notice or other matter issued for the information of the public by or on behalf of any government department, officer

of state, local authority or chief officer of police is privileged subject to explanation or contradiction (para 12).

General Conditions of s7 Privilege
9.58   In order that a report in a programme included in a programme service may be privileged under s7 of the Defamation Acts certain conditions must be satisfied. The report must be fair and accurate. The judge determines whether there is some evidence of unfairness or inaccuracy to go to the jury to determine whether, in fact, the report was unfair or inaccurate. The protection does not extend to matter, the publication of which is forbidden by law, or which is not of public concern and public benefit (s7(3)) of the Defamation Acts). The report must not be maliciously included in a programme service. The accuracy of a report is no defence if the motive of the defendant was to expose the plaintiff to hatred, ridicule or contempt and the desire to inform the public of the proceedings was merely a secondary consideration (s7(1) of the Defamation Acts). Additionally, where the report falls with Part II of the Schedule to s7, the defendant must, if so requested, publish in the programme service in which the original publication was made, a reasonable letter or statement by way of explanation or contradiction (s7(2)).

Application of s3 of the Defamation Acts to Slander of Title etc (s166(2))
9.59   The rule in s166(1) [1] that false defamatory words in a programme included in a programme service constitute a libel applies also for the purposes of s3 of both the Defamation Act 1952 and the Defamation Act (Northern Ireland) 1955 (sub-s(2)) [2] . The wording of s3 in each Act is identical. It provides that in an action for slander of title, slander of goods, or other malicious falsehoods, it is not necessary to prove special damage if (a) the words upon which the action is founded are calculated to cause pecuniary damage to the plaintiff and are published in writing or other permanent form or (b) those words are calculated to cause pecuniary damage to the plaintiff in respect of any office, profession, calling, trade or business held or carried on by him at the time of the publication (s3(1)). To maliciously disparage the audience of a rival station in a programme included in a programme service so as to discourage advertisers is a malicious falsehood, just as if the circulation of a rival newspaper is similarly disparaged [3], and is regarded as made in permanent form.

1   See para 9.48.
2   Section 166(1) and (2) does not extend to Scotland (s166(2)).
3   See *Lyne v Nicholls* 1906 23 TLR 86.

Chapter 10

RESTRICTIONS ON THE HOLDING OF LICENCES

Introduction

10.1   In the White Paper 'Broadcasting in the '90s: Competition Choice and Quality' (Cmnd 517) the Government stated its determination that ownership in the independent sector should be, and remain, widely spread [1]. The pre-1990 Act controls on takeovers are removed. The policy now is that the ITC and Radio Authority's regulation should 'bite' more on performance rather than through extensive and rigid disqualifications, although some are necessary and are found in Sch 2. These rules impose limits on concentration of ownership and on excessive cross-media ownership. Their purpose is to keep the market open for newcomers and prevent undue editorial uniformity or domination by a few groups. Schedule 2 reflects the government's proposal to make substantial use of subordinate legislation for these rules so as to enable a flexible response to changing circumstances. This chapter looks at the provisions of Sch 2 which are referred to in ss5 [2] and 88 [3].

1   See para 6.48.
2   See paras 3.20 to 3.26.
3   See paras 8.21 to 8.23.

Part I of Sch 2 – General

10.2   Para 1(1) of Part I of Sch 2 gives meanings to a number of key concepts found in the media ownership regulations. The meaning of the term 'national' in relation to the United Kingdom is not given. This follows the recent convention not to define United Kingdom nationals in legislation which relies on that concept. It is considered possible for the body responsible for administering the legislation to find out, without a definition, what that concept means and then apply it. It is also considered unnecessary to incorporate into United Kingdom legislation definitions of nationality relating to other EC countries [1].

1   House of Commons Committee, col 298.

10.3   'Advertising agency' means an individual or a body corporate who carries on business as an advertising agent [1] (whether alone or in partnership) or has control over any body corporate which carries on business as an advertising agent. Any reference to an advertising agency includes a reference to an individual who (a) is a director or officer of any body corporate which carries on that business or (b) is employed by any person who carries on that business (para 1(1)).

1   For the purposes of the 1990 Act (a) a person is not to be regarded as carrying on business as an advertising agent, or as acting as such an agent, unless he carries on a business involving the selection and purchase of advertising time or space for persons wishing to advertise (b) a person who carries on such a business is to be regarded as carrying on business as an

advertising agent irrespective of whether in law he is the agent for those for whom he acts (c) the proprietor of a newspaper is not to be regarded as carrying on business as an advertising agent by reason only that he makes arrangements on behalf of advertisers whereby advertisements appearing in the newspaper are also to appear in one or more other newspapers (d) a company or other body corporate is not to be regarded as carrying on business as an advertising agent by reason only that its objects or powers include or authorise that activity (s202(7)).

10.4 'Associate' in relation to a body corporate, means a director of that body corporate or a body corporate which is a member of the same group[1] as that body corporate (para 1(1)). In relation to an individual, certain persons are regarded as associates of each other. They are (a) any individual and that individual's spouse (b) any individual and any body corporate of which that individual is a director (c) any person in his capacity as trustee of a settlement and the settler or grantor and any person associated with the settler or grantor (d) persons carrying on business in partnership and the spouse and relatives of any of them (e) any two or more persons acting together to secure or exercise control of a body corporate or other association or to secure control of any enterprise or assets. 'Relative' means a brother, sister, uncle, aunt, nephew, niece, lineal ancestor or descendant (the stepchild or illegitimate child of any person or anyone adopted by a person whether legally or otherwise, as his child, being regarded as a relative or taken into account to trace a relationship in the same way as that person's child). References to a spouse include a former spouse and a reputed spouse (para 1(2)).

1   For the purposes of para 1 two bodies corporate are treated as members of the same group if (a) one of them is a body corporate of which the other is a subsidiary or (b) both of them are subsidiaries of another body corporate (para 2(2)). 'Subsidiary' has the meaning given by s736 of the Companies Act 1985 (para 2(3)).

10.5   'Control' in relation to any body other than a body corporate means the power of a person to secure, by virtue of the rules regulating that or any other body, that the affairs of the first-mentioned body are conducted in accordance with the wishes of that person (para 1(1)). A person controls a body corporate if (a) he has a controlling interest in the body or (b) (although not having such an interest in the body) he is able, by virtue of holding shares or the possession of voting power in or in relation to the body or any other body corporate, to secure that the affairs of the body are conducted in accordance with his wishes or (c) he has the power, by virtue of any powers conferred by the articles of association or other document regulating the body or any other body corporate, to secure that the affairs of the body are so conducted. For this purpose a person has a controlling interest in a body corporate if he holds, or is beneficially entitled to, more than 50% of the equity share capital in that body, or possesses more than 50 per cent of the voting power in it (para 1(3)). A person may be regarded as controlling a body corporate by virtue of para (3)(b) above despite the fact that (a) he does not have a controlling interest in any such other body corporate as is mentioned in that paragraph or (b) any such other body corporate does not have a controlling interest in the body in question or (c) he and any such other body corporate together do not have a controlling interest in that body (para 1(4)). For the purposes of Sch 2 provisions which refer to a body controlled by two or more persons or bodies of any description taken together, those persons or bodies are not to be regarded as controlling the body by virtue of para 1(3)(b) above unless they are acting in concert (para 1(5)). References in para 1 to a person (a) holding or being entitled to shares, or any amount of these shares or equity share capital, in a body corporate or (b) possessing voting power, or any amount of the voting power, in a body corporate, is a reference to his doing so, or being so entitled, whether alone or jointly with one or more other persons and whether directly or through one or more nominees (para 2(1)).

10.6   'Equity share capital' has the same meaning as in the Companies Act 1985 (para 1(1)).

10.7   'Local authority' (a) in relation to England and Wales, means the council of a country, district or London borough, the Common Council of the City of London and the Council of the Isles of Scilly (b) in relation to Scotland, means a regional, islands or district council and (c) in relation to Northern Ireland, means a district council (para 1(1)).

10.8   A 'local delivery licence' is a licence to provide a local delivery service which is defined in s72(1) [1] (para 1(1)).
1   See para 7.2.

10.9   'Participant', in relation to a body corporate, means a person who holds or is beneficially entitled to shares in that body or who possesses voting power in that body (para 1(1)). In Sch 2 any reference to a participant with more than a 5% or (as the case may be) 20% interest in a body corporate is a reference to a person who (a) holds or is beneficially entitled to more than 5 or (as the case may be) 20% of the shares in that body or (b) possesses more than 5 or (as the case may be) 20% of the voting power in that body. Where such a reference has been amended by an order under Sch 2 varying the percentage, this provision has effect in relation to it subject to the necessary modifications (para 1(6)).

10.10   Schedule 2 imposes certain limits or degrees of financial interest in a body corporate, some as low as 5%, others 20%. These prevent a controlling interest but are significant enough to permit companies to have cross-media holdings without that degree of dominance that becomes contrary to the public interest [1].
1   House of Commons Committee, col 301.

10.11   For the purposes of Sch 2 certain persons are connected with each other in relation to a particular licence. They are (a) the licence holder (b) a person who controls the licence (c) an associate of the licence holder or of a person falling within (b) above and (d) a body which is controlled by the licence holder or by an associate of the licence holder (para 3).

10.12   An order made under Sch 2 can only be made by the Secretary of State if a draft of it has been approved by a resolution of each House of Parliament (para 4). Examples of this affirmative resolutions provision are orders made imposing limits on participation by holders of licences in bodies licensed to provide services of the same category (Part III, para 4) and restrictions on proprietors of newspapers (Part IV para 2(5)).

Part II of Sch 2 – Disqualification from Holding Licences

General Disqualification of Non-EEC Nationals and Bodies having Political Connections (para 1)

10.13   Certain persons are disqualified persons in relation to a licence granted by the ITC or the Radio Authority. They are (a) an individual who is neither (i) a national of a member state who is ordinarily resident within the European Economic Community (EEC) nor (ii) ordinarily resident in the United Kingdom, the Isle of Man or the Channel Islands (b) a body corporate which is neither (i) a body formed under the law of a member state which has its registered or head office or principal place of business within the EEC nor (ii) a body incorporated under the law of the Isle of Man or the

190

Channel Islands (c) a local authority (d) a body whose objects are wholly or mainly of a political nature (e) a body affiliated to a body falling within (d) above (f) an individual who is an officer of a body falling within (d) or (e) above (g) a body corporate which is an associate of a body corporate falling within (d) or (e) above (g) a body corporate which is an associate of a body corporate falling within (d) or (e) above (h) a body corporate in which a body falling within any of paragraphs (a) - (e) and (g) above is a participant with more than a 5% interest (i) a body which is controlled by a person falling within any of paragraphs (a) - (g) above or by two or more such persons taken together and (j) a body corporate in which a body falling within (i) above, other than one which is controlled by (i) a person falling with (a), (b) or (f) above or (ii) two or more such persons taken together, is a participant with more than a 5% interest (para 1(1)).

10.14 The above rules apply as if paragraphs (a) and (b) (and the reference to those paragraphs in para (1)) were omitted in relation to a (a) local delivery licence (b) licence to provide a non-domestic satellite service (c) licence to provide a non-domestic satellite radio service within the meaning of the 1990 Act which is not provided on any frequency allocated to the United Kingdom for broadcasting by satellite (d) licence to provide a licensable programme service (e) licence to provide a licensable sound programme service or (f) licence to provide additional services (within the meanings of the 1990 Act) other than a licence to provide the teletext service referred to in s 49(2) [1] (para 1(2), (3)).
1   See para 4.154.

10.15 Paragraphs 1(1)(a) and (b) seek to prevent ITC or Radio Authority licences being granted to non-EEC nationals and in effect carry forward rules found in the 1981 and 1984 Broadcasting legislation. These prohibitions do not apply, for example, to a licence to provide a non-domestic satellite service. The White Paper (Cmnd 517) considered that although licensing such services would subject them to consumer protection regulation of programme content, their development should be left to the market [1]. However, the owners of non-direct broadcasting by satellite services are prevented from having excessive interests in other UK Channels. Part III para 6(2) [2] limits such an interest to 20%. The government considered that it would be undesirable to prevent non-EEC control of local delivery licences because such licences do not normally exercise editorial control over the content of channels that they relay [3]. This permits the large investment interest shown before the 1990 Act in cable franchises to be unthreatened.
1   Para 6.31.
2   See para 10.33.
3   House of Commons Committee, col 311.

Disqualification of religious bodies (para 2)

10.16 Certain persons are disqualified persons in relation to a licence granted by the ITC or Radio Authority. They are (a) a body whose objects are wholly or mainly of a religious nature (b) a body which is controlled by a body falling within (a) above or by two or more such bodies taken together (c) a body which controls a body falling within (a) above (d) a body corporate which is an associate of a body corporate falling within (a), (b) or (c) above (e) a body corporate in which a body falling within any of paragraphs (a) - (d) is a participant with more than a 5% interest (f) an individual who is an officer of a body falling within (a) above and (g) a body which is controlled by an individual falling within (f) above or by two or more such individuals taken together (para 2(1)).

10.17 If on an application made to them (a) the ITC are satisfied that it is appropriate for a person who would otherwise be disqualified by virtue of para 2(1) to hold a licence to provide (i) a non-domestic satellite service or (ii) a licensable programme service or (b) the Radio Authority is satisfied that it is appropriate for an otherwise similarly disqualified person to hold a particular kind of licence that may be granted by it under the 1990 Act, other than a national licence, they must make a determination that they are so satisfied. As long as the determination remains in force in relation to that person, he is not a disqualified person in relation to that licence (para 2(2)).

10.18 The exemption to the ban on religious bodies in relation to non-domestic satellite services, licensable programme services and Radio Authority licences other than for a national service relies on the ITC and Radio Authority operating an 'appropriateness' test. The policy is to enable those bodies to disqualify cults which might exploit the audience [1].
1   House of Lords Committee, col 70.

10.19 The ITC and Radio Authority must each publish, in the manner they consider appropriate, general guidance to applicants for a para 2(2) determination as to the principles to be applied by them in determining whether it is appropriate for them to hold those categories of licence (para 2(3)).

Disqualification of publicly-funded bodies for radio service licences (para 3)

10.20 The following persons are disqualified persons in relation to any licence granted by the Radio Authority other than a licence to provide a restricted service - (a) a body (other than a local authority) which has, in its last financial year, received more than half its income from public funds (b) a body which is controlled by a body falling within (a) above or by two or more such bodies taken together and (c) a body corporate in which a body falling within (a) or (b) above is a participant with more than a 5% interest (para 3(1)). Money is received from public funds if it is paid by (a) a Minister of the Crown out of money provided by Parliament or out of the National Loans Fund (b) a Northern Ireland department out of the Consolidated Fund of Northern Ireland or out of money appropriated by Measure of Northern Ireland Assembly or (c) a body which itself falls within para 3(1)(a), including a body which falls within that provision because of para 3(2). However, in each case, any money paid as consideration for the acquisition of property, supply of goods or services or as remuneration, expenses, pensions, allowances or similar benefits for or in respect of a person as the holder of an office must be disregarded (para 3(2)).

General disqualification on grounds of undue influence (para 4)

10.21 A person is a disqualified person in relation to a licence granted by the ITC or Radio Authority if in the opinion of that body (a) a relevant body is, by giving financial assistance or otherwise, exerting influence over the activities of that person and (b) that influence has led, or is leading or is likely to lead to results which are adverse to the public interest (para 4(1)). A 'relevant body' in relation to a licence granted by the ITC is a body falling within para 1(1)(c) - (h) or (j) [1] above or a body which is controlled (i) by a person falling within para 1(1)(c) - (g) [1] above or (ii) by two or more such persons taken together (para 4(2)(a)). A 'relevant body' in relation to a licence granted by the Radio Authority, means a body falling within para 1(1)(c) - (h) or (j) [1] or 3 [2] above or a body which is controlled as mentioned in para 4(2)(a)(i) or (ii) above (para 4(2)(b)).
1   See para 10.13.
2   See para 10.20.

General Disqualification of Broadcasting Bodies (para 5)

10.22 Certain persons are disqualified persons in relation to a licence granted by the ITC or Radio Authority. They are (a) the BBC (b) the Welsh Authority (c) a body corporate which is controlled by either of those bodies and (d) a body corporate in which either of those bodies or (ii) a body corporate falling within (c) above is (to any extent) a participant (para 5).

General Disqualification of Advertising Agencies (para 6)

10.23 Certain persons are disqualified persons in relation to a licence granted by the ITC or Radio Authority. They are (a) an advertising agency (b) an associate of an advertising agency (c) a body which is controlled by a person falling within (a) or (b) above or by two or more such persons taken together (d) a body corporate in which a person falling within (a) - (c) above is a participant with more than a 5% interest (para 6).

Part III of Sch 2 – Restrictions to Prevent Accumulations of Interests in Licensed Services

Preliminary (para 1)

10.24 In Part III 'relevant services' means the services mentioned in para 1(2) and (3) below. They are divided into 12 categories (para 1(1)). In the case of services licensed by the ITC, the categories are (a) regional and national Channel 3 services and Channel 5 (b) domestic satellite services (c) non-domestic satellite services (d) licensable programme services (e) additional services (f) local delivery services (para 1(2)). In the case of services licensed by the Radio Authority, the categories are (a) national radio services (b) local radio services (c) restricted radio services (d) satellite radio services (e) licensable sound programme services and (f) additional services (para 1(3)).

Limits on the Holding of Licences to Provide Particular Categories of Services (para 2)

10.25 The maximum number of licences which may at any time be held [1] by any one person to provide relevant services falling within each of the following categories is (a) two in the case of regional Channel 3 services (b) one in the case of national Channel 3 services (c) one in the case of Channel 5 (d) one in the case of national radio services (e) 20 in the case of local radio services and (f) six in the case of restricted radio services (para 2(1)). The Secretary of State may, in the case of any category of relevant services not falling within para 2(1) by order prescribe the maximum number of licences which may at any time be held [1] by one person to provide relevant services falling within that category (para 2(2)). He may by order (a) amend para 2(1) by substituting a different limit for the limit specified there (b) impose, in relation to any category of relevant services specified in or under para 2(1) and (2) limits on the holding of licences to provide relevant services falling within that category which are additional to any limits specified there and are framed (i) by reference to any specified circumstances relating to the licence holders in question or to the services to be provided by them or (ii) (in the case of licences granted by the ITC) by reference to matters determined by it under the order (para 2(3)). An order made in pursuance of this provision may impose on the licence holder to provide any specified category of relevant services limits framed (directly or indirectly) by reference to either or both of the following matters. These are (a) the number of licences of any one or more specified descriptions which are held by him or by any body controlled by him and (b) his participation, to any specified extent,

in any body corporate which is the holder of any licence(s) of any one or more such descriptions (para 2(4)).
1   A person is treated as holding a licence if the licence is held by a person connected with him (para 2(8)).

10.26   A person is permitted to control two regional Channel 3 licences but the government is committed to bringing forward subordinate legislation to supplement this limit so that a person could not control two large licences or two contiguous ones. It is proposed that the ITC may permit a takeover by a contiguous licencee only if it is satisfied that the licence area had become unviable, that no company would be interested in owning the licence either by takeover or through a further competitive tender and that the separate regional identity of the two licences would be maintained notwithstanding that they were in the same ownership [1].
1   House of Lords Report, col 187.

10.27   Where a person holds a licence to provide a local radio service which, in accordance with s86(2) [1], authorises the provision of a multi-channel service, he must be treated for the purposes of para 2(1) as holding [2] such number of licences to provide local radio services as corresponds to the number of channels on which the service may be provided (para 2(5)). Likewise, where a person holds [2] a licence to provide a (a) domestic satellite service (b) non-domestic satellite service or (c) a satellite radio service which in accordance with s44(2) [3], 45(3) [4] or 86(2) [5], authorises the provision of a multi-channel service, he must be treated for the purposes of any order made under para 2(2) as holding such number of licences to provide domestic satellite services, non-domestic satellite services or (as the case may be) satellite radio services as corresponds to the number of channels on which the service may be provided (para 2(6)). A 'multi-channel service' means a service which to any extent consists in the simultaneous transmission of different programmes on different frequencies. The references to the number of channels on which that service may be provided is a reference to the number of different frequencies involved (para 2(7)).
1   See para 8.24.
2   A person is treated as holding a licence if the licence is held by a person connected with him (para 2(8)).
3   See para 4.123.
4   See para 4.129.
5   See para 8.24.

10.28   Most of the pre-1990 Act radio stations broadcast under a single contract on at least two frequencies [1]. The rules provide that it is the number of channels rather than the number of licences which are important. Before the 1990 Act there were over 130 independent radio channels (as opposed to contracts) and that number is set to increase rapidly.
1   House of Lords Report, col 174.

Limit on the Holding of Licences to Provide Different Categories of Services (para 3)

10.29   Where any restriction is imposed by or under paras 5 [1] or 6 [2] below on the holder of a particular kind of licence in relation to participation in a body corporate which is the holder of another kind of licence, any person who holds one of those kinds of licence must not also hold the other kind of licence (para 3).
1   See para 10.31.
2   See paras 10.32 - 10.38.

Limit on Participation by Holders of Licences in Bodies Licensed to Provide Services of Same Category (para 4)

10.30 The Secretary of State may by order prescribe restrictions on the extent to which the holder of a licence to provide a relevant service falling within a particular category may be a participant in (a) a body corporate which is the holder of another licence to provide a relevant service falling within that category or (b) two or more such bodies corporate (para 4).

Special Rules Relating to Participation by Holders of Television Broadcasting Licences (para 5)

10.31 For the purposes of para 4 [1] above and this paragraph the services specified in para 1(2)(a) [2] above must be divided into three categories (a) regional Channel 3 services (b) national Channel 3 services and (c) Channel 5 (para 5(1)). Where a person is the holder of a licence to provide a service falling within one of those categories, he must not be a participant with more than a 20% interest in a body corporate which is the holder of a licence to provide a service falling within either of the other two categories (para 5(2)). The Secretary of State may be order (a) amend para 5(2) by substituting a different percentage for the percentage specified there (b) prescribe restrictions on the extent to which the holder of a licence to provide a service falling within one of the categories specified in para 5(1) may be a participant in two or more bodies corporate which are the holders of licences to provide services falling within either of the other two specified categories (para 5(3)).

1   See para 10.30.
2   See para 10.24.

Limits on Participation by Holders of Licences in Bodies Licensed to Provide Services of Different Category (para 6)

10.32 Where a person is the holder of a licence to provide a relevant service falling within one of the categories specified in para 1(2)(a) or (b) or (3)(a) [1] above, he must not be a participant with more than a 20% [2] interest in a body corporate which is the holder of a licence to provide a relevant service falling within either of the other specified categories (para 6(1)).

1   See para 10.24.
2   The Secretary of State may by order substitute a different percentage (para 6(10)).

10.33 Where a person (a) is the holder of a licence to provide a non-domestic satellite service or (b) provides a satellite television service (other than a non-domestic satellite service) which is provided on a non-allocated frequency and appears to the ITC to be intended for general reception in the United Kingdom (whether or not it appears to it to be also intended for reception elsewhere), he must not be a participant with more than a 20% interest in a body corporate which is the holder of a licence to provide a relevant service falling within one of the categories referred to in para 6(1) [1]. Where a person is the holder of a licence to provide such a relevant service, he must not be a participant with more than a 20% [2] interest in a body corporate which is the holder of a licence mentioned in (a) above or which provides the service mentioned in (b) above (para 6(2)). A service is disregarded for the purposes of (a) and (b) above if the programmes included in the service are at all times the same as those which are for the time being broadcast in a Channel 3 service or on Channel 5. A 'non-allocated frequency' is a frequency other than one allocated to the United Kingdom for broadcasting by satellite.

'Satellite television service' is a service consisting in the transmission of television programmes by satellite (para 6(3)).
1   See para 10.32.
2   The Secretary of State may by order substitute a different percentage (para 6(10)).

10.34   Nothing in para 6(2) [1] imposes a restriction on the extent to which (a) an excluded licensee may be a participant in a body corporate which is the holder of a licence to provide a domestic satellite service or (b) the holder of such a licence may be a participant in a body corporate which is an excluded licensee. An 'excluded licensee' is a person who is the holder of a licence to provide a non-domestic satellite service and (i) is licensed under s7 of the Telecommunications Act 1984 to provide a specialised satellite service and (ii) is so licensed (or, as the case may be, was first so licensed) by virtue of a licence granted under that section before the commencement of para 6(2) and (iii) is not connected with any other person who is the holder of a licence to provide a non-domestic satellite service (para 6(4)).
1   See para 10.33.

10.35   Where a person is the holder of a licence to provide a satellite radio service, he must not be a participant with more than a 20% [1] interest in a body corporate which is the holder of a licence to provide a relevant service falling within para 1(2)(a) or (3)(a) [2] above. Where a person is the holder of a licence to provide such a relevant service, he must not be a participant with more than a 20% [2] interest in a body corporate which is the holder of a licence to provide a satellite radio service (para 6(5)).
1   The Secretary of State may by order substitute a different percentage (para 6(10)).
2   See para 10.24.

10.36   Where a person is the holder of a licence to provide a satellite radio service which is provided on any frequency allocated to the United Kingdom for broadcasting by satellite ('a domestic licence') he must not be a participant with more than a 20% [1] interest in a body corporate which is the holder of a licence to provide a satellite radio service which is not provided on any such frequency ('a non-domestic licence'). Where a person is the holder of a non-domestic licence, he must not be a participant with more than a 20% [1] interest in a body corporate which is the holder of a domestic licence (para 6(6)).
1   The Secretary of State may by order substitute a different percentage (para 6(10)).

10.37   Where a person is the holder of a licence to provide a relevant service falling within one of the categories specified (a) in para 1(2)(f) (local delivery services) or (3)(b) [1] (local radio services) or (b) in para 5(1)(a) [2] (regional Channel 3 services), he must not be a participant with more than a 20% [3] interest in a body corporate which is the holder of a licence to provide a relevant service falling within either of the other specified categories if each of the services in question is provided for an area which is to a significant extent the same as that for which the other is provided (para 6(7)).
1   See para 10.24.
2   See para 10.31.
3   The Secretary of State may by order substitute a different percentage (para 6(10)).

10.38   The Secretary of State may by order prescribe restrictions on two matters. First, the extent to which (i) the holder of a relevant national or satellite licence or (ii) a person providing a service mentioned in para 6(2)(b) [1] may be a participant in a body corporate who is the holder of a relevant local licence, or in two or more such bodies corporate (para 6(8)(a)). Second, the extent to which the holder of a relevant local licence may be a participant in a body corporate which (i) is the holder of a relevant national or satellite licence or (ii) provides a service mentioned in para 6(2)(b) [1], or in two or more such bodies corporate (para 6(8)(b)). A 'relevant local licence' is a licence to provide a relevant service falling within either of the categories specified in para 1(2)(f) (local delivery services) or (3)(b) [2] (local radio services). A 'relevant national or satellite licence' is a licence to provide a relevant service falling within one of the categories specified (a) in para 1(2)(b) (domestic satellite services) or (c) (non-domestic satellite service) or (3)(a) (national radio services) or (d) (satellite radio services) [2] or (b) in para 5(1)(b) (national Channel 3 services) or (c) (Channel 5) [3] (para 6(9)).

1   See para 10.33.
2   See para 10.24.
3   See para 10.31.

Limits on Participation in Bodies Holding Licences to Extend to Participation in Bodies Controlling Such Bodies (para 7)

10.39 Any restriction imposed by or under paras 4 [1], 5 [2] or 6 [3] on participation (a) in a body corporate which is the holder of a particular kind of licence or (b) in two or more such bodies, apply equally to participation in (i) a body corporate which controls the holder of such a licence or (ii) two or more bodies corporate each of which controls the holder of such a licence, as the case may be (para 7(1)).

1   See para 10.30.
2   See para 10.31.
3   See paras 10.32 - 10.38.

10.40   Any restriction imposed under para 6(8)(b) [1] on participation in a body corporate providing the service mentioned in 6(2)(b) [2] applies equally to participation in a body corporate which controls a body providing that service (para 7(2)).

1   See para 10.38.
2   See para 10.33.

Attribution of Interests of Connected Persons (para 8)

10.41   Any restriciton on participation imposed by or under paras 4 [1], 5 [2] or 6 [3] on (a) the holder of a licence or (b) a person providing a service as mentioned in para 6(2)(b) [4], apply to him as if he and every person connected with him were one person (para 8(1)).

1   See para 10.30.
2   See para 10.31.
3   See paras 10.32 - 10.38.
4   See para 10.33.

10.42   For the purposes of paras 8 and 9 [1] certain persons are treated as connected with a person providing such a service as is mentioned in para 6(2)(b) [2]. They are (a) a person who controls that person (b) an associate of that person or of a person falling within (a) above and (c) a body which is controlled by that person or by an associate of that person (para 8(2)).

1   See para 10.43.
2   See para 10.33.

Restrictions Imposed by Orders (para 9)

10.43   Without prejudice to the generality of para 4 [1] or 6(8) [2], an order made in pursuance of that provision may impose restrictions framed by reference to the number of bodies corporate in which the holder of a licence, or any person connected with him, is a participant. An order made in pursuance of para 6(8)(a)(ii) [2] may impose restrictions framed by reference to the number of bodies corporate in which a person providing such a service as is mentioned in para 6(2)(b) [3], or any person connected with him, is a participant (para 9(1)). Paragraph 8(2) [4] applies for the purposes of para 9 (para 9(2)).

1   See para 10.30.
2   See para 10.38.
3   See para 10.33.
4   See para 10.42.

Power to Impose Restrictions on Participation by Persons other than Licence Holders (para 10)

10.44   Where by virtue of any provision in Part III of Sch 2 any restriction applies in relation to participation in any body or bodies corporate of a particular description, the Secretary of State may by order provide for further restrictions to apply in relation to participation in any such body or bodies. The restrictions are ones which (a) are imposed on persons to whom the first-mentioned restriction does not apply and (b) are framed by reference to the number of bodies corporate in which such persons, or persons connected with them, are participants (para 9(1)). For the purposes of para 9 certain persons are treated as connected with a particular person. They are (a) a person who controls that person (b) an associate of that person or of a person falling within (a) above and (c) a body which is controlled by that person or his associate (para 10(2)).

Part IV of Sch 2 – Restrictions on Controlling Interests in both Newspapers and Licensed Services

Preliminary (para 1)

10.45   References to a national or local newspaper are references to a national or local newspaper circulating wholly or mainly in the United Kingdom or in a part of the United Kingdom. The relevant authority may determine that a newspaper which would not otherwise be a national or local newspaper for the purposes of Part IV of Sch 2 is to be so treated for the purposes of any restriction imposed by or under Part IV if this appears to them appropriate having regard to its circulation or influence in the United Kingdom or (as the case may be) in a part of the United Kingdom. The relevant authority in relation to a restriction having effect in relation to any licence which may be granted (a) by ITC, means the ITC and (b) by the Radio Authority, means that Authority. The following persons are connected with each other in relation to a particular national or local newspaper. They are (a) the newspapers' proprietor (b) a person who controls the proprietor (c) as associate of the proprietor or of a person falling within (b) above and (d) a body which is controlled by the proprietor or his associate. Any reference in Part IV, in relation to a local newspaper, a relevant local radio service or a relevant local delivery service is a reference to a local radio service or a local delivery service which serves an area which is to a significant extent the same as that served by the newspaper.

Restrictions on Proprietors (para 2)

10.46   The proprietor of a national or local newspaper can be a participant with more than a 20% interest in a body corporate which is the holder of a licence to provide (a) a Channel 3 service or Channel 5 or (b) a national radio service (para 2(1)). This does not impose a restriction on the proprietor of a local newspaper as respects participation in a body corporate which is the holder of a licence to provide a regional Channel 3 service except where the newspaper and the service each serve an area which is to a significant extent the same as that served by the other (para 2(2)). No person who (a) is a national newspaper proprietor and (b) is a participant with more than a 5% interest in a body corporate falling within para 2(1) (but in accordance with it is not a participant with more than a 20% interest in it), can be a participant with more than a 5% interest in any other such body corporate (para 2(3)). No person who is a local newspaper proprietor can be a participant with more than a 20% interest in a body corporate which is the holder of a licence to provide a relevant local radio service or a relevant local delivery service (para 2(4)).

10.47 The Secretary of State may by order (a) amend para 2(1), (3) or (4) by substituting a different percentage for that specified there (b) prescribe restrictions (in addition to that imposed by para 2(3)) on the extent to which a national or local newspaper proprietor may be a participant in two or more bodies corporate which are the holders of licences to provide services falling within para 2(1)(a) or (b) (c) prescribe restrictions on the extent to which a national newspaper proprietor may be a participant in a body corporate which is the holder of a licence to provide a relevant service falling within para 1(2)(f) or (3)(b) in Part III [1], or in two or more such bodies corporate (d) prescribe restrictions on the extent to which a local newspaper proprietor may be a participant in two or more bodies corporate which are the holders of licences to provide relevant local radio services or relevant local delivery services (e) prescribe restrictions on the extent to which the proprietor of a newspaper of any specified description may be a participant in a body corporate which is the holder of a licence to provide any specified description of a service falling within para 1(2)(b) or (c) or (3)(d) in Part III [1] or in two or more such bodies corporate (para 2(5)).
1   See para 10.24.

10.48 Para 7(1) in Part III [1] has effect in relation to any restriction imposed by or under paragraph 2 as it has effect in relation to any restriction imposed by or under paras 4 [2], 5 [3] or 6 [4] in Part III (para 2(6)).
1   See para 10.39.
2   See para 10.30.
3   See para 10.31.
4   See paras 10.32 to 10.38.

Restrictions on Holders of Licences (para 3)

10.49 No person who is the holder of a licence to provide (a) a Channel 3 service or Channel 5 or (b) a national radio service, can be a participant with more than a 20% interest in a body corporate which runs a national or local newspaper (para 3(1)). For the purposes of para 3 a person runs a national or local newspaper if (a) he is the proprietor of such a newspaper or (b) he controls a body which is the proprietor of such a newspaper (para 3(6)). This does not impose a restriction on the holder of a licence to provide a regional Channel 3 service as respects participation in a body corporate which runs a local newspaper except where the service and the newspaper each serve an area which is significantly the same as that served by the other (para 3(2)). No person who (a) is the holder of a licence mentioned in para 3(1) and (b) is a participant with more than a 5% interest in a body corporate which runs a national newspaper (but, in accordance with paragraph 3(1), is not a participant with more than a 20% interest in it), can be a participant with more than a 5% interest in any other such body corporate (para 3(3)). No person who is the holder of a licence to provide a relevant local radio service or a relevant local delivery service can be a participant with more than a 20% interest in a body corporate which runs a local newspaper (para 3(4)).

10.50 The Secretary of State may by order (a) vary para 3(1),(3) or (4) by substituting a different percentage for that specified there (b) prescribe restrictions (in addition to that imposed by para 3(3)) on the extent to which the holder of such a licence as is mentioned in para 3(1) may be a participant in two or more bodies corporate which run national or local newspapers (c) prescribe restrictions on the extent to which the holder of a licence to provide a relevant service falling within para 1(2)(f) or (3)(b) in Part III [1] may be a participant in a body corporate which runs a national newspaper, or in two or more such bodies corporate (d) prescribe restrictions on the extent to which the holder of such a licence as is mentioned in para 3(4) may be a participant in two or more bodies corporate which run local newspapers (e) prescribe restrictions on the extent to which the holder of a licence to provide any specified description of a service falling within para 1(2)(b) or (c) or (3)(d) in Part III [1] may be a participant in a body corporate which runs a national or local newspaper, or in two or more such bodies corporate (para 3(5)).

1   See para 10.24.

Attribution of Interests of Connected Persons (para 4)

10.51   Any restriction on participation imposed by or under para 2 [1] or 3 [2] on the (a) proprietor of any newspaper or (b) holder of any licence, applies to him as if he and every person connected with him were one person.

1   See paras 10.46 to 10.48.
2   See paras 10.49 to 10.50.

Restrictions Imposed by Orders (Para 5)

10.52   An order made in pursuance of paras 2(5) [1] or 3(5) [2] may impose restrictions framed by reference to the number of bodies corporate in which (a) the proprietor of a newspaper or (b) the holder of a licence, as the case may be , or any person connected with him, is a participant.

1   See para 10.47.
2   See para 10.50.

Part V of Sch 2 – Restriction on Holding of Licences by Operators of Public Telecommunications Systems

10.53   The Secretary of State may by order specify categories of licences granted by the ITC or the Radio Authority which may not be held by all or any of certain persons. They are (a) a national public telecommunications operator or a national public telecommunications operator of any description specified in the order (b) a person who controls such an operator (c) an associate of such an operator or of a person falling within (b) above and (d) a body which is controlled by such an operator or his associate. A 'national public telecommunication operator' is a public telecommunications operator (within the meaning of the Telecommunications Act 1984) who is authorised to run a telecommunication system for the whole, or substantially the whole, of the United Kingdom.

Index

Additional payments
additional services licence,
  conditions, 4.166 8.105
  generally, 4.165 8.104
Channel 3 licence, for. *See* CHANNEL 3
local delivery services licence,
  conditions, 7.28
  generally, 7.27
national service licence,
  conditions, 8.62A
  generally, 8.60
  qualifying revenue, 8.61-8.62
Additional services
additional payments,
  generally, 4.165
  licence conditions, 4.166
independent local radio, 8.15
licence ,
  additional payment, conditions relating to,
    4.166
  application, 4.160
  conditions,
    no interference, 4.173
    renewed, 4.172
  consideration of application, 4.162
  duration of, 4.167
  enforcement,
    financial penalty, imposition of, 4.174
    revocation of licence, powers relating to,
      4.175
  person submitting highest cash bid, award
    to, 4.163
  proposal notice, 4.159
  publication of application, 4.161
  renewal of,
    formal, 4.171
    generally, 4.168
    refusal to renew, 4.169
    renewed licence conditions, 4.172
  revocation of, 4.175
  scope of, 4.157
licence holder, authorisation of another to
  provide local delivery services, 4.158
licensing authority, 4.151-4.153
meaning, 4.150 8.92
post grant awards, determination of, 4.170
refusal to begin, 4.164
single teletext service, 4.154-4.156

Additional services – *continued*
sound broadcasting frequencies. *See* SOUND
  BROADCASTING FREQUENCIES
spare capacity, meaning, 4.152
telecommunication signals, meaning, 4.152
Advertisements
code. *See* ADVERTISEMENTS AND
  SPONSORSHIP CODE
ITC, regulation by, 3.33-3.38
Radio Authority, powers of, 8.36-8.38
religious, 3.35
Welsh Authority,
  code, 4.191
  generally, 4.190
  Secretary of State, directions from, 4.192
Advertisements and sponsorship code
compliance with, 3.38
ITC, powers of, 3.36-3.37
Welsh Authority, 4.191
Advertising agency
general disqualification of, 10.23
meaning, 10.3
Allocated frequency
meaning, 3.8
Announcements
Broadcasting Act 1990, relating to, 1.4
Apology
broadcast of,
  Channel 3, 4.111
  Channel 4, 4.111
  Channel 5, 4.111
  non-domestic satellite service, 4.131
  Radio Authority, powers of, 8.80
Apparatus
meaning, 5.15
sharing of, by operators of
  telecommunications systems, 5.37-5.38
telecommunication apparatus, meaning,
  5.37*n*
wireless telegraphy, deemed to be for, 5.19-
  5.20
Archive
national television, contributions towards
  maintenance of, 5.27-5.28
Assets
Cable Authority, of, vesting in ITC, 2.22
IBA, of, division of, 2.3-2.14
Associate
meaning, 10.4